Political Risk Management for the Global Supply Chain

Political Risk Management for the Global Supply Chain

Ralph L. Kliem PMP, CBCP

CRC Press
Taylor & Francis Group
Boca Raton London New York

CRC Press is an imprint of the
Taylor & Francis Group, an **informa** business
AN AUERBACH BOOK

First edition published 2022
by CRC Press
6000 Broken Sound Parkway NW, Suite 300, Boca Raton, FL 33487-2742

and by CRC Press
2 Park Square, Milton Park, Abingdon, Oxon, OX14 4RN

CRC Press is an imprint of Taylor & Francis Group, LLC

ISBN: 978-0-367-47733-2 (hbk)
ISBN: 978-1-032-04537-5 (pbk)
ISBN: 978-1-003-03624-1 (ebk)

Typeset in Minion
by SPi Global, India

Contents

List of Figures

Preface

The global business environment has never been so complex, making supply chains more fragile than ever. A stable business environment seems like a distant dream in today's global marketplace; instability, not stability, has become the norm. Albeit global supply chains have never been stable, they have become less so today. Anti-globalization and nationalization coupled with populist movements and transnational terrorism, just to name a few targeting global supply chains, now pose significant challenges and risks when doing business across the globe, not only in less developed countries but also in developed ones. Fortunately, global business enterprises have ways to manage, survive, and prosper in the current political environment by applying the concepts, tools in techniques of political risk management.

Discussions about politics can be an emotional topic, often because it involves exchanging, even imposing, beliefs and values, such as when seeking maintaining political power or using ideological persuasion. This book deliberately tries to avoid such an orientation. Instead, it addresses the topic of political risk management from the perspective of an ophthalmologist, focusing on seeing reality as it is, not how it ought to be.

This book begins with an overview on why political risk management is an important, yet overlooked, topic and the corresponding consequences if it is ignored or overlooked on enterprises and their global supply chains. It also provides an overview of the many risks that can impact supply chains and, ultimately, the performance of global enterprises.

Next, this book provides systemic and systematic perspectives on political risk management and explains why the topic is more important than ever. Most importantly, it provides a framework that enterprises, regardless of nationality, can use to develop and deploy to manage political risks – political risk management. It also provides insights on supply chain, project management, change implementation, and business continuity to make political risk management a reality in an enterprise.

Finally, this book discusses the full spectrum of developing, deploying, testing, and maintaining processes to conduct political risk management. It also contains a case study that demonstrates applying the processes.

The objectives of this book are to:

- Provide an overview of basic political terminology and political risk management
- Present the basic processes of political risk management
- Understand the current and future impacts of political events on global supply chains

Some specific topics discussed in this book include narratives on:

- Defining political risk management
- Understanding why you should care about political risk management
- Identifying different categories of political risk
- Understanding the relationship of political risk management, enterprise risk management, supply chain, project management, change management, and business continuity
- Laying the groundwork for efficient and effective political risk management
- Understanding the current political environment
- Identifying potential political risks
- Determining the priority and impact of political risk
- Developing and applying appropriate responses
- Evaluating the effectiveness of responses, and
- Improving political risk management performance

The following chapters will help to achieve the objectives.

Chapter 1 describes some of the key political events that have had an impact on the global supply chain. It also introduces some basic concepts of political science; what makes political risk management so difficult to apply; and its drivers and goals.

Chapter 2 begins with a discussion on the global supply and its relationship with globalization. It presents the basic elements of a global supply chain; its relationship not with just politics but also economics, and sociology; and the political impacts both disciplines have on the global supply chain.

Chapter 3 begins with a discussion on governance. The topic is followed by another one on planning and implementing political risk management using the disciplines, tools, and techniques of program and project management.

Chapter 4 provides an in-depth discussion of the basics of political risk management, to include the basic processes of the framework: identify strategic goals and objectives; identify stakeholders; prepare the political risk management plan; identify risks; assess risks; prepare risk responses; perform risk monitoring and controlling; perform risk reporting; and maintain political risk management processes.

Chapter 5 introduces the political risk management process, identify strategic goals and objectives. It discusses approaches for collecting, compiling, and reviewing facts and data to determine the enterprise-wide goals and objectives along with its corresponding benefits and challenges of the process. It also discusses the key points, benefits, approaches, and challenges of this process.

Chapter 6 discusses the political risk management process, identify stakeholders. It involves determining which people and organizations have an interest in and will be impacted by political risk management. It also discusses the key points, benefits, approaches, and challenges of this process.

Chapter 7 presents the political risk management process, prepare political risk management plan. It describes the content of the plan, which includes the procedures, tools, and techniques use when employing political risk management. It also discusses the key points, benefits, approaches, and challenges of this process.

Chapter 8 discusses the political risk management process, identify risks. It discusses and presents techniques for identifying political risks that can impact the global supply chain. It also discusses the key points, benefits, approaches, and challenges of this process.

Chapter 9 presents the political risk management process, assess risks. It discusses and presents techniques to determine the probability or likelihood of risks, their impacts, and, ultimately, their priorities. It presents two approaches to analyze risks, qualitative and quantitative risk analysis. It also discusses the key points, benefits, approaches, and challenges of this process.

Chapter 10 introduces the political risk management process, prepare risk responses. It discusses strategies and corresponding tactical actions to apply when responding threats and opportunities. It also discusses the key points, benefits, approaches, and challenges of this process.

Chapter 11 presents the political risk management process, perform risk controlling and monitoring. It discusses the techniques for determining the status of risks and the effectiveness of responses to them. It also discusses the key points, benefits, approaches, and challenges of this process.

Chapter 12 discusses the political risk management, perform risk reporting. It presents techniques for communicating status to stakeholders both at the detail and summary levels. It also discusses the key points, benefits, approaches, and challenges of this process.

Chapter 13 introduces the political risk management process, maintaining political risk management processes. It presents techniques for keeping the other process and the risk management plan current. It also discusses the key points, benefits, approaches, and challenges of this process.

Chapter 14 provides an overview of political risk management as described in this book. It also provides seven keys for its successful implementation as it relates to an enterprise's global supply chain.

The Appendix provides a case study is applied to demonstrate developing and implementing political risk management in a global enterprise. It shows what is required to succeed, the pitfalls to avoid, and the challenges to overcome.

Ignoring political risk management for a global enterprise can prove disastrous for its supply chain. Events can pop up just about anywhere around the globe, causing a supply chain to collapse like a row of dominoes, impacting an enterprise's profitability and even jeopardizing its very existence. Political risk management provides the necessary framework to increase its survivability.

Ralph L. Kliem PMP, CBCP

About the Author

Ralph L. Kliem, *PMP* (Project Management Professional) and *CBCP* (Certified Business Continuity Professional), is founder and president of LeanPM, LLC, and has over 30 years of combined experience in the private and public sectors as a project manager and internal auditor. He holds an M.A. in Political Science, a member of social, history, and political honor societies, a former legislative intern, and artillery officer. He retired from The Boeing Company where he conducted enterprise risk assessments and audits of its political action committee; evaluated lobbying activities; managed the development of business continuity plans for its major airplane programs; and taught professional seminars and workshops throughout the corporation and its clients, such as Ford, General Motors, Department of Defense, Internal Revenue Service, and other corporations and public institutions. He has authored more than 15 books with major publishers and over 300 articles for leading business and information technology magazines.

He is a frequent speaker at PMI chapters and other events. He has developed and delivered project management courses for Cascadia Community College and Bellevue College. He also delivers seminars and workshops for corporate clients through Key Consulting, Inc., and the Business Productivity Center, Inc. throughout the United States, Canada, and the Caribbean. He is an Instructor at City University of Seattle and a former adjunct faculty member with Seattle Pacific University.

His book publications include:

- *Business Continuity Planning* (CRC Press., ISBN: 978-1-4822-5178-4)
- *Creative, Efficient, and Effective Project Management* (Auerbach, ISBN: 9781466576926)
- *Effective Communications for Project Management* (Auerbach, ISBN: 978-1-4200-6246-5)
- *Ethics and Project Management* (Auerbach, ISBN: 978-1439852613)
- *Leading High Performance Projects* (J. Ross Publishing, ISBN: 1-932159-10-X)

- *Managing Lean Projects* (CRC Press, ISBN: 978-1-4822-5182-1)
- *Managing Projects in Trouble* (Auerbach, ISBN: 978-1-4398-5246-0)
- *Tools and Tips for Today's Project Manager* (Project Management Institute, ISBN 1-880410-61-3)

1

Politics and the Global Supply Chain

Global supply chains are operating in an unstable international environment. The relative predictability that has occurred over the last 70 years or so is disappearing. The solid alliances that the US once enjoyed are crumbling, disrupting and, in some cases, destroying the Pax Americana that enterprises enjoyed in the past. No longer can Fortune 500 or smaller firms assume that they can focus on making profits while ignoring political activities occurring in other countries. Enterprises treating politics as something to ignore in a remote region on the other side of the globe is simplistic, naïve, and even detrimental especially if it affects global supply chains transcending political boundaries. Whether an event impacts, for example, the supply chain like the COVID-19 pandemic or the airplane crashes of the 737 Max 8, politics gets involved. Both examples have shown that politics is inevitable and can disrupt global supply chains and often require, ironically, political action to mitigate the impacts.

STRANGE BED FELLOWS

Politics and global supply chains are, therefore, tightly interlinked. They are inseparable. Here are some other reasons why politics cannot be ignored.

Global supply chain thinking predicates itself on predictability. Just about any book on the supply chain in general emphasizes streamlining to increase efficiencies. The rational, logical thinking behind supply chain management seeks to reveal how well the supply chain operates to satisfy a customer by eliminating redundancies, waste, and rework. This understanding is completely rational and logical. However, the political environment often throws a curve seemingly out of nowhere, disrupting the supply chain. In other words, an unanticipated political decision often affects, for example, the rational mental model of a global supply chain; a political decision from a supply chain perspective can appear irrational. Better put: the rational mind meets the seemingly irrational, whimsical mind.

Somewhat connected to the last point, a supply chain emphasizes facts and data. Measurements are taken and metrics are accumulated to address topics like inventory levels, cycle times, etc. The idea is to reduce costs and increase efficiencies to address the needs of a customer. In politics, facts and data matter but there is a third factor that is often not considered: power. Power and politics are what facts and data are to the supply chain. Sometimes power and politics mix well with facts and data and the supply chain; frequently they do not. A government can make a policy decision that disrupts a global supply chain and increase inefficiencies and decrease customer satisfaction bewildering the most astute executive team of a global enterprise.

The supply chain model often looks for outliers, that is, anomalies which can upset its flow. Often, the anomaly is treated as waste and must be removed. Six Sigma or Lean thinking are two such examples that frequently looks askance at anomalies. Nothing wrong with that. From a supply chain perspective, it makes complete sense. The political environment can, however, introduce many outliers that seem to make no sense to the supply chain model. Public policies may require certain participants, e.g., manufacturers, in a supply chain, for example, to comply with regulations that appear to lack value but being noncompliant may result in facing penalties. Many outliers can arise seemingly out of nowhere from a government which can impact the efficiency and effectiveness of a global supply chain. However, outliers do not have to originate from a government. They can originate from organized groups that can present a significant challenge to a supply chain, such as environmental groups or other nongovernmental organizations.

The global supply chain often operates in a dynamic, unstable environment. Think about the impact of politics on a global level. Frequent conflicts arise in the Middle East, such as between Israel and some Arab states, or even among the Arab states themselves, e.g., Saudi Arabia and Yemen, or in central Asia, e.g., China and India. These conflicts are as much political as they are economic, perhaps more so. Other conflicts that are often viewed as economic also have a political flavor to them, such as tariff wars between the United States and China. Corruption within emerging countries can have an impact on developing nations, such as Russia, Ukraine, and the United States regarding global supply chains. All these and many other conflicts can have an impact on global supply chains, either directly or indirectly. The COVID-19 pandemic is an example whereby political tension between China and the United States impacts the latter's ability to have the supply chain provide personal protective equipment (PPE) and ventilators from the former.

Enterprises with global supply chains are being forced to reconcile with the political environment because they must. The power of nation states, regions, and global entities, such as the European Union and the United Nations, respectively, can make policy affecting global supply chains within a specific industry. Brexit, for example, cannot help but have, for better or worse, an impact on supply chains between Britain and continental Europe. Even on a nation-to-nation level, global supply chains can be impacted, positively or negatively. The political renegotiations over NAFTA among the United States, Canada, and Mexico impacted global supply chains; the renegotiations had a strong political tone to it, largely in part to satisfy populist movements.

Internationally, politics can play an important role on the efficiency and effectiveness of a global supply chain. Unfortunately, politics can often become a volatile discussion in a corporate environment, largely because these models are so different. The subject of politics in a corporation is often ignored because of the intense emotions that arise. Yet, politics exist, and it has a big influence on business enterprises and their global supply chains. That is why international companies must engage in political activities at the regional, national, and international levels. Ignoring this topic is to their detriment. Companies must become politically involved individually and through associations. The ones that do not will fail and face a roadblock on their way to success. Many companies, like Microsoft, had to eventually engage in the political arena to compete successfully. Companies, like Boeing, have and continue to recognize the importance of understanding the politics and realize the need to acknowledge the impact of politics on them. The success of global supply chains requires it. Unfortunately, when the subject of politics surfaces in conference rooms, emotions run high, ending in comments like "they are all crooks" or "they are only looking out for themselves." Such expressions only reveal a naivete about politics, and frustration with the subject.

SOME BASIC DEFINITIONS

Before addressing going any further on the topic of politics, a few terms need definition.

To many people, politics is often construed as something akin to a dirty word. Some people take a Machiavellian perspective of the subject while others simply view it as valueless. Regardless of one's perspective, the reality is that politics has always existed. Even inside today's corporate environment, politics exists. Little value exists in denying its existence.

So what is meant by politics? From the context of this book, politics is defined as the art and science of one or more political actors seeking, holding, or accumulating power to achieve tangible or intangible goals. A political actor can be an individual, business, government, nongovernmental organization (NGO), and international government organization (IGO) that can interact in a complex, nonlinear manner. Politics is, therefore, purpose-driven and power is the means to an end. Power is, in other words, the enabler to satisfy a desire. But exactly what is power? It is the capability or authority to execute actions to achieve some tangible or intangible goal or goals. A tangible goal might be allocating financial resources among different strata throughout the public or stop an action by people in the government from executing a specific policy. An intangible goal might impose a political or religious set of values on the general population. Regardless, a political actor exercises power to achieve a specific goal. A political actor might be an individual or group that holds formal or informal power. Formal power might be a regime ruling a government while an informal one could be a political actor representing a large portion of the population to prevent a government from adopting and executing a policy adverse to the public interests. The actual exercise of power by political actors is called political action, that is, behavior exhibited by an individual or group to influence or impose its will either upon segments or all of the public to achieve its goals either through cooperation or conflict with others.

Most businesses have a supply chain under the purview of a home government which is a set of authoritative institutions, e.g., executive, legislative, and administrative entities that have the authority and capacity to impose desired behaviors and values on the public. A supply chain consists of an integrated network of suppliers, manufacturers, warehouses, distribution centers, and retail outlets that either operate within the political jurisdiction or boundaries of a government or across several governments, necessitating compliance with laws, regulations, decrees, etc. of these public entities. These laws, regulations, decrees, etc. reflect values deemed important by a regime in power. Sometimes, a regime change can pose a risk to a supply chain because the rules and norms have changed dramatically. The risk posed may be positive or negative, meaning the former may present an opportunity or it may impose additional burdens when executing the supply chain. Risk in this context means a condition or event that introduces uncertainty, such as a sudden regime change in a developing country, e.g., Brazil, Russia, India, China (also grouped as BRIC) or a less developed country, such as Libya. These types of uncertainties pose what are known as political risks obviously due to their political nature.

Here are some different perspectives on what political risks are. Louis Wells, Jr. in *Managing International Political Risk* refers to political risks as: "Those risks that are principally the result of forces external to the industry and which involve some sort of government action or, occasionally, inaction."[1]

Condoleezza Rice and Amy Zegart in *Political Risk* describes it differently: "Put in its most elemental terms, twenty-first-century political risk is the probability that a political action could affect a company in significant ways."[2]

A political risk, therefore, is an event or condition that can negatively or positively affect a business investment and has some probability of occurrence.

Understanding political risk requires looking across a time continuum, as shown in Figure 1.1. It requires studying the past, understanding present, and anticipating the future.

Looking into the past, such as events, and attempting to understand their causes and impacts is important, especially by inquiring about the

FIGURE 1.1
The Continuum of Political Risks.

causes and the effects. Take the following example. What were the causes attributed to the expropriation of manufacturing plants in South America? What were the risks? What were the responses and how effective were they? In which country or countries did it occur? Who were the major political actors? When did the event occur? How long did the event last? Just as importantly, why did it occur? What were the short- and long-term impacts to doing business in these countries, especially from a global supply chain perspective?

Obtaining solid understanding of present events also requires asking questions. What are the important political issues concerning potential expropriation of manufacturing plants in one or more countries today in South America? What are the causes of the expropriation? What current events are occurring? When and for how long? What are the impacts to businesses operating there today, especially from a global supply chain perspective? Who are the significant political actors? What are the current issues? Are any political risk responses being implemented and, if so, how effective are they?

Looking into the future requires anticipating potential threats and opportunities and the trigger events that could reflect their existence. What could be the impact on businesses operating in one or more countries, especially from a global supply chain perspective? What does the future look like for manufacturing plants in South America? Who could be the major political actors? When could expropriation occur? What is the likelihood of it occurring? What could be the causes for the risks? How will the risks be managed?

Political risk management is, therefore, understanding context, accumulating facts and data, assessing situations, and responding effectively to political behavior in a manner that minimizes loss and maximizes gain. The whole idea is to have good situational awareness; that is, having knowledge and understanding of an environment, in this case the political environment, and avoid reacting to it in a way that is detrimental to the performance of an enterprise whether its supply chain occurs locally, e.g., within one country, or multiple countries in a global economy. In a global economy, the risks, more specifically the threats, to supply chains can be especially acute if an integrated network of processes transcends several governmental jurisdictions and interlinks with other businesses across the globe. Globalization adds a whole new level of complexity that augments the threats but can also provide opportunities to enhance a supply chain performance. The ability of a corporation to respond or recover from conditions or events is called resilience which involves applying the disciplines of risk management in general and political risk management in particular when identifying and responding to political events that affect operations and a supply chain. Through political risk management, companies do not have to feel they are simply victims of politics as is so often expressed in boardrooms and other venues. Strategic and operational leadership can enhance their political situational awareness by acquiring an understanding on how politics affects their enterprises and how to best adapt to the circumstances.

A simplistic view of political risk management might look like a Roman or Greek temple. The base of the temple is the enterprise. On top of the enterprise (base) are five pillars. The first pillar is probability or likelihood which is the chances of a political risk occurring. The second pillar is the impact of a political risk. The third pillar is the priority of a political risk relative to others. The fourth pillar is the response to manage a political risk. All four pillars support the roof of the temple, which represents a political risk management. If any of the pillars lack the strength necessary to protect uphold the roof, then the temple could collapse, smashing the base, or more.

UNIQUENESS OF POLITICS

So what makes politics so frustrating or difficult for people to understand or tolerate in the business world?

Politics often involves a high degree of uncertainty. Even governmental institutions dealing with foreign policy or intelligence have difficulty predicting what will happen in the world of politics. History is replete with examples of governments failing to predict a political event. The overthrow of the Shah of Iran is an example. No one predicted that the US embassy would be overtaken, let alone the Shah being exiled. No one anticipated the Arab Spring of 2010. No one predicted that it would start in Tunisia and work its way across northern Africa and into the Middle East. Or that the Egyptian president, Mubarak, would be removed and imprisoned. The point is that a political environment is enveloped in considerable uncertainty. Rarely is a government, business, or individual is going to have enough facts and data to anticipate political conditions or events; calculations or exercise or pure logic often fails in this regard. Enterprises seem to do no better.

Closely tied to the last point, facts and data are not always explicitly available or reliable. This situation does not mean understanding politics is hopeless. It just means research must that go beyond what is reported in papers and journals. It requires people on the ground who are familiar with a government, region, NGO, or IGO. Even then, facts and data may be unavailable. Sometimes available facts and data need additional investigation, such as about a guerrilla movement in a country or obtaining intelligence on a regime to ascertain the likelihood that a major event or condition could occur and affect a global supply chain. Nigeria is a perfect example where the foreign oil industry must maintain constant awareness of the activities of fundamentalist groups, like Boko Haram, which threatens their operations. Or the shipping industry must maintain awareness of pirate activity off the coast of Somalia. Such facts and data may not be explicitly or discrete enough to be of any value to act to protect a global supply chain from a political condition or event.

Political terminology makes it difficult to manage political risk due to the difficulty in defining it in the context of an environment and because of its abstractness. For example, people use terms like liberal and conservative from an American perspective when in another country the same terminology can mean something entirely different. Even using terms like "freedom" and "equality" may have different meanings from one country or culture to the next, let alone from one era to the next. Terminology is often used loosely to simplify understanding of what is going on as opposed to accounting situational nuances. Many Americans view Iranians, for example, as all being Arabic, not realizing that another substantial percentage of the population are Persians and Kurds. Throughout the Middle East, of course, the tension between the Sunni and the Shia has presented many challenges to keep supply chains open for the oil industry; many people naively lump both groups as Moslem fanatics.

Understanding politics is often skewed with biases and prejudices. For example, many people confuse being Arabic and Muslim as one in the same which is another incorrect assumption. Or people form visual stereotypes of other cultures which influences their interpretations of political conditions or events and decisions about what actions to pursue. Some people hold certain perceptions about Mexicans, Italians, or Israelis, for example, that may simplify interpretations of political events or conditions but could lead to miscalculations when responding to a situation. The anti-Chinese perceptions that prevailed over the COVID-19 pandemic have caused a strain between the United States and China which has affected directly or indirectly the supply chain for personal protective equipment, such as masks. Unfortunately, stereotyping prevails due to the simplicity it provides in handling complexity surrounding political situations.

Since facts and data are often tarnished or unavailable, politics often relies on intuition or instinct. Personal relationships among political leaders and business leaders are important. Facts and data may be too unreliable or the political circumstances so unstable, resulting in a lack of confidence when in decision-making. Yet, the "gut feel" may be the only reliable bellwether for decision makers of a global enterprise. Of course, a "left brain" culture within an enterprise will look askance at doing business this way; the truth is, however, that there will never be enough facts and data to make a final decision. That is a major reason why politics involves building relationships either through cooperation or conflict and involves as much intuition and instinct as it does facts and data. Successful companies often have a government affairs department that places a high priority on building relationships with political leaders across the globe, not just to improve sales, but also to ensure the supply chain continues to build and deliver a product. Aerospace, oil, and pharmaceutical companies have such departments with one of their goals being to maintain good relationships with political leaders.

Because politics involves considerable uncertainty, it is often an exercise in forecasting rather than predicting. Predictability is more useful when dealing with facts and data that are measurable. The relationship among datum is determinable with some degree of reliability and validity; both facts and data can be either time dependent or time independent. When it involves politics, political conditions or events may, of course, lend themselves to predictability, such as when a certain party or political movement has a strong probability of occurring, such as a ninety percent chance of occurrence, coming into power. Such circumstances lend itself to measurability. Forecasting is, however, much more difficult because facts and data are often vague or unreliable and the timeframe unknown, resulting in difficulty determining the likelihood of a condition or event existing. Often, forecasting involves using what are commonly known as warning signs, or signals, to indicate the possibility, not probability, of future conditions or events. Forecasting does not guarantee absolute assurance, only the potential to occur. An example of a forecast is the overthrow of Venezuelan regime, which many political experts have indicated would happen but has yet to occur as of this writing. In the case of Venezuela, warning signs might be violent protests, labor problems, etc.

Seemingly unrelated external factors can influence decisions or actions of political actors which could eventually affect an enterprise's global supply chain. External factors, such as a political decision in the United States can affect less developed countries by imposing tariffs to protect its domestic labor force. For example, the United States may impose a tariff on an Asian country, such as Vietnam, to protect textile workers in a certain region in the US. This could hurt the global supply chain for certain US companies that manufacture and distribute clothes from Vietnam. The reason may be simply due to foreign lobbying interests in the District of Columbia being not as strong as the ones countering the labor movement in the domestic textile industry. On a more global scale, an external factor might involve an IGO, such as the Security Council of the United Nations, deciding to enforce a boycott against a certain country which, in turn, impacts the global supply chains of enterprises. The difficulty with external political factors is their impact on global supply chains can go undetected for a substantial time. For example, the oil war between Russia and Saudi Arabia in 2020 has caused a dramatic drop in the price of a barrel of oil which also affected the United States oil market. The impact on the global supply chain of the petroleum industry, from a US perspective, was unanticipated, resulting in political as well as economic consequences; less developed countries that depend on oil for revenue had negative financial and political impacts. Essentially, external political decisions and actions are difficult to manage. They are likened, in many cases, as the butterfly effect in Chaos Theory, whereby a small change in a nonlinear system can have a large impact somewhere else.

Politics, due to its nonlinearity, can become complex as the number of political actors become involved. For example, politics is easier to understand when two political actors are analyzed to determine political risk than when three or more actors get reviewed. The complexity is likened to the three-body problem in physics. According to the three-body problem, predictability becomes much more difficult to understand, analyze, and predict results (usually producing an approximate solution) when three or more physical bodies are involved; the relationship among all three bodies becomes more complex and nonlinear as opposed to the relationship between two of them. In politics, the same situation occurs. When the leaders of the United States and North Korea met, the relationship, despite the disagreements between both, appeared manageable despite speculations. However, mixing China, South Korea, and Japan into the equation increased the complexity of the meetings, such as raising questions whether North Korea was negotiating as a proxy for China or acting independently. Tensions increased in the region, causing political strains among South Korea, China, Japan, and United States. The results have become an approximate position regarding the relationship between the United States and North Korea. For a while, the global supply chains from South Korea was a concern due to fear of war resulting from missile fires by North Korea. Hence, the more political actors became involved, the greater the chances the situation became increasingly complex and potentially dangerous.

The existence and impact of politics may not be readily apparent. The decisions or actions of political actors may not be known, especially if facts and data are vague or non-existent. A prime example, of course, is the risks associated with the leadership of North Korea even with US intelligence. Or take the relationship with China. During the COVID-19 crisis, questions arose over the cause of the virus and the number of people affected. Even a question arose whether China defeated the virus. The same applies to companies doing business in China as it relates to the global supply chains. The lack of openness of the Chinese government and the facts and data about the performance of its economy puts many enterprises ill-at-ease since it manufactures many components used by western countries. Due to the lack of reliable facts and data, countries and enterprises alike often must second guess the purpose of the Chinese regime's policies and their effect on the global supply chains and even the world economy. Again, the COVID-19 pandemic is a perfect example over whether the Chinese could recover enough to provide personal protective equipment, such as masks. The previous and current "tariff wars" between the United States and China have led to questions over the risks that may be realized among different industries within the US, e.g., aerospace or agriculture sectors.

Politics is often not an island onto itself. Politics is also interlinked with economics and sociology. Their relationships overlap. If political actors make a decision, they can also affect the performance of an economy and have sociological consequences. For example, Congress in the United States may decide to pass strict regulations on fracking (the forcing of pressurized liquid into the ground to force oil or gas to come to the surface). These regulations can significantly impact the oil industry's supply chain as well as cause unemployment to rise which, in turn, adds to social problems, e.g., drug and alcohol abuse. Economic and sociological problems can also cause political problems, too. The economy of a country can collapse and create many social problems, such as severe unemployment, and cause political upheaval, thereby threatening the stability of the current regime in power. The Arab Spring served as an example whereby poor economic performance and huge unemployment among educated youth, resulting in political upheaval in Egypt and the removal of Hosni Mubarak.

Politics poses yet another challenge: distinguishing between causal and dependent variables. This challenge exists due to a lack of reliable and valid facts and data that exists in a political environment as well as the abstruse nature of political definitions. Relationships among the variables, while not always impossible to distinguish between both types of variables, require considerable vigor to ascertain which one is the cause and which one is the effect. For example, is political instability in a government the cause of rebellion in the outlying areas of a country or is it the other way around, such as between the Colombian government or FARC (Armadas Revolucionarias de Colombia)? Is an unpopular government due to poor efficacy by the public or the other way around? The point is that unlike other disciplines, such as in economics, it is sometimes very hard to determine, analyze, and manage risks when the variables and their relationships are hard to distinguish between which ones are causal and which are the dependent ones with any reasonable confidence.

Politics often makes it difficult to test assumptions. Politics requires making many assumptions about a political environment, such as within a country, throughout a region, or even across the globe. These assumptions are often considered real until proven otherwise. Politics often requires developing assumptions about the present and future based upon what has occurred in the past. For example, a company assumes that a current regime or political system will remain stable for a substantial time based upon its history, expecting one of its manufacturing operations will be ongoing for a considerable time. However, a series of events may suddenly arise that find the political situation deteriorating in the country as a radical opposition party has an unexpected electoral victory which could result in kicking out foreign manufacturing operations. Obviously, the assumptions under this circumstance need revisiting. Or take another example. Manufacturers in China building technical products eventually land on US retail counters. The US then threatens to impose higher tariffs. The Chinese, in retaliation for anti-Chinese actions by the United States, decides to restrict imports of agricultural goods, such as soybeans. This sudden change in events requires making different political assumptions about future trade relationships between the United States and China. Some new assumptions might require asking: Will trade resume? Will the new trade relationship negatively impact the US economy? Or will the relationship return to normal? These and other assumptions and questions will likely change depending on the context of the political situation. Facts and data from a political perspective may be unavailable or unreliable since the relationship involves two different political systems may change.

In many disciplines, such as science, an assumption about the world is testable to determine whether accurate; data can be verified in a way that proves or disproves the assumption. In economics, testing an assumption is usually easier because facts and data are often tangible. In politics, as just discussed, that is not often the case. In politics, the testing of an assumption occurs when a condition or event occurs. While governments occasionally test each other, a slight miscalculation can have cataclysmic results. For example, the Russians often test American naval presence in the Black Sea. Or Russia sends a Bear bomber into the US airspace in Alaska to test American resolve to protect itself; the US sends a scramble of F-22 jet fighters to intercept the bomber. Businesses, rarely if ever, often do not have that opportunity to test assumptions about a regime. They can only plan for some potential condition or event and respond according to contingency plans to deal with such a potential eventuality.

Politics is a mixture of qualitative and quantitative facts and data. Qualitative facts and data are frequently anecdotal and historical coupled with intelligence from governments and other political actors; realistically, it is often part fact, part interpretation, and even part fiction being mixed with bias and misinformation. Quantitative facts and data are proven either by previous studies, such as political science studies at universities, governments, and think tanks, having a high confidence level of being reliable and valid; ideally, the facts and data are devoid of bias unless, of course, the studies are skewed purposely in a certain way to further some policy. An example of purposely skewing qualitative facts and data might include a study by a think tank subscribing to a "liberal" or "conservative" ideology. Ideological bias might influence the results, that is, by interpreting and presenting facts and data a certain way. An example of quantitative facts and data might include a study by a reputable think tank that looks at the relationship between political efficacy and demographics; the study will likely be devoid of ideological influence. Businesses when performing political analysis should rely on both qualitative and quantitative facts and data.

When conducting political analysis, businesses find it difficult to ascertain what motivates leaders in a political environment. Most political actors are multi-faceted, meaning they may have many reasons to seek or remain in power. In other words, businesses often have difficulty determining what makes political actors tick. Are they motivated only for self-aggrandizement? Power? Money? Historical greatness? Ideological purity? Many reasons exist for why a political actor seeks or seizes a significant position within a government, NGO, or IGO. Businesses assume political actors operate on what they perceive as a rational basis, often seeing as something akin to game theory whereby making choices among competitors that maximizes payoff relative to the others. However, not all political actors make such rational decisions; they may be motivated by something other than pure material payoff. The motivation of a political actor may be the result of a previous experience with a company, such as in Cuba where Fidel Castro expropriated the holdings of the United Fruit Company or other actions by political leaders in Latin American countries, e.g., Colombia and Guatemala. Not all political leaders act rationally from an economic perspective as is often presumed when enterprises perform political analysis.

Game theory presumes that people are motivated by self-interest which in politics may not necessarily be the case. Ideologies and political retributions are just two examples of motivations of political actors can go beyond self-interest. Such perspectives of political actors may appear irrational to economists and business professionals who subscribe to the perspective or paradigm of a Paul Samuelson or Milton Friedman.

Ultimately, the biggest challenge to understanding political motivation is the nature of a business the leadership occupying it. Observes Theodore Moran in *Managing International Political Risk*: "Contemporary managers...may be less well prepared to deal with political risks than their predecessors of two decades ago...Many of these managers...come from the ranks of deal makers whose business depend upon closing international investment negotiations successfully in the present rather than worrying about changes that may not emerge for a number of years in the future."[3]

Although simplistic in theory, one way to understand the degree of uncertainty when trying to ascertain the motivation of political actors is to consider the distinction between stimulus-response and stimulus-organism-response. Stimulus-response takes the perspective that an individual, for example, reacts to its environment in a predictable, causal way to a stimulus, such as a physical one. Stimulus-organism-response recognizes that an individual responds in a less than predictable manner which is largely psychological in nature; it involves an individual's interaction with the environment based upon how she or he views the world. The distinction helps in understanding the variability of human response to environmental stimulus as opposed to just reacting to it.

For many enterprises, dealing with a host country's government can be the most difficult, simply because it is a political institution. Like all political institutions, its behaviors and actions reflect those of the people who occupy its leadership positions and run it. However, understanding government is not that easy. Its dynamics when dealing with its environment make predicting current and future behaviors difficult due to the wide range of internal and external influences affecting it.

THE DRIVERS FOR POLITICAL RISK MANAGEMENT

What are the drivers that enterprises want to understand and manage political risks?

Globalization is a major driver and with that sometimes comes an unstable global supply chain. The world, as mentioned earlier, is no longer bipolar world but a multipolar whereby several countries have risen in power to challenge the dominance of the United States. Despite the United States being still the premier military and economic power (albeit some people say it is declining), it now faces growing challenges from other countries, such as Russia and China, across the globe. Russia, as it once did under the Soviet Union, has a lurking presence in the European arena while China has grown in stature in Asia, Africa, and the Middle East. The collapse of communism in the USSR and its transformation in China has now enabled these two countries to rise in international stature that 30 years ago people never thought possible. Other countries are growing as well in terms of political, economic, and military power, such as India in central Asia and Brazil in South America. The impacts to global supply chains are immense. Enterprises with supply chains that cut across multiple countries can face significant distribution challenges. For instance, the oil war between Saudi Arabia and Russia had upset the supply chain of the major oil companies, causing their stocks and overall performance to decline. The COVID-19 event of 2020 had shown the stresses to the global supply chain for PPE that hindered the US ability to recover from the pandemic. China, being a key manufacturer of PPE, especially the components of ventilators and medicines, has hindered enterprises' ability to adapt to the stresses of the circumstance as the political and economic relationship between the United States and that country have become strained.

The rise of nationalism is a driver of the need for political risk management. As less developed countries grow economically and politically, they have become more assertive in their regions, such as Myanmar in Southeast Asia, Pakistan in Central Asia, and Iran in the Middle East. Adding to this challenge doing business with less developing countries is their political instability as they go through a transition economically, politically, and socially. Sri Lanka has experienced intense fighting between Hindus and Muslims as well as within Turkey between Kurds and Muslims. Internal instability can lead to aggressive behavior between neighboring countries, such as between Pakistan and India or Iran and Saudi Arabia. Under these circumstances, despite the price of cheap labor relative to a developed country, such as the United States or Great Britain, it is difficult to establish and execute a global supply chain. Within the United States, a growing nationalist movement has arisen that threatens to rise tariffs against countries perceived as being treated unfairly has impacted supply chains north and south of its border. Outsourcing, for example, has become an emotional rallying cry to protect jobs in the United States. However, the United States is not the only country experiencing such nationalism; countries in Europe, such as Great Britain adopting and executing Brexit or continental European countries, such as Sweden, insisting on having their own currency rather than adopting the Euro.

Related to the rise of nationalism is the movement toward greater democratization or populism in many countries, whether in a developed or less developed country. The Arab Spring is perhaps the most pertinent example of the cry for greater democratization, whereby particularly virulent political movements and risen in nations like Tunisia and Egypt. The Arab Spring had become a fight between authoritarian leadership and forces seeking greater democratization within the countries of north Africa and the Middle East. However, currently only Tunisia has become a constitutional democracy while the Muslim fundamentalists have taken the reign of power in other countries or caused continuing instability, such as in Libya and Syria. Political instability has not only been a problem in the Middle East but also in Africa where many groups exist which challenge the stability of a government from an even more violent perspective, such as Boko Haram in Nigeria, and the spread of Al-Shabaab in Somalia, Kenya, and Uganda. Even developed countries in Europe and the United States have experienced the rise of greater democratization or a virulent form of populism which has the potential to impact a global supply chain, such as the National Rally in France and the League in Italy. Anger is often directed toward "elites" both in the government and throughout the economy which can lead to greater tariffs and regulations impacting business transactions as well as greater regulatory oversight. Business must be aware of such situations to survive economically in such environments.

Demographics are a driver. In some countries, a population is getting older, such as in Japan; in others, the population is becoming younger, such as in many Arab countries. Demographics can have a considerable impact on the politics of a nation; aging of a population can have economic and social as well as political consequences. Countries with an older population require greater social services and tend to support the status quo; countries with younger populations tend to experience more political instability, especially with high youth unemployment. In the former, the younger people often assume a financial burden to support an older population and, if coming from the middle and upper classes, tend to challenge the status quo. The United States experienced this during the tumultuous 1960s. Revolutionaries in the United States and in Europe, such as the Baader–Meinhof Gang, and the Red Brigades in Italy, were middle- and upper-class youths. Even in Africa and Asia, some of the more radical groups are primarily young, such as Al-Qaeda in the Islamic Maghreb and the Moro National Liberation Front (MNLF) in the Philippines, respectively. Many of these groups are vying for power in their country or region against other groups. Businesses need to know about their existence of such groups to determine the impacts on their trade and foreign direct investments (FDI) in these countries as well as on their global supply chain.

Corruption can be either explicit or implicit, such as bribery, is a driver. Corruption can occur involving employees operating in a foreign country or even in an enterprise's host country. Regardless of source, corruption can cause problems for an enterprise. It can tarnish an enterprise's reputation and become entangled in the internal politics of another country, face fines, expropriation, or other threats. It can also get an enterprise in trouble with its host country, such as the United States, if it violates the Foreign Corrupt Practices Act (FCPA). While corruption is quite prevalent in less developing countries, such as in Africa, by no means do they have a monopoly on it. Countries in Europe, such as Airbus bribery incidents in the United Kingdom and France, and Boeing within the United States, can prove disastrous to the reputation of an enterprise. Corruption imperils an enterprise in other ways, too, such as leading to inefficiencies in operations and the global supply chain.

Wealth distribution is a driver. It can potentially have a big impact on business performance, especially the supply chain. If the wealth gap is wide, that is, the disparity between the rich and poor, the purchasing power of a population will be less than under a more equitable distribution of wealth. Countries with wide disparities of wealth tend to experience political instability, especially if it depends on few resources for export while the global economy slows. Companies invested in those countries often become a target for political violence or nationalization especially if that country is viewed as "representative" of its home country. A prime example is the many US oil companies operating in Venezuela; most of these companies currently comply with US sanctions but have become political targets of successive ruling regimes in that country. Poverty and the poor distribution of wealth have contributed, to violence and unstable business environment, raising the prospect of some companies facing severe political risk. Naturally, managing political risks is an effective tool that businesses can use to identify political risks and develop appropriate responses should they arise. Some companies have successfully sought or had alternative sources of oil to lessen the impact to their supply chain.

Domestic issues having international consequences is a driver. Regulatory decisions made by political leaders in the United States, for example, can significantly impact an enterprise's global supply chain. Regulations by the Department of Commerce, such as the Export Administration Regulations (EAR), Department of State's International Traffic in Arms Regulations (ITAR), and the Treasury Department's Office of Foreign Assets (OFAC) are three examples whereby domestic regulations can impact an enterprise's complex supply chain. Regulations can also come from other countries and regions which can affect a global supply chain. Europe has stringent frameworks that require financial compliance, such as Basel, to strengthen rules regarding global capital and liquidity of financial institutions to avoid situations like the 2007–2008 financial crash. The European Union (EU) has also passed regulations on data privacy and security by placing stringent controls via the General Data

Protection Regulation (GDPR). The GDPR affects information technology intensive companies, such as Google and Facebook. The lesson is that companies can be affected by their home and host countries and, therefore, need to assess the political risks that impact their supply chains.

Technology is a driver. Companies, domestic or international, increasingly rely on the Internet to conduct business. While it plays a significant role on operations and the global supply chain, it may be vulnerable to cyberattacks. Attacks can come from other governments or political groups. Some governments are well known to conduct cyberattacks against other companies, such as North Korea against SONY and Russian cyberattacks, such as against JPMorgan Chase. Even the French government is known to perform "cyber spying." Generally, such attacks seek privacy and financial information as well as crash a system. Not just governments get involved in cyberattacks; so do private groups with political motives, such as Anonymous, which has attacked governments and businesses alike, such as Airplex Software (an Indian firm). Attacks by government and private groups can have devastating effects on global supply chains of enterprises. Being aware of the risks and mitigation strategies, coupled with information technological security can go a long way to protect and recover from a cyberattack.

Immigration is a major driver. Currently, it is a volatile topic that can have profound consequences for an enterprise and its global supply chain. Illegal immigration from Mexico into the United States is an example. The topic has become very politicized to the extent that it has strained trade relations between both countries. Although the United States and Mexico have recently renegotiated the North American Free Trade Agreement (NAFTA) with Mexico (and Canada), the relationship between the two countries remains strained over immigration and has affected the other issues. The United States continues to rebuild and extend a wall demarcating the boundaries between the countries; it also threatens and, in many cases, has returned aliens to Mexico and central American nations. The United States, however, is not the only country raising the immigration issue. Many European countries, too, have done so, to include Italy, Hungary, and France. Some European nations perceive North African and Middle Eastern immigrants as threatening to take jobs and as well as drain resources to the extent that it increases the debt burden of these countries. Democracies, such as Italy and Hungary, are slowly moving toward authoritarianism with immigration providing a political lever to advance certain political interests. Anti-immigration can encourage xenophobic behavior in regimes that may impact foreign business operations, and the corresponding global supply chains, especially if enterprises hire immigrants as a substitute for native workers.

Many more drivers exist, especially now in a multipolar world where many nations compete economically and politically. Some other salient ones include pandemics, rare earth minerals, international capital, intellectual property, space exploration, information, democratization, climate change, technology, demographics, terrorism, energy, and immigration. All these drivers are regional or global in scope and involve many of the 180-plus countries to one degree or another. Just as importantly, they have as much political implications as they do economic and social. Take climate change. Putting aside all the controversy about the topic, climate change has real political consequences across the globe. Some companies find they must operate in some countries according to carbon free regulations, such as ones in Europe, while in others the regulations are weak or nonexistent, such as in less developed countries. Reinsurance companies, such as Munich Re and Swiss Re, recognize the impact of climate change on their ability to serve their clients. A global enterprise may find itself in political trouble because one element of its global their supply chain, such as in the extractive industries, is not complying with certain environmental regulations. Democratization can serve as a driver. It is increasing in developing and less developed countries, such as the Middle East, resulting in a political "contagion" effect elsewhere, impacting, even threatening, the efficiency and effectiveness of a global supply chain.

GOALS OF POLITICAL RISK MANAGEMENT

Political risk management is a framework that can help manage the complexities of politics that face global supply chains. But just what does political risk management hope to achieve for a global enterprise?

The most important goal is, of course, to enable a global enterprise to have a profitable rate of return from their supply chains. Naturally, enterprises want to have a profitable relationship with the countries affecting global supply chains by avoiding retaliatory actions like expropriation or exchange rate manipulation. Other goals exist, too, besides making a profit.

Having a sustainable global supply chain. Some investments in a few countries are short term while others, like capital investments, are long-term. Heavy investments related to construction or manufacturing often require a long-term commitment to realize a gain. Enterprises in these and other industries will not likely find themselves profitable if they disregard political risks impacting an element in their global supply chain. These seek to anticipate and respond accordingly to any threats that arise. They may also want to seize any opportunities, too.

Avoiding or responding to a public relations disaster, especially one with political consequences. A major disaster, such as the Bhopal disaster in 1984 where Union Carbide India Limited had a pesticide accident that injured hundreds of thousands of people and killed thousands, was both a reputational and health disaster, resulting in severe political consequences with the Indian government. The 2010 Deepwater Horizon spill in the Gulf of Mexico created a political firestorm, too, for British Petroleum, Transocean, and Halliburton. The plane crashes of the Boeing 737 Max 8 which was a reputational disaster and resulted in severe political consequences between governmental institutions and the company.

Having the ability to assess, minimize the impact of, and respond to a threat. Unfortunately, many enterprises do risk assessments thinking about economics but fail to pay attention to the political consequences of an event and are unable to respond to them. They consider the technical and financial impacts, but few recognize the political ones. Instead, they react to a condition or event and then find themselves on the defensive, either with governmental or other political institutions. For example, during the first term of the Trump administration, many companies involved in the agricultural supply chain, especially in respect to the soybean industry, did not anticipate the impact the tariff conflict between the United States and China. Many agribusinesses and small farmers found themselves unprepared for such an event and how to respond to it. The Administration ended up providing financial assistance to the industry while other countries filled the void in the supply chain.

Determining political consequences of nonpolitical events. These nonpolitical events include earthquakes, pandemics, hurricanes, tornados, and plane crashes to name a few. Frequently, companies do not think about the political consequences of such events. Again, take the COVID-19 pandemic. Many pharmaceutical companies discovered that their supply chains were heavily dependent on China to deliver not just PPE but also medicine. Many American citizens could not understand how the

United States had become dependent on another country, China, for medicines like ibuprofen, hydrocortisone, and acetaminophen. One company, 3M, as a result of a shortage of respirator masks, found itself in political trouble from the presidency of the United States due to its supply chain sending masks out of the US, e.g., to Latin America, during a time of shortage.

FINAL THOUGHTS

Political risks are different from many other kinds of risks, most of all being mercurial in nature. The topic of politics is riddled with a high degree of ambiguity and uncertainty. Facts and data are often scarce and of questionable validity and reliability, making it difficult to determine the impacts on enterprises' global supply chains. Yet, it is not impossible to manage if enterprises take a systemic and systematic approach by applying political risk management.

GETTING STARTED QUESTIONS

Questions	Yes	No
1. Have you thought about how political risks and events have or may have impacted your global supply chain?		
2. Have you identified the major assets of your enterprises global supply chain? The assets' locations across the globe? Which locations present the biggest challenges in terms of political risks and events?		
3. What has been the history of your enterprise when dealing with political risks and events?		
4. What are some of the major political risks and events in the recent past that have impacted the global supply chain? What was their impacts? How effectively were they handled?		
5. What are some major drivers for political risk management in your enterprise?		
6. What are the major goals of political risk management in your enterprise as they relate to the global supply chain?		

NOTES

1. Louis T. Wells, "God and Fair Competition: Does the Foreign Direct Investor Face Still Other Risks in Emerging Markets?" in *Managing International Political Risk*, ed. Theodore H. Moran (Oxford: Blackwell Business1998), 15.
2. Condoleezza Rice and Amy B. Zegart, *Political Risk* (New York: Twelve, 2018), 5.
3. Theodore H. Moran in "The Changing Nature of Political Risk, in *Managing International Political Risk*, ed. Theodore H. Moran (Oxford: Blackwell Publishers, 1998), 8.

2

Global Supply Chain and the Rise of Globalization

The global economic environment is highly integrated and interdependent. Nation states can no longer, contrary to the cries of some politicians, operate independently even if they wanted to do so. Pandemics alone have proven that. So is the case with supply chains, regardless of industry. Supply chains have turned into an intricate weave across the world, from the point of extraction to the delivery of a product to a customer, thanks largely to the rise of globalization. A disruption of an enterprise's global supply chain on one side of the world can have a cascading effect on the other.

SUPPLY CHAIN: AN OVERVIEW

One cannot discuss globalization without an understanding of the basics of a supply chain; the two are intrinsically interconnected.

As with globalization, definitions of supply chains vary.

David Simchi-Levi, Philip Kaminsky, and Edith Simchi-Levi in *Managing the Supply Chain* define "the supply chain...consists of suppliers, manufacturing centers, warehouses, distribution centers, and retail outlets, as well as raw materials, work-in-progress inventory, and finished products that flow between the facilities."[1]

Donald Bowersox, David Closs, and M. Bixby Cooper in *Supply Chain Logistics Management* take a broader perspective by subsuming supply chain under supply chain management which "consists of firms collaborating to leverage strategic positioning and to improve operating efficiency. For each firm involved, the supply chain relationship reflects a strategic choice."[2]

David Blanchard in *Supply Chain Management* provides this definition of a supply chain: "A supply chain, boiled down to its basic elements, is the sequence of events and processes that take a product from dirt to dirt…It encompasses a series of activities that people have engaged since the dawn of commerce…extends from the ultimate supplier or source…to the ultimate customer."[3]

A supply chain consists, therefore, of an interconnected set of assets, or elements. From a generic standpoint this means a supply chain consists of these assets: suppliers, manufacturers, warehouses, distribution centers, customers, raw materials, inventory, and finished products. The process of producing and delivering a product to a customer generally flows in this manner: raw materials are procured to incorporate into components. The components are then shipped to one or more warehouses. The components are eventually shipped to a final assembly facility. From the final assembly, the product is shipped to the customer. The supply chain involves a host of business processes to include network planning, inventory control, supplier management, distribution, and product design. In the end, the goal is to deliver a product that meets the requirements of a customer.

An important point is needed to make here. The categories of the assets of a supply chain consist of elemental assets, or sub-assets, that comprise them. An example of a sub-asset is a warehouse. It can consist of some or all these elemental assets:

- Data
- Equipment
- Information systems
- Knowledge
- Materials
- People
- Subproducts
- Supplies

These elemental assets contribute to the value of an asset in a global supply chain. Indeed, their failure to add value may impact the performance of an asset, such as a warehouse, which, in turn, impacts a global supply chain.

Ideally, a supply chain operates efficiently and effectively. To do so requires that all parties be integrated and interdependent throughout a supply chain, resulting in delivery that satisfies a customer. Realistically, a supply chain rarely operates efficiently and effectively. An asset of a global supply chain may fail to perform for many reasons. It may be late in developing and delivering a component due to labor unrest, for example, which can affect a supply chain downstream. Or materials may be unavailable due to international tensions making it difficult to obtain access to raw material. Regardless, a supply chain can experience many problems, some controllable, others not. Some examples of problems include late shipments of raw materials, poor communications, substandard product quality, and part shortages at warehouses. Many issues contribute to problems, such as marrying supply and demand as well as synchronizing transportation times between manufacturers and warehouses.

Many of the problems just mentioned result from the inherent complexity and uncertainty that exists in a supply chain. Something can easily go awry affecting the integration and independence of a supply chain, especially as the number of assets and the flows become more complex in a global supply chain. The combination of uncertainty and complexity makes running an efficient and effective global supply chain increasingly difficult. The chances of something going awry increases and so does its impact to a global enterprise. If an enterprise fails to prepare itself to deal with this uncertainty and complexity risk increases and so do the challenges.

Adding to the complexity and uncertainty are the quality movements that have occurred over the years. Total Quality Management, Lean, Just-in-Time, and Kanban may have streamlined and tightened the supply chain. While these focused on satisfying the customer by eliminating waste, increasing standardization, reducing cycle time, lowering inventories and other gains, the ultimate effect has been "tightening" a global supply chain. When one asset of a supply chain fails to perform, circumstances can result in exceeding lead times, causing miscommunication, or creating a bull whip effect. These and other impacts to a global supply chain and an enterprise can range from minimum to maximum consequences, depending on the magnitude of a failure.

Today, a key enabler to an efficient and effective supply chain is information. Thanks to rise of information technology, which includes both hardware and software, all the assets of a global supply chain can access and share information about their respective activities. The parties at each point of the global supply chain can provide the necessary information regarding status, from procuring raw material to delivering a product to a customer. The technology has enabled sharing information in a manner that allows for advanced exchanges of facts and data. In developed countries, at least, business-to-business (B2B) and business-to-consumer (B2C) are something taken for granted. However, such is not the case in many developing and less developed countries where standards differ from one another and the supporting infrastructure is not robust, even nonexistent.

Facts and data can provide a strategic perspective regarding the layout of a supply chain, such as, technical aspects like purchasing and transportation decisions; or operational activities, like scheduling deliveries and loads for vehicles. Much of facts and data, of course, is very left-brain dominant to use a crude dichotomy. The facts and data are highly tangible and discrete. Mathematical formulas can be applied to help forecast regarding required lot sizes at warehouses, lead times, etc. to produce an optimized supply chain. Often, developing an optimized supply chain requires making tradeoffs, such as cost vs. customer service or lot vs. inventory. Such calculations are necessary and allow forecasting with some reliability, despite some variability in the calculated results, and can even use simulations to achieve optimization.

As a supply chain expands globally, an enterprise will likely have to form strategic alliances with other private and public entities to create and deliver a product to its customer base. Assuming an enterprise has identified its strengths and core competencies, it can go on to form relationships that can capitalize on their strengths. These strategic alliances can perform all or part of an enterprise's global supply chain processes either on a short- or long-term basis. Outsourcing is one approach which recently in the United States has come under fire. Alliances offer several advantages, to include capitalizing on one another's strengths and compensating for weaknesses, taking advantage of economies of scale, and pooling risks. Alliances also pose several potential disadvantages, to include loss of control and fractured relationship as well as a partner eventually becoming a competitor.

Product modularity has been a significant enabler of the global supply chain. Components, thanks to process and product standards adopted throughout an enterprise's supply chain, can be produced in different countries, and then shipped to subassembly and assembly facilities prior to delivery to the customer. Components from one country can be mixed and matched with components from another country and so on to form a final product, thanks to standard interfaces. The configuration of the components can also be changed to meet customer needs. No longer does the phrase the "customer can have whatever he wants as long as its black" apply. Additionally, product costs decrease by reducing overhead and material costs as well as increase delivery to the customer.

In addition to product modularity and standardization is the rise of the process standardization and modularity. Thanks in part to international standards organizations; alliances among multinational corporations; and maturity models, global supply chains, in theory, can operate more efficiently and effectively. All parties across a global supply chain can communicate easier with one another, resolve conflict more easily, provide technical expertise, and share resources by adopting common standards. Additionally, process costs decrease by reducing operational complexity and redundancy as well as increase delivery to the customer. Naturally, cultural, language, and historical differences will add complexity to relationships throughout a global supply chain.

The combination of standardization and modularity of products and processes has led to an interesting supply chain philosophy that has been adopted throughout several industries. Mass customization has become popular in the last decade or so. It is essentially a mixture of craft production and mass production, allowing the ability to change the configuration of a product to meet unique customer requirements quickly, efficiently, and effectively. Additional features and functions are added to components or the final product based upon customer requirements.

All this progress may have facilitated establishing new supply chain arrangements like the ones identified by David Simchi-Levi, Philip Kaminsky, and Edith Simchi-Levi in *Managing the Supply Chain*[4]

- Manufacturing is domestic; however, other functions, such as distribution occurs outside the host country.
- Materials and components procured from suppliers outside the host country; however, assembly occurs in the host country.
- The product is procured and manufactured outside the host country in one country; however, both are shipped to a warehouse in the host cost country for eventual sale and distribution.
- The product is the result of a fully integrated supply chain spanning the globe.

The authors take a slightly different perspective on the causes of the new arrangements. These four arrangements according the authors are the result of four forces. The first are global market forces, such as the presence of foreign enterprises in the market and similar products wanted across the globe. The second are the technological forces, such as the availability of specific technical expertise across the globe and the ability to obtain resources quickly. The third force is global cost forces, such as inexpensive labor located across the globe. The fourth is the political and economic forces, such as regional trade agreements and government support for or against trade. All four forces interplay with one another; none of them are mutually exclusive. For the most part, global market, technological, and global cost forces are easier to understand than the political and economic forces as they apply to the global supply chain. This does not mean they are easier subjects to comprehend; quite the contrary. All four forces are a challenge to understand but the predictability and forecasting of the political and economic forces are more unstable and less tangible as applied to the global supply chain. For example, one can with greater confidence determine the impact of higher prices of raw materials and labor costs on the end product or see the tangible benefits of technology on the performance parties involved in the supply chain or the impact, for example, of declining global market share of a multinational company. However, it is much more nebulous to determine the political impact of a military coup d'etat in a country that provides a crucial component for an airliner being built in a less developed country.

Ila Manuj and John Mentzer in the *International Journal of Physical Distribution and Logistics Management* identifies four categories of global supply chain risks: supply, operational, demand, and security.[5]

Supply risks pertain to inbound supplies coming into a global enterprise can impact an enterprise's ability to meet customer requirements. Operational risks affect the internal performance of an enterprise to produce goods and provide services which can ultimately affect its profitability. Demand risks relate to outbound flows to satisfy customer requirements. Security risks pertain to ones concerning personnel, information systems, and other functional responsibilities of an enterprise.

These categories of risks simply reflect one way of carving up a global supply chain. Unfortunately, they typically reflect a narrow economic perspective. The reality is that there is another category of risks that are often ignored – political risks. In fact, one could argue that a political risk can be a primary risk and causes the other risks to become secondary risks. By the same token, one of the four risks can be the primary risk and a political risk to become a secondary one. Manuj and Mentzer mention the "interconnectedness" among the four risks but the same occurs with political risks with them. The point is that political risk is not an isolated phenomenon with economics.

Regardless of the arrangement, a global supply chain faces many risks. The interplay of a multiple categories of risks, from customers, suppliers to competitors to technology to government adds a high level of complexity and uncertainty. Direct and indirect actions by parties on a national, regional, and international level can present a host of risks to a global enterprise. Customers purchasing power can decrease due to ravaging inflation, eating away their purchasing power which can reduce the demand for an enterprise's product. Suppliers of a raw material confiscated by a government can force a price rise that could impact profitability of an enterprise. A foreign source of cheap labor may no longer be available due to a pandemic, causing a delivery delays of medical supplies in an enterprise's global supply chain. A government facing xenophobic fervor among its citizens has no choice but to impose tariffs against or taxes on foreign entities, again hurting an enterprise's profitability.

Depending upon the circumstance, the impact of each risk can cripple a global supply chain. Some risks are easier to detect than others. Many risks are easier to detect than others when they occur to include ones that related to natural disasters (e.g., earthquakes), pricing (e.g., exchange rate fluctuations), technology (e.g., computing infrastructure incompatibility), and even many of the economic ones (e.g., gross domestic product). The less tangible ones are ones pertaining to political risks. The impacts of such risks are frequently long-term (not that many of the other ones just mentioned are not) making their effects on an enterprise difficult to detect. In addition, it is difficult to determine among the variables which ones are the risk and which ones are the effect, thereby making it a challenge to determine one or more strategic responses and contingencies to employ. Even then it may take a while to ascertain whether risk responses and contingencies are effective and if they spawned secondary risks.

Understanding a global supply chain can seem complex, uncertain, and even fragile. A single political event can seem overwhelming. An appropriate analogy is dominoes falling, causing a cascading disruption in the performance of a global supply chain, from the point of collapse onward. Political risk management is a means to help prevent or anticipate the falling of dominos. If a domino does fall political risk management can help set it up right to avoid collapsing the entire global supply chain. Or it can take action to save the other dominos from falling. Not an easy accomplishment when considering how difficult it was to recover the global supply chain for personal protective equipment (PPE) during the Covid-19 crisis, especially the global supply chain for US enterprises. Not only were there technical and economic issues but political ones, too, that strained relations with one country, China.

Other issues add to the complexities and uncertainties affecting a global supply chain. These issues include differences in culture. Not only do cultural differences exist among nations but also within each one. Some differences may be based upon dialects, religion, history, and race, or other factors. Even what was once referred to as socio-economic status conditions can differ throughout regions and within countries. These can result in peaceful relations among the inhabitants or violent conflict, adding risks to the supply chain. These differences not only exist with the developing and less developed countries but also within developed ones. Other differences include, which reflects cultural differences among countries and regions, are laws and regulations, for example, ones involving accepting business courtesies. Other issues that add to the complexities and uncertainties of a global supply chain are differences in technological and transportation infrastructures, and contractual arrangements and interpretations, all of which can reflect culture. Eventually, all these issues can create political risks.

After World War II, in retrospect, the global supply chain appears simplistic when compared with what exists today. After World War II, the globe was essentially divided into two superpowers, the United States and the Soviet Union. Nowadays, global supply chains face a multipolar world resulting from the collapse of the Soviet Union and Soviet Bloc. Complexities and uncertainty have skyrocketed. The United States is but one of several countries with enterprises involved in the global supply chain. What adds to the complexities and uncertainty to the global supply chain is not only an approximate "equalization" among other nations but also a diffusion of power from nation states to other actors, notes Fareed Zakaria in *The Post-American World*:

> The 'rest' that is rising includes many nonstate actors. Groups and individuals have been empowered, and hierarchy, centralization and control are being undermined…Power is shifting away from nation-states…the traditional applications of national power, both economic and military, have become less effective…the distribution of power is shifting, moving away from American dominance. That does not mean we are entering an anti-American world. But we are moving into a post-American world.[6]

Under these circumstances, one can see that the global supply chain is facing greater complexity and uncertainty from a political perspective. Hence, political risk management, if an enterprise is going to survive in a global marketplace, must play an integral role in supply chain management. Notes Robert McKellar in *A Short Guide for Political Risk*, "Competition for markets, labor and supplies has become intense with globalisation (sic). A firm capable of extending beyond its comfort zones is better positioned to achieve its global objectives than many competitors. In the global context, political risk management is a strategic enabler."[7] Condoleezza Rice and Amy Zegart agree, noting that "companies that want a competitive edge need to manage the risks generated by this widening array of global political actors, from documentary film makers to international institutions like the European Union."[8]

THE RISE OF GLOBALIZATION

Today, one cannot discuss global supply chain without talking about globalization. Many definitions exist on just what is meant by globalization. Here are a few contemporary definitions.

...the expansion and intensification of social relations and consciousness across world-time and world-space.
– Manfred Steger in *Globalization: A Very Short Introduction*[9]

Globalization is "the process of expanding and intensifying linkages between states, societies, and economies.
– Patrick O'Neil in *Essentials of Comparative Politics*[10]

Those processes that knit people everywhere together, thereby producing worldwide interconnectedness and interdependence and featuring the elimination of borders and the rapid and large-scale movement of persons, things, and ideas across sovereign borders.
– Richard Mansbach and Kirsten Taylor in *Introduction to Global Politics*[11]

> Globalization encompasses many things: the international flow of ideas and knowledge, the sharing of cultures, global civil society, and the global environmental movement.
>
> – Joseph Stiglitz in *Making Globalization Work*[12]

> The global economy has become interconnected than ever before. More goods and services are produced in one country and sold in other countries. More people migrate between countries. More investors around the world are sending their funds to other countries.
>
> – Timothy Taylor in *America and the New Global Economy*[13]

From the quotes above, it is quite clear globalization entails more than simply an economic perspective of a supply chain transcending from country to country, region to region, or continent to continent. With globalization comes complex relationships among all the entities involved, such as governments, business enterprises, and nongovernmental groups. When a global supply chain becomes "globalized," the challenges to operate more efficiently and effectively increase dramatically. Just one event – economic, social, or political – can have a severe impact on a global supply chain. Manfred Steger further observes that globalization goes beyond economics: "...the transformative powers of globalization reach deeply into the economic, political, and cultural technological and ecological dimensions of contemporary social life."[14]

Manfred Steger refers to three drivers of globalization: economics, politics, and cultural drivers.

Economics is the first dimension, which is basically the profit motive. Ultimately, economics is fundamentally improving the efficiency and effectiveness of a firm when pursuing profits and the global supply chain is a way to achieve that. Social is the second dimension, covering not just the cultural in the content of this book but also the stratification of society, its demographics. Social goes beyond what Manfred Steger refers to as cultural, noting it as "...the intensification and expansion of cultural flows across the globe."[15] He then ascribes the economic "with the productive exchange, and consumption of commodities" and the political as "practices related to the generation and distribution of power in societies."[16] Once again, he stresses the characteristics of interconnection and interdependence. In the context of this book, the preference is to use the word "social" rather than "cultural" to include a much greater breadth of content than the latter. Social goes beyond just his three elements of language,

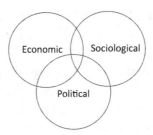

FIGURE 2.1
The Drivers of Globalization.

music, and images. The social incorporates other elements like demographics and psychological considerations which can interrelate with the economic and political dimensions.

Figure 2.1 shows the relationships among the three dimension which is represented in a Venn diagram, shown in Figure 2.1. As one can see, all three drivers are not mutually exclusive. The economic dimension by itself deals with such topics as the profitability of a firm. The social dimension deals with the sociological and psychological characteristics. The political dimension deals with power in terms of its acquisition and exercise within government and throughout society. Where all three dimensions overlap in the diagram represents their impact on each other. The relationships are dynamic and, under most circumstances, are inseparable.

Figure 2.2 demonstrates at a simplistic level how all three levels interact. Notice the double headed curved arrow between each of the following relationships: economics and political; political and social; and social and economic. The relationships can be explained in the following manner: an economic condition affects a political condition; the latter, in return, affects an economic condition. An economic condition affects a social condition; the latter affects, in return, an economic condition. A political condition affects a social condition; the latter affects, in return, a political

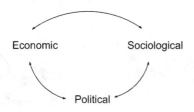

FIGURE 2.2
Relationship of Three Drivers of Globalization.

condition. The double headed arrow indicates that one condition can be the cause under certain circumstances and under other situations be the result of one of the other drivers.

Figure 2.3 demonstrates the same logic regarding the relationships from a risk perspective. A political risk can increase social risk and a social risk can increase economic risk. Conversely, a decrease in political risk impact can decrease social risk and social risk can decrease economic risk. Again, the diagram illustrates, albeit simplistically, the dynamic relationship among the three dimensions, reflecting the difficulty in separating them.

Figure 2.4 can apply the same logic within the political dimension. At the international level, tensions can exist between two developed countries,

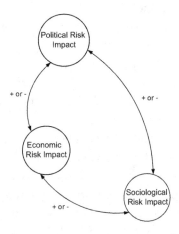

FIGURE 2.3
Relationship of Political, Economic, and Sociological Risks Impacting Each Other.

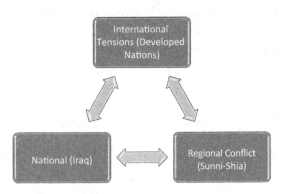

FIGURE 2.4
Political Dynamics Example.

in this case the United States and Russia. This tension can cause regional conflict in the Middle East, especially between the Shia and the Sunni. This conflict between Shia and Sunni can cause conflict at a national level, in this case in Iraq. In turn, the Iraqi conflict causes tension between the US and Russia. Going counterclockwise, the tension between the US and Russia can be the result of the conflict in Iraq which, in turn, can be the result of regional conflict which can be the result of conflict between the US and Russia. Looking at the logical relationships, one can then determine the impact of the conflict at the international, regional, and national levels on the economic dimension, such as the supply chain for the petroleum industry, and the social dimension, such as displaced citizens flooding refugee camps.

Consider the economic side of the globalization. It involves the exchange of goods and services among different countries. For example, a global supply chain may allow components to be designed in one country, developed in another one, assembled in still another, and distributed in yet another. The assets in each country throughout a global supply chain capitalizes on the strengths of each country. Assuming all assets throughout the global supply chain perform efficiently and effectively the product arrives according to requirements. Of course, often one of the assets in a country has trouble, for example, manufacturing a component, and impacts the global supply chain downstream. Or the problem could be a slowdown of economic performance within a country.

Social considerations can impact a global supply chain, too. Ideally, a workforce within a country that is educated and motivated, major labor issues are nonexistent. Employees of a global enterprise understand the entire supply chain and their role in ensuring that it functions efficiently and effectively. Employees, too, have a deep cultural understanding of other enterprises participating in the global supply chain, acknowledging such differences linguistically and a time perspective, demonstrates a willingness to work with everyone. Now consider what is often reality in a global supply chain, even as globalization grows. An enterprise within a global supply chain may lack access to an educated workforce to produce a component. The enterprise within that country may be riddled with criminal behavior to such an extent it affects its performance, such as theft of important materials or deliberate use of substandard materials and embezzlement of the difference in cost of the higher quality ones. Or the failure to deliver a product may be due to a virus spreading among employees. Or enterprises in a global supply chain may close for holidays and vacation periods that exceed that of other enterprises in other countries, causing delays in transportation to assembly or distribution warehouses.

What is often overlooked is how politics can also affect globalization. Indeed, politics may have been the primary driver for globalization since the end of World War II although other periods of globalization existed. Organizations formed with governmental encouragement that has furthered the growth of globalization. Institutions that encouraged globalization include the General Agreement on Tariffs and Trade (GATT) to reduce trade barriers, learning from the disastrous trade wars of the 1920s; GATT evolved into the World Trade Organization (WTO). The International Monetary Fund (IMF) was formed to facilitate the flow of capital among countries; the International Bank for Reconstruction and Development (IBRD), or World Bank, provided loans to countries. The United States played an instrumental role in encouraging the successful growth of these and other organization in the post-World War II period in part to further its business interests but also to contain communism. With this political support came the rise of a massive military establishment that provided the "muscle" to allow for free trade arise and blossom among its allies.

Ideally, politics plays a significant, proactive role in furthering globalization. Countries followed liberal trade policies through lower tariffs, thanks to unimpeded flow of financial capital; formation of regional and international trade agreements; and reduction of taxes on foreign entities. Under such conditions, enterprises in the global supply chain became interdependent and integrated with little interference thanks to the banking of political actors, such as governments of developed countries, to include the United States, and nongovernmental organizations. Today, US dominance has declined due to challenges from developing nations, such as Brazil, Russia, India, and China (BRIC), and regional organizations like the European Union, which present significant political challenges that can impact the global supply chain.

Many political challenges confront a global supply chain, thanks in part to globalization. Over the years, globalization has faced some criticism, even to the point of sparking riots throughout the world. The WTO riots in Seattle (US), Geneva (Switzerland), and Milan (Italy) experienced extreme protests opposing globalization, reflecting the tarnished perception of globalization. These protests represent reaction against globalization, as observed by Manfred Steger who says that political globalization is an "intensification and political interrelatedness across the globe," dealing with issues concerning sovereignty, NGOs, and governance.[17] It is understandable how these issues can engender anger among populations across the globe, challenging legacy of globalization.

Some of the more common political complaints against globalization include:

- Causing financial instability to destabilize a democratically elected regime
- Circumventing regional and international oversight or visibility on issues like climate change, labor exploitation, human rights violations, economic injustice, and financial malfeasance, especially in less developed countries
- Corrupting political leaders
- Encouraging ethnic divisions or the opposite, by destroying ethnic identities
- Exacerbating social conditions which could lead to political instability
- Exploiting a country by a foreign enterprise by encouraging economic dependency
- Fomenting governmental instability
- Fostering and exploiting conflict between countries
- Fostering domestic political division
- Ransacking national resources
- Threatening, directly or indirectly, to isolate a country from being integrated into the global trade and financial system
- Weakening democratic institutions by wrestling away local control from the body politic
- Weakening of domestic political institutions by usurping power from local authorities and shifting it to regional and international organizations

Whether these complaints and others are real or imagined, they can add complexity when executing a global supply chain. Governments and nongovernmental organizations can retaliate with political action against a global enterprise, adversely impacting its global supply chain. Political actions include:

- Anti-business sentiment augmentation
- Bureaucratic delays

- Business pursuits with another enterprise or country
- Corporate espionage
- Currency inconvertibility
- Default on loans
- Deliberate contract violations
- Expropriation, including creeping expropriation
- Fiscal and monetary inflexibility
- Foreign hiring restrictions
- High tax imposition on foreign enterprises
- Kidnapping
- Labor strikes
- Noncompliance with contractual obligations
- Piracy
- Production stoppages
- Regulatory actions increased
- Restrictions imposed on foreign investments
- Restrictive repatriation policies
- Tariffs and non-tariff barriers implemented
- Trade quotas imposed

Additionally, political conditions or events, such as the ones below, can surface that have nothing to do directly with the global supply chain having an impact, nonetheless. These include:

- Assassinations of key political actors
- Civil war
- Corruption in business dealings
- Embargo
- Extensive black market
- Military takeover
- Regime instability
- Religious conflict
- Riots and demonstrations
- Territorial conflict
- War between and among countries
- Xenophobia

An intriguing perspective of the global market is described by Pankaj Ghemawat in his book *Redefining Global Strategy*. He describes relationship complexities among countries as being one of "distance" which manifests itself in four areas: cultural, administrative, geographic, and economic. Hence, the acronym CAGE. Some examples of cultural distances include language and ethnicity; for administrative distances, governmental policies and stability; for geographical distances, climate and size; and for economic distances, financial and infrastructure. These distances underpin the difficulties global enterprises have when dealing with other countries. Observes Ghemawat: "...the CAGE framework not only helps identify the key differences in particular settings; it also affords insights into differences in difference by providing a basis for distinguishing countries that are relatively close, along the key dimensions, from those that are relatively far."[18]

It would be a mistake to assume that the four distances are mutually exclusive; they are not. Figure 2.5 shows the overlaps among the four distances. From a political risk management perspective, this insight is important. Cultural distances can create political threats resulting from different values and norms that can lead to unstable or mistrustful relationships with a key country which, in turn, can impact a global supply chain. Geographic differences, such as environmental, can lead to epidemics that can expand to pandemics which, in turn, can impact the global supply chain. Economic distance, such as differences in infrastructure, can lead to xenophobia and extreme nationalism resulting in higher tariffs and quotas between two countries which, in turn, can impact a global supply chain. Administrative distance, such as ideology

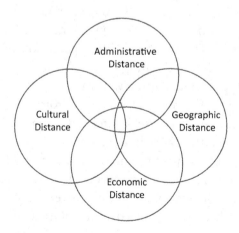

FIGURE 2.5
CAGE Venn Diagram.

and regulatory oversight, can result in a tense and unstable political and military environment which can, in turn, impact a global supply chain. The overall result is something akin to the volatile differences between major economic powers, sandwiching a global enterprise and its supply chain.

Globalization, then, is wrought with complexity and face precarious situations. In addition to the above list, many countries, especially with developing and less developed countries, must confront a tradeoff between stability and growth. Moving from one extreme to the other (such as from stability to growth or vice versa), which happens frequently on a national or regional basis, presents many political risks to a global supply chain. The degree of intensity between stability and growth has a substantial impact to a global supply chain. If the intensity is high, the legitimacy of a regime may become questionable as it confronts considerable popular unrest; the odds increase that a global supply chain can be impacted. For example, if a regime experiences political instability in the midst of a growing revolutionary rebellion, a global supply chain will be impacted, such as the case with Cuba and the United Fruit Company and the government in Yemen being racked with conflict which threatens international oil trade.

A perfect example of the complexities surrounding globalization, albeit regional in scope, is the experience of the European Union (EU). Originally, an outcrop of the European Coal and Steel Community (Treaty of Paris in 1951), the European Community (1957 Treaty of Rome), the EU has evolved from a handful of nations, e.g., France, Germany, Belgium, Netherlands, and Luxembourg, to a group of about 25 or more countries, with members spreading from Western to Eastern Europe, thanks to the collapse of the Soviet Union. The EU offers peace and stability among its members but not without exhibiting some political and economic tension over the years. The original tension was over the role of Germany among its members, mainly the result of its legacy from two world wars, and Britain's reluctance to find itself bonded to continental Europe but nevertheless joined in the 1970s until recently departing due to Brexit. The transition to the European Union through the Maastricht Treaty in 1993 and subsequent others are an expression of common goals sought by European powers; however, not without controversy: economic integration via a common market resulting in a decrease of trade barriers and quotas; security via peaceful reconciliation of historical differences, and restoration of European influence around the world. They agreed to address common issues, such as the environment and injustice while at the same time allowing member states to pursue their own national interests. The pursuit of these and other goals have not been smooth, considering a legacy of centuries of economic, political, and military conflict. An institutional structure eventually came to fruition, consisting of a European council, parliament, commission, court of justice, bank, and common currency (for the most part) along with other treaties (such as the Amsterdam Treaty) concerning the distribution of power vis-à-vis the EU and member nations and membership enlargement (such as the Nice Treaty). Growing membership obviously has its benefits as the number of members has grown despite the earlier reluctance of countries like Norway, Denmark, Britain, Switzerland, and Ireland to join.

Two additional endeavors, to further membership cohesiveness and overall economic performance, are the Single Market Project and the Lisbon Agenda. The Single Market Project addresses what the EU calls the four freedoms which are the free flow of goods, services, workers, and financial capital. The Lisbon Agenda embraces a policy consisting of four tasks: invest in people and modernize labor markets; unlock business potential; invest in knowledge and innovation; and focus on energy and climate change.

The organizational structure appears complex at first sight. At the top of the pyramid is the European Council which provides guidelines and consists of heads of states and the president of the EU; it resolves issues from the Council of Ministers. The Council of ministers consists of members representing each state, has considerable power, and ministers attend meeting of "forms" depending on the subject. The parliament consists of elected members from each of the member states using proportional representation; it plays an important role in supervising the expenditures of monies and shares power with the commission. The commission performs an executive role by executing EU policies, proposing text for laws to parliament as well as present initiatives to parliament and the council of ministers, submits general policies for the European Council, and ensures treaties and laws are applied inside member states with the option to pursue action in the Court of Justice for violations. The Court of Justice has the role of ensuring that the member states observe the laws and treaties of the EU, such as judging legality of actions by a member state or between member states. Even individuals and companies can bring action to the Court of Justice but only after being tried in the applicable member's court and only if a need arises to provide interpretation of the law. Efforts have been made to simplify the complexity of the relations through the Reform Treaty of 2007. The European Central Bank was established, too, consisting of an executive board and governors of member states' banks to form a governing council. The bank has the primary goal of fostering economic and monetary union by maintaining price stability and issuing currency. In addition to the European Central Bank to maintain economic and monetary union is the Euro. Adopting a single currency enabled overcoming risks dealing with exchange rates and cross-border investments. To participate in the Euro, states had to meet certain criteria related to inflation and public debt. In the end, some countries elected not to participate, such as Britain. Still, the Euro is a major achievement and reflects the growing presence of globalization among many countries in Europe as well as serve as a challenge to the primacy of the US dollar.

Oddly enough, despite the historical and political differences among the current member nations and the complex governmental structure, the EU has become just that, a union. While economic performance lags when compared with the United States, the EU has risen in stature to the point that it poses a challenge to the dominance of the global supply chain of the United States. The EU has also raised issues that affect global supply chains. These issues include privacy laws; aerospace manufacturing; accounting and reporting practices; environmental laws; immigration; health; trade; and nationalism (on both sides of the Atlantic). Yet, from what existed before, dealing with the EU holistically has made its global supply chain more efficient and effective; otherwise, global supply chains of each state would add greater complexity and uncertainty. The relationship between the EU and other nation states has become strained, particularly with such countries as the United States and Australia over certain trade practices related to information technology and agriculture, respectively. Nonetheless, the EU is a good example of how the relationships of localities, regions, and global jurisdictions and issues can overlap in a transformative and dynamic way. Interdependence and integration, from economic, political, and social perspectives. It is not difficult to see the impacts of an economic, social, or political event can have on a global supply chain.

One more thought about globalization. Interestingly, Manfred Steger discusses two main categories of thinking concerning globalization: hyperglobalists who believe globalization signifies the decline of the state as a natural occurrence and the sceptics who view it as a deliberate decision by states to make globalization a reality.[19] Whatever side one chooses, the reality is globalization is a fact although not to the extent that hyperglobalists believe and no doubt states have been instigators in pushing globalization to further their own interests. One thing for sure is that globalization involves a strong relationship among the social, economic, and political processes in a way that can negatively or positively affect the global supply chain of an enterprise.

FINAL THOUGHTS

An enterprise's global supply chain has become increasingly complex. Political conditions and events can add to the degree of complexity. A political condition or event at one point can cause significant disruption to an enterprise's global supply chain, causing all the subsequent assets to fall like dominoes. Not all political conditions or events are negative; some present opportunities but an enterprise must be prepared to take advantage of such situations. Whether facing a threat or an opportunity an enterprise must be prepared to respond and the means to accomplish that is political risk management.

NOTES

1. David Simchi-Levi, Philip Kaminsky, and Edith Simchi-Levi, *Managing the Supply Chain* (New York: McGraw-Hill: 2004), 1.
2. Donald Bowersox, David Closs, and M. Bixby Cooper, *Supply Chain Logistics Management* (New York: McGraw-Hill/Irwin: 2010), 4.
3. David Blanchard, *Supply Chain Management* (Hoboken, NJ: John Wiley & Sons: 2007), 7.
4. Simchi-Levi, Kaminsky, and Simchi-Levi, *Managing the Supply Chain*, 223–224.
5. Ila Manuj and John Mentzer, "Global Supply Chain Risk Management Strategies," *International Journal of Physical Distribution and Logistics*, vol. 3, 2008), 197–198.
6. Fareed Zakaria, *The Post-American World* (New York: W. W. Norton & Company: 2008), 4–5.
7. Robert McKellar, *A Short Guide to Political Risk* (Surrey, England: Gower Publishing, Ltd.: 2010), 115.
8. Rice and Zegart, *Political Risk*, 5.
9. Manfred Steger, *Globalization: A Very Short Introduction* (New York: Oxford University Press: 2009), 15.

10. Patrick O'Neil, *Essentials of Comparative Politics* (New York: W. W. Norton & Company: 2013), A-18.
11. Patrick Mansbach and Kirsten Taylor, *Introduction to Global Politics* (London: Routledge: 2012), 577.
12. Joseph Stiglitz, *Making Globalization Work* (New York: W. W. Norton & Company: 2007), 4.
13. Timothy Taylor, American and the New Global Economy (Chantilly, Virginia: The Teaching Company: 2008), 1.
14. Steger, *Globalization*, x.
15. Steger, *Globalization*, 71.
16. Steger, *Globalization*, 71.
17. Steger, *Globalization*, 58.
18. Pankaj Ghemawat, *Redefining Global Strategy* (Boston: Harvard Business School Press: 2007), 33.
19. Steger, *Globalization*, 63–64.

3

Political Risk Management: The Basics

The approach to political risk management is not as unique as one would think. It follows largely the basic principles of enterprise risk management. What is unique is the subject matter for all the reasons discussed earlier. Many tools and techniques of enterprise risk management are applicable to political risk management. Because of its unique nature, political risk management is usually conducted at the enterprise level, that is, at the higher levels of an enterprise, supported by the business unit or subsidiary levels. What follows are the basics of political risk management predicated on using the framework of enterprise risk management. The application of these basics will be expanded in the following chapters.

KEY POINTS

Keep the following points in mind about political risk management.

Take a systemic view of an enterprise. That is, view the enterprise as an interacting set of components working together to achieve strategic goals. These components consist of actors, data, signals, deliverables (or artifacts), and controls that result in internal behavior but, just as importantly, interact with the external environment, too. These components share facts and data among each other and can affect one another. A change in the facts and data can affect the decisions made by key stakeholders. Frequently, an enterprise operates in equilibrium but sometimes an internal or external event, such as a political action by a government, occurs that causes disequilibrium. How an enterprise deals with the event reflects its ability to adapt and have resilience.

Integrate political risk management with business strategies and operations. It is not developed and deployed in a void. Successful political risk management requires a strong linkage between what happens at the higher levels of an enterprise with what occurs at a business unit or subsidiary level. While the strategic focus is mainly at the top of an enterprise, the failure to understand what goes at the lower levels can result in something like a layered cake effect where the top layer is misaligned with the lower levels. Integration throughout an enterprise, both vertically and horizontally, is crucial for successful political risk management.

Take a systematic approach. That is, employ a framework that all stakeholders agree to follow to avoid inconsistency in results. If it just is a hodgepodge of activities, then political risk management only produces confusing results. In the end, all relevant stakeholders need to feel confident in the results and see the output as meaningful and useful to manage risks related to the strategic goals of the enterprise. A political risk management plan should help in this regard.

Recognize political risk management deals with considerable uncertainty which implies imprecision, meaning that a lot is unknown about a political risk. Since risk deals with what might happen in the future, it uses probability, even only possibility. For some stakeholders looking for precision, this characteristic of political risk management can make them nervous. But such is the nature of political risk management. If an enterprise fails to experience any known political risk that situation does not necessarily mean political risk management was a wasted effort; it may be precisely because the results of political risk management have worked. In other words, an enterprise had effectively prepared in advance to deal with political risks before their becoming an issue.

Political risk management is no "guarantee" any of the results exist. It does not guarantee a risk will become a reality. Nor does it guarantee that any responses will deal with political risks effectively. Political risk management can only offer reasonable assurance that a risk might occur and that the corresponding response will be effective. Such is the nature of political risks being dynamic, and unpredictable. New risks will arise while others fade from the attention span of stakeholders.

BENEFITS

Oddly enough, many enterprises do not perform political risk management despite the benefits. What follows are some common benefits.

Enables an enterprise to perform proactively, not reactively. It provides a means to determine in advance any potential risks that could arise and prepare to respond accordingly. In other words, it helps in avoiding being reactive, that is, constantly putting out fires. When an enterprise constantly reacts, the behavior reflects an inability to operate efficiently and effectively. Also, its reaction to an event or conditions may aggravate the enterprise's situation. Not all risks, of course, are easily anticipated. Some risks are black swans, that is, events that are totally unanticipated, explainable only in hindsight, and have a catastrophic impact; however, these occurrences are rare. Not all unanticipated events have the same impact as black swans and these events or conditions are known as unknown unknowns (or unk unks).

Providing for better decision-making by accounting for risks, regardless of industry. Most decisions have consequences, positive and negative. While not all risks are identifiable, good decision-making accounts for as many of them as possible before acting and having a potential response ready. In other words, good decisions about risks require preparation. The best way to accomplish that is to anticipate what could go awry and what may go well. When a threat arises, executive and senior management can respond; if an opportunity arises (that is something positive), then executive and senior management can seize the opportunity. The fundamental point here is that political risk management should be an integral part of decision-making at strategic and operational levels.

Generates confidence when a business goes into unknown territory. Risk involves uncertainty and political risk management provides an effective means to deal with it. Executive and senior management should feel more confident if they have an idea of what potentially could go wrong and well. They can prepare in advance for any potentiality that arises. The future will not necessarily seem insurmountable since they should have some reasonable assurance of being ready to meet whatever confronts them. Obviously, this does not mean that unanticipated events or conditions will occur but at least they have an awareness of that possibility.

Enables executive and senior management to be aware of their own vulnerabilities. Political risk management helps executive and senior management to have a greater awareness of their strengths but, just as importantly, their weaknesses. By knowing the vulnerabilities, executive and senior management can take compensatory action to protect themselves and their enterprise from an unwanted event or condition. For example, it might consider preparing contingency plans if a vulnerability appears uncontrollable.

Allows executive and senior management to think not only about the present but also the future. Political risk management can examine the present to determine future risks. Technically, if a risk exists it is no longer one, it has become an issue and an identified response is deployed. It requires looking into the future to determine what could negatively and positively occur. Peering into the future depends on the availability of facts and data, valid assumptions made, and the nature of an event or condition confronting an enterprise. In a sense, political risk management provides the means to act similar to a clairvoyant but with one difference. A clairvoyant predicts the future; executive and senior management are not predicting the future but rather anticipating what could possibly happen and being prepared to respond with certain events or conditions should they arise.

Requires taking a broad, strategic perspective, meaning viewing the entire enterprise as one integrated system albeit often consisting of multiple subsystems. Executive and senior management applies political management in a way that accounts for the strategic goals of an enterprise. It also requires understanding how all the subsystems, such as business units and subsidiaries, interact to achieve its goals. Ideally, the subsystems are integrated and interdependent but, realistically, that is usually not the norm, especially for large enterprises. Political risk management enables identifying the risks that potentially many impact achieving goals due to inefficient and ineffective performance within an enterprise's environment.

Related to the previous benefit necessitates taking a multi-disciplinary approach, such as involving people from various organizational silos, e.g., information technology, logistics, transportation, and expertise. Many executives and senior managers moved up the ranks in these silos. It becomes easy to fall into the trap of viewing one's own discipline or silo as the most important. If it is to prove of value, political risk management requires executives and senior managers to put on their "big hat," and consider all the disciplines when identifying, assessing, and responding to risks. That means considering all components and activities of an enterprise from the perspective of achieving the strategic goals of an enterprise.

Helps to further communications among executive and senior management. Often, it is at the executive ranks where communication becomes a challenge. Many reasons exist; the most common ones are competition among peers; vying for political ascendancy to a higher position; fighting for one's area of responsibility; and seeking greater financial rewards. While none of these reasons are bad per se when taken to the extreme they can tear an enterprise apart. Political risk management provides a means for executive and senior management to communicate with each other when continually identifying enterprise-wide risks. Political risk management, if it is to be successful, requires good communication among all the participants, up and down and across the chain of command as well as monthly, quarterly, or annually.

Requires people to be continuously aware and involved if the results are to remain of value. If executive and senior management simply go through the mechanics without follow-up, then the contents will eventually be irrelevant, outdated, and unfocused. In other words, political risk management is not a one-time affair. Participants' continuous involvement means that the enterprise will be able to adapt to changing circumstances, for example, by modifying its strategic goals or responding to political risks. Consistent and continuous feedback are key to ensure stakeholders maintaining awareness of the effectiveness of managing political risks.

Encourages executives and senior management to focus on the strategic goals of an enterprise. Because it requires taking a broad perspective, political risk management helps prevent executives and senior managers from falling within the comfort zone of their silos, that is, focusing on their own organization's goals at the expense of the overall ones of the enterprise. Political risk management, therefore, facilities – not guarantee – that every silos' goals align with the enterprise's goals. Sometimes both sets of goals do not align. Political risk management will often reveal this misalignment, necessitating corrective action.

APPROACH

Basically, political risk management involves applying risk management at the executive and senior levels of an organization. It is an integrated approach applied to identify, analyze, monitor and control, and respond to risks potentially occurring at a strategic level. The fundamental processes are: identify the strategic goals; identify stakeholders; prepare risk management plan; identify risks; assess risks; prepare risk responses; perform risk monitoring and controlling; perform risk reporting; and maintaining political risk management processes.

Identify strategic goals. This process entails collecting, compiling, and reviewing facts and data to ascertain an enterprise's overall goals. The strategic goals provide direction and parameters to orient the application of political enterprise risk management. Knowing the goals will help to determine scope and guide the other political risk management processes at the business unit or subsidiary level. It also helps in performing the next process.

Identify stakeholders. This process identifies the right people and organizations to engage when performing political risk management. It also helps encourage teaming, trust, buy-in, and commitment.

Prepare a risk management plan. This process documents the overall approach, tools, and techniques to apply when performing political risk management. It describes how to conduct all processes of political risk management.

Identify risks. This process takes the facts and data and to develop a list of possible risks impacting strategic goals. The purpose is to have a working set of risks to proceed to the next phase. It does not preclude removing or adding risks later.

Assess risks. This process determines which risks are more important than others. The usual determinants of the importance of a risk relative to another is probability or likelihood and impact.

Prepare risk responses. This process identifies the strategies and specific actions to take should a risk becomes a reality. Strategic approaches potentially help to alleviate the impact of a threat to seize an opportunity.

Perform risk controlling and monitoring. This process monitors whether a risk has occurred and implements the requisite response to deal with it. The idea here is to respond, not react, to conditions or events and to determine the effectiveness of responses.

Perform risk reporting. This process compiles facts and data about of the effectiveness of managing political risks. It looks at current status as well as presents new risks and potential responses to them.

Maintain political risk management. This process keeps the other processes relevant to the needs of an enterprise. It also documents updates in a risk management plan.

While these processes are described sequentially in this book; in reality, they occur nonlinearly. Often a risk management plan is developed during identify strategic goals and even during identify risks. Identify strategic goals can occur while identifying risks and assessing risks while more facts and data become available. Likewise, assess risks can occur while preparing risk responses. Inherently, prepare risk responses should be completed prior to perform risk control. Risk reporting often occurs sometimes in parallel with perform risk control.

The entire set of processes are repeatable. That is, the flow can reiterate as time progresses and as more facts and data become available. Usually, this reiteration leads to a more refined, improved risk management approach and a better understanding of the risks that may arise and the responses to deal with them.

CHALLENGES

Despite the benefits of political risk management, several challenges must be overcome.

Desire to work under the radar. Sometimes people rise through the ranks by avoiding visibility unless advantageous to do so. They distance themselves from organizational conflict, riding the coattails of others. Regardless, operating under the radar proves of value to the people doing so but not for the enterprise. Political risk management makes it difficult to do so since it requires taking a broad, multi-disciplinary perspective to focus on the strategic goals. Other executives and senior managers will likely hesitate to raise concerns about risks that could affect their own organizational goals.

Not perceived as not having value. Many people view risk management in general as lacking value, at best being only an administrative requirement to check off. A main reason for this perspective is the results are often not immediate, but rather, long-term. Also, a risk may or may not surface. Some people find it, too, difficult to apply, finding it a challenge to think about what could happen in the future. All they may see is a colorful matrix or a chart reflecting possible events, their likelihood or probability, impact, and priority.

Distorting or "massaging" facts and data. Organizational and group pressure surfaces in any organization but it is especially present when performing political risk management. The pecking order or a common set of beliefs are two ways that negatively affect the quality of facts and data. The results of a political risk management activity, for example, may be skewed toward a group of related risks while discounting or disregarding others, resulting in a flawed result. For example, a risk report may go before an audit or risk committee and wordsmithing may give the appearance that a political risk is not as negative as it appears. Such occurrences only give the impression that political risk management lacks any objective value which may not be the case.

Fear, which may permeate an organization due to internecine warfare resulting from a merger; the threat of outsourcing; or the coming of executive and senior management dismissals. When it arises, fear inhibits sharing of facts and data, reflecting distrust. People may not speak their minds about a certain risk. When that happens, the results of political risk management may not prove its value. Not surprising, some members of executive and senior management may not want to participate in any political risk management session for fear that some facts and data may reflect on their performance.

Unable to clearly identify an enterprise's goals. In many enterprises, only a few people may have an idea of what the strategic goals are, others see them as vague or conflicting, or, quite frankly, do not care. Ideally, the goals appear in a vision or mission statement and the financial statement, the objectives, which are more definitive, are often unknown unless people have access to an operations plan. When people have only a vague notion of the strategic goals, they may find it difficult to participate in a worthwhile manner during a political risk management exercise. This lack of knowledge or enthusiasm may result in going off on a tangent or their thinking is based upon misinterpretation of or inaccurate assumptions. Knowing the strategic goals enable performing meaningful political risk management.

Poor attendance at political risk management meetings or working sessions. Political risk management, despite its obvious value, can be time consuming. Executive and senior managers' time is valuable and often insufficient or unavailable. For that reason, some of them may not want to devote the time and effort to participate in political risk management or they will send a substitute but who lacks the knowledge, expertise, or power to be involved effectively.

Follow an inconsistent approach. This situation is especially the case when working groups consisting of executive and senior management are grouped into sub-teams, each one covering a separate political topic. One team might rely on literature review while another on interviews with subject matter experts. The results are then compiled but the facts and data may not have validity or reliability. "Apples mixed with oranges" may be the result. Inconsistency in approach can lead to a lack of credible results. This circumstance often arises when a supporting staff member is unavailable or has insufficient time to do a thorough job.

Unavailability of facts and data.to perform meaningful political risk management. Many reasons explain this circumstance. People may be reluctant to share facts and data because distrust permeates the chain of command; layoffs are looming in the horizon; or resources are scattered about an enterprise making it difficult to find and compile facts and data. If solid facts and data are unavailable, performing meaningful political risk management becomes quite a challenge. Facts and data are the lifeblood of political risk management.

Intolerance of different perspectives. Dialogue is critical for effective political risk management; however, if the participants are shunned because they provide a perspective variant to others on a team, it can lead to overlooking key political risks. People must feel comfortable sharing their thoughts and stepping outside their comfort zones to identify and assess political risks. Their insights may not be popular but should be worthy of consideration. One of the biggest dangers to political risk management is for one silo or discipline dominating any risk-related working session. In the world of corporate politics, tolerance is not always embraced, especially if a clique dominates and embraces a certain paradigm.

Lack of education and awareness about political risk management. Some executive and senior managers may never have the time or desire to learn about the topic. Political risk management at the strategic level requires a different mindset from leading at an operational level. It requires, as mentioned earlier, removing their silo hat and seeing the enterprise from a holistic perspective and the environment in which it operates. They will likely have to think about issues that do not apply to them directly now or in the past. They need to put on a different hat, which is not easy for anyone who has worked in a silo or discipline their entire career. They may be, for instance, good convergent thinkers but have rarely exercised divergent thinking.

Organizational structure and its accompanying cultural resistance. In a traditional hierarchical company, power relationships can influence the performance of any political risk management endeavor. A strong, cohesive executive team may be good under certain conditions; however, it can also lead to challenges when performing political risk management. Participants during the sessions may reluctantly speak their minds, function as bobbleheads, or play the political game by taking sides, to further a hidden agenda. In other organizational structures and cultures, cliques may form, such as after a merger between two companies, which can result in taking sides, thereby causing the political risk management to appear as a power play rather than an objective assessment and analysis of the strategic risks affecting an enterprise.

A tendency to act first and think later. Many people at the strategic level emphasize doing over just thinking. They think, of course, but they often want to see tangible results from thinking. They also have other goals that they must meet. Political risk management may seem an endeavor that removes them from activities that furthers their goals despite acknowledging the importance of political risk management; political risk management must be conducted efficiently and effectively if it is to prove of value to an enterprise.

SHOWSTOPPERS

The challenges described above, if not addressed, can result in major showstoppers when implementing political risk management.

Treating all risks as independent from each other is one major showstopper. The reality is many risks are integrated and interdependent. One risk may lead to another risk; they may be linked. If a risk occurs (now being an issue), it may cause another risk to become an issue which, in turn, causes another one to become an issue, and so on. In other words, a domino effect results. The cumulative effect can be very destructive simply because the complexity is too difficult to understand or manage.

Not looking at an enterprise as an integrated system. A change in one component of a system, e.g., department, can impact another component, e.g., a department, even if others are more important. If a risk becomes an issue, it may impact other components, causing other risks to arise, ones seemingly unrelated to a risk. The complexity can increase dramatically. Take a political example. A labor strike occurs in one country; it results in a failure to build a subproduct in another which, in turn, impacts building the final product is still another for delivery to a customer.

Poor situational awareness, which is being cognizant of what is happening in an environment. From a political risk management perspective, poor or no situational awareness can prove disastrous. Enterprises should be aware of their environment and the political risks that may potentially arise. That means being aware of the potential events in their environment; their significance; basic information (such as who, what, when, where, why, and how); and their impact on itself and others. Situational awareness depends largely on information, communication, coordination, and objectivity when dealing with political risks.

Inability to learn from an event. Some enterprises seem to repeat this one whether at the strategic or operational levels. Some enterprises experience the same phenomenon, every so often partly due to continual change in leadership; denial of reality; cultural intransigence; and arrogance. Failure to learn from a risk event can hurt an enterprise's and leadership's reputation as well as lead to lack of effectiveness in achieving strategic goals and efficiency in its operations. These firms make the same mistakes especially while expecting different results.

Not anticipating what political risks could happen in the future. Executive and senior management do not perform political risk management (or any risk management for that matter) and instead decide to deal with any risk as it arises. This attitude is often a result of arrogance, viewing political risk management as not value-added, or relying on its financial reserves to deal with a political risk if, and when, it occurs. This failure often reflects a reactive management style.

Unable to adapt to changing political circumstance. In most environments, change is, ironically, the only constant. Like all systems, enterprises need to adapt to changing circumstances, especially if events have a significant impact. This inability to adapt can mean disaster, turning an enterprise into an anachronism. Not performing enterprise risk management can cause a firm to hop into the past rather than leaping into the future.

FINAL THOUGHTS

Political risk management requires taking a strategic perspective on its impact to an enterprise's global supply chain. To do so involves being systemic and systematic to deal effectively with the political uncertainty that surrounds a global business environment.

GETTING STARTED QUESTIONS

Questions	Yes	No

1. If your enterprise decides to develop and deploy political risk management, does it have the capacity to perform the following processes?
   a) Identify strategic goals?
   b) Identify stakeholders?
   c) Prepare a risk management plan?
   d) Identify risks?
   e) Assess risks?
   f) Prepare risk responses?
   g) Perform risk controlling and monitoring?
   h) Perform risk reporting?
   i) Maintain political risk management processes

2. Are you keeping the following points in mind?
   a) Take a systemic view of the enterprise?
   b) Integrate political risk management with business strategies and operations?
   c) Take a systematic approach?
   d) Recognize political risk management deals with considerable uncertainty?
   e) No guarantee of any results from political risk management

3. Are you expecting to experience any of the following challenges and, if so, determining how to deal with them?
   a) Desire to work under the radar?
   b) Not perceive political management as having value?
   c) Distorting or massaging facts and data?
   d) Fear?
   e) Unable to clearly identify an enterprise's goals?
   f) Poor attendance by stakeholders at political risk management meetings?
   g) Follow an inconsistent approach?
   h) Unavailability of facts and data to perform meaningful political risk management?
   i) Intolerance of different perspectives?
   j) Lack of education and awareness about political risk management?
   k) Organizational structure and cultural resistance?
   l) Tendency to act first and think later?

4. Have you determined how your enterprise can avoid these big failures?
   a) Trusting all risk independent from each other?
   b) Not looking at an enterprise as an integrated system?
   c) Poor situational awareness?
   d) Inability to learn from a political event?
   e) Not anticipating what political risks could happen?
   f) Unable to adapt to changing political circumstances?

4

Establish Infrastructure and Project

Political risk management does not happen in a vacuum. In fact, it is likely to be implemented after a risk management governance infrastructure is already in place. Political risk management in an enterprise often operates as a subset within a larger risk management organization. This chapter and the entire book assume that political risk management is part of a larger organization responsible for risk management.

GOVERNANCE

Governance within an organization, indeed an entire enterprise, entails establishing a functional unit, preparing supporting procedures, determining goals, implementing strategies, and monitoring performance to achieve desired results as identified by a governing body, such as an executive steering committee. There are two parts to governance, the infrastructure and training.

The infrastructure for political risk management is an organization that is a component of a much larger risk organization. The supporting infrastructure entails creating a political risk organization that develops, deploys, and maintains strategies and procedures that aligns with a parent risk management organization which, in turn, supports an entire enterprise. It develops and implements procedures to support ongoing identifying, assessing, monitoring, controlling, and reporting political risks impacting an enterprise as well as determining the effectiveness of responses.

A political risk organization has two fundamental goals. The first one is to support the overall strategic goals of an enterprise. The second one is to ensure effective execution of its responsibilities to enable resilience in a dynamic political world.

It achieves the two goals by developing, implementing, and maintaining 11 processes listed below:

- Establish a governance infrastructure
- Identify strategic goals for the enterprise
- Identify stakeholders
- Prepare a project or program management plan
- Prepare a political risk management plan
- Identify political risks
- Assess political risks
- Prepare political risk responses
- Perform political risk monitoring and controlling
- Perform political risk reporting
- Maintain political risk management

A key distinction needs clarification at this point. The relationships among the political risk management processes is often thought to be linear whereby one process logically follows one after another, as shown in Figure 4.1. For simplistic purposes, they are presented linearly in this book albeit that may not necessarily be the case in real life as discussed soon.

The first process is to establish a governance infrastructure which entails setting up a governance structure to develop and deploy political risk management within an enterprise. The second and third processes occur concurrently, with identify strategic goals (which give overall direction to an enterprise) and identify stakeholders (which is identifying people and organizations having an interest in political risk management). The fourth process is to prepare a project or program plan to develop and deploy political risk management for an enterprise; it includes, but not limited to,

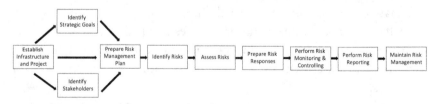

FIGURE 4.1
Political Risk Management Processes.

preparing a charter, identifying scope, building a schedule, tracking and monitoring performance, and reporting on progress. The fifth process is to prepare a political risk management plan which describes the processes and procedures to conduct political risk management; it describes the procedures, tools, and techniques to use. The sixth process is to identify political risks possibly occurring which can affect an enterprise's ability to achieve its strategic goals. The seventh process is to assess the political risks identified in the previous process; the results from this process are to determine the probability or likelihood of political risks, their impacts, and priorities. The eighth process is to prepare political risk responses to manage any significant risks if they become issues (that is, realized); these responses take the form of strategic responses and tactical actions. The ninth process is to perform political risk monitoring and controlling which is determining which political risks that have occurred and their effectiveness of the responses managing them. The tenth process in the sequence is to perform political risk reporting; it requires compiling facts and data from perform political risk monitoring and controlling and communicating the results to applicable stakeholders. The final process is to maintain the political risk management which involves keeping the political risk management plan current. One important point. Rarely do these processes occur linearly. Rather, they often occur nonlinearly and are iterative.

As one progresses through all the processes more facts and data become available which may require making changes to one or more processes.

KEY POINTS

To achieve the two goals for an infrastructure requires keeping these key points in mind.

Understand how political risk management should fit within the existing organization. Often the hierarchy is the following. The board of directors sets the overall strategic direction of an enterprise. The board of directors has an audit or risk committee which receives and reviews risk reports. The committee often has a senior risk management executive who serves as an advisor to the committee; he or she may function in the role of a process owner responsible for strategic oversight of risk management throughout an enterprise, ensuring risk management procedures are followed, reports are generated, and monitors overall effectiveness. A chief risk officer does the reporting as well as manages the risk management organization, at the corporate level. In turn, each of the business units may have their own risk management organization with its own chief risk officer feeding data and information to the corporate level.

Obtain executive sponsorship. An executive sponsor is essential to facilitate successfully implementing political risk management throughout an organization. Ideally, this sponsorship should be at the highest levels of the organization, such as at the C-suite level; this person may also function as the process owner for political risk management. This executive ensures not only financial support is available but also internal political assistance, if necessary. The chief risk officer who is responsible for the risk management organization may serve in this role but he or she might not be as effective when dealing with cross functional issues at the enterprise and business unit levels.

Prepare a business case demonstrating the value of political risk management to an enterprise. When preparing the business case, think about leveraging the successes of other risk management in furthering the strategic goals of an enterprise. The business case covers the tangible benefits of the political risk management, such as payback or shareholder value, but also intangible benefits, such as the ability to respond to political events that may not be quantifiable. Much of the business case can be extracted from what is called the Situation-Target-Proposal.

Usually, executives and senior managers become interested in a project after they decide it has potential. They often require some type of preliminary analysis and recommendations before performing a thorough business case. A situation-target-proposal, shown in Figure 4.2, is a common tool used for that purpose. The situation describes the issue or

Situation	Target	Proposal

FIGURE 4.2
Situation, Target, Proposal (STP).

problem that needs addressing. The target is the best or ideal state to address the situation, and the proposal is actions to address the situation. The proposal may include several proposals with a recommendation. The whole idea with an STP is to verify that a problem really exists before investing considerable resources into a project, such as creating and implementing a political risk management organization. If executive and senior management decide in favor of a proposal, the next action is to perform a cost-benefit analysis to determine whether a political risk management project should proceed.

Identify the relevant stakeholders either having a direct or indirect interest in the outcome of political risk management. The most obvious stakeholders are the members of the board of directors or an audit or risk management committee. Other obvious ones are the chief risk officer and other stakeholders in his or her chain of command. Less obvious stakeholders are shareholders or owners, suppliers, vendors, business unit executives, business risk officers, consultants, etc. Knowing and involving the stakeholders helps to reduce resistance over implementing a risk management office. The key is to obtain their engagement and keep it throughout when deploying political risk management.

Establish and maintain visibility about the importance of political risk management. With so much going on in a global enterprise, a political risk management project can be easily overlooked even by the most committed stakeholders. This situation is especially the case when resources are scarce. It can also be the case if political risk management participation is charged to overhead, meaning that other organizations must absorb the costs. Under such circumstances, attention can easily shift to what is perceived as more important matters. The importance of an executive sponsor can help provide further visibility with members of the board of directors and other senior executives. This visibility, along with other approaches, should be continuous and occur throughout an enterprise, vertically and horizontally.

Tied closely to the last point is to draft a vision statement for the political risk management group. A vision, formulated by key stakeholders, can serve as a powerful tool to gain buy-in and commitment from them. Additionally, all efforts and resources should be directed toward achieving the vision. Regular feedback to stakeholders on progress toward achieving the vision is critical and, if necessary, seek suggestions for improvement.

Use the vision to develop and document processes to turn political risk management into a reality. All processes should be predicated upon supporting the achievement of the vision. The processes, in turn, are supported by procedures and guidelines for political risk management. These policies and procedures should clearly articulate the relationship with the parent risk management organization and with other relevant organizational entities, e.g., internal audit. These documents should be available, preferably online nowadays.

Hire a competent team for the political risk management group. A tendency is to bring on board people with strictly a business background at the exclusion of other disciplines. This narrow focus could pose a serious problem as discussed earlier. Political risk management requires a different set of skills and often involves a different paradigm to interpret global political issues. All differences can be a strength if both backgrounds complement one another. Employees in the political risk management group should have a broad background in the social sciences (such as political science and economics) as well as some background in global business operations. Additional knowledge and background in supply chain management, project management, risk management, and business continuity are important, too. The number of people in the group should be relatively small. It might also be useful to have members having a good background in a region or country where the global supply chain touches, e.g., Central America or China, respectively.

Be open to suggestions for improvement from key stakeholders. Other groups in the risk management organization, legal department, internal audit, procurement management, security, and others may have substantial political or global experience that can provide insight on the processes and procedures. Gaining this input can help avoid making mistakes, such as oversights, as well as gain an emotional connection with political risk management being adopted in an enterprise.

Since political risk management will be new to an enterprise, conflict with other organizations may arise, even with other groups within the risk management organization. Many reasons can contribute to this conflict; typical examples include jurisdictional issues, battles over a tight budget, and a threat to empire building. Regardless of the reason, this conflict, if it arises, will require the support of an executive sponsor and other key stakeholders to manage such conflicts. They should address any serious conflict as early as possible to avoid escalation even before building and deploying a political risk management group begins. Being open to suggestions for improvement can help.

Coordinate or integrate with other organizations that may have touchpoints with the political risk management group. By doing so, the political risk group can help address conflict discussed in the last point and connect with allies. Coordination and integration will assure efficient and effective deployment of a political risk management group. It also builds a greater relationship with these organizations. These organizations to coordinate and integrate include security, legal, other groups within a risk management organization, internal audit, procurement, and risk management organizations inside business units and subsidiaries operating in countries touching a global supply chain.

Identify a portfolio of investments and projects potentially affected by political risks, whether threats or opportunities. This portfolio can be used to demonstrate the value of political risk management by identifying possible events or scenarios that may impact, for instance, a global supply chain involving certain countries and any corresponding strategic responses and contingencies to manage them. Having this portfolio will provide an idea of the potential size of the political risk management group and the skills, knowledge, and experience of the people to staff it.

Adopt a framework to perform political risk management. This framework could be developed inhouse or adopted from some other organization. A framework provides the structure and discipline for people to follow. It is often best to follow the framework used by the parent organization so that the political risk management group will conflict less with the parent risk management organization.

Condoleezza Rice and Amy Zegart in their book, *Political Risk*, identify a four-part framework to manage political risk:

- Understand
- Analyze
- Mitigate
- Respond

Understand involves looking at the risk appetite of stakeholders and increasing alertness about "blind spots." Analyze entails collecting and evaluating information about political risk and then using that information to make business decisions. Mitigate is about managing exposure to risks, such as implementing a system to alert when a risk occurs and respond accordingly to lessen damage. Respond is learning from what they call "near misses," by asking about the effectiveness of a response and identifying ways to improve.[1]

To a large extent, their framework corresponds with the processes of political risk management described by the author of this book (which, in

Process	Understand	Analyze	Mitigate	Respond
Establish Governance Infrastructure and Project	N/A	N/A	N/A	N/A
Identify Strategic Goals	✓			
Identify Stakeholders	✓			
Prepare Risk Management Plan				
Identify Risks		✓		
Assess Risks		✓		
Prepare Risk Responses			✓	
Perform Risk Monitoring and Controlling			✓	
Perform Risk Reporting				✓
Maintaining Risk Monitoring Processes	N/A	N/A	N/A	N/A

FIGURE 4.3
Rice and Zegart Framework and Political Risk Management Relationship.

turn, is based upon the concepts of enterprise risk management). Figure 4.3 shows the relationships between the Rice and Zegart framework and the political risk management. Understand roughly corresponds with identify strategic goals; identify stakeholders; and prepare risk management plan; analyze with identify risks and assess risks; mitigate with prepare risk responses; and respond corresponds with risk reporting.

The impression from Rice and Zegart's book is the process in linear, that is, one part of the framework follows the other. In political risk management, the flow realistically is often nonlinear as discussed earlier. Another difference is political risk management requires additional processes establishing a governance infrastructure, prepare a project or program management plan, and maintain the political risk management processes.

PLANNING AND IMPLEMENTING A POLITICAL RISK MANAGEMENT PROJECT

The best way to develop and deploy political risk management in a global enterprise is to apply project management. What follows is the rudiments of project management.

A project is a set of processes performed to achieve a specific result, e.g., service or product. It has these characteristics:

- Logical sequence
- Series of actions
- Start and stop date
- Unique, final product or service

In addition, a project involves these four elements, often interacting with one another:

- People: individuals working to achieve the vision of the project, e.g., team members, customers
- Processes: an integrated set of activities required to achieve a specific result, e.g., develop a project plan
- Systems: the automated and manual integrated set of processes, tools, and techniques to complete a project, e.g., information systems
- Data: a grouping of datum used to apply processes, tools, and techniques on a project and the subject being addressed

KEY POINTS

Keep the following points in mind when applying project management.

Adapt project management disciplines, tools, and techniques to the culture of an organization. Some organizations view project management as administrative overhead, and like all overhead, should be reduced. Not all enterprises, fortunately, reflect this attitude toward project management. In some organizations, however, project management might be as difficult to implement as political risk management. If this circumstance exists, applying project management on a small scale may help and, if the results are positive, expand its application on a larger scale.

After creating plans, ensure that everyone follows them. Sometimes, and too often, so much attention is on building plans which subsequently sit on a shelf and are never referenced until the project nears completion or the auditors arrive. The idea behind plans is to help a project proceed efficiently and effectively. Referring to plans after the fact is akin to looking at a map after arriving at an unknown destination.

Obtain participation from stakeholders when building plans. If participating in planning, stakeholders will have a greater willingness to follow plans. It also provides an opportunity to give visibility of their contributions after successfully implementing political risk management in an enterprise. Additionally, it provides stakeholders with the opportunity raise concerns, issues, challenges, etc. rather than wait to the last minute and cause havoc.

Provide a way to bring visibility to stakeholders whether they want it or not. Many people prefer to work under the radar, as an old saying goes. That is why it is important to remember the previous point – obtain their participation. Given the opportunity, many people will follow the line of least resistance and keep a low profile about their work, especially if it potentially has a negative result. By having, for example, group planning sessions stakeholders will find it very hard to disappear within the ranks because the success of a political risk management project requires integration with several people and organizations; any stakeholder who fails to deliver can impact others.

Be consistent and persistent when collecting status on cost, schedule, and quality performance. Consistency and persistency both require following a pattern of behavior. From a consistency perspective, collect the same categories of facts and data about project performance in ongoing, regular reporting about the project. From a persistency perspective, do whatever is required to obtain the same facts and data about project performance from the same stakeholders.

Give visibility of plans to stakeholders. Make them available to all pertinent stakeholders and tailor them to the needs of the recipients. The more visibility given to a project plan, the less likely people will be noncompliant and probably more supportive of a political risk management project.

Communicate, communicate, communicate. All successful project managers have one characteristic in common: they communicate with all stakeholders. Their communication goes beyond just sending reports. They meet regularly with stakeholders and go beyond just talking; they also listen to issues and concerns, which includes the project manager, from team members to executive and senior management. In fact, all stakeholders need to listen.

BENEFITS

Applying project to develop and deploy political risk management, offers several benefits.

Implements a project more efficiently and effectively. Rather than everyone scurrying, all stakeholders know what the goals are and, just as importantly, the path to achieve them. Rework and waste of resources is minimal in comparison to a risk management project without employing project or management. A well-defined, documented description of the goals and the path that all relevant stakeholders follow enhances performance synergistically.

Educates stakeholders on what constitutes success. With the goals defined for the project and plans related to cost, schedule, and quality stakeholders know when a project is over and whether it was truly a success. Without definitive goals for a project or program, stakeholders, to include the customer, e.g., the board of directors, for which a political risk management project exists, will have a difficult time determining whether a project is complete or a success.

Engenders greater stakeholder confidence when proceeding into the future when implementing political risk management. Most projects require marching into a future filled with unknowns. Having well-defined plans gives stakeholders the confidence that, they are prepared to deal with the unknown. Of course, some unknowns will exist as they do for just about every project. With the disciplines, tools, and techniques of project management stakeholders have the means to face the unknown and adapt accordingly.

Helps avoid some of the frequent problems plaguing many poorly managed or led projects. Some problems include unclear authority and responsibility; lack of scope definition; decision delays; underestimated time and costs to complete a project; unclear requirements; poor planning, and disengagement by team members. Applying project management disciplines, tools, and techniques, such as scheduling, responsibility assignment matrices, progress reporting, and a charter are just a few of the deliverables that can help overcome problems on the way toward completing a political risk management project with fewer problems.

Enables stakeholders to proact rather than react to circumstances. Situations will arise that impact the performance of a political risk management project. Unanticipated issues and concerns will always arise. Unfortunately, without project management some stakeholders treat all issues and concerns as equal when, realistically, they are not. Project management enables identifying and prioritizing issues and concerns. The whack-a-mole approach is no longer the norm, thereby enable applying resources efficiently and effectively.

Allows for greater interdependence and integration among specialties project or program. Sometimes, specialists on a project team perceive phenomena from a narrow vantage point, even to the extent of only thinking issues related to their specialty as being important. A political risk management project typically involves many disciplines, to include political science, security, law, economics, and information technology professionals. Project management helps to build a team of stakeholders from different disciplines to work together by focusing on common goals and path. In other words, they step out of the boundaries of their disciplinary field, producing synergistic results.

Enables better communication among all stakeholders on a project. Stakeholders are formed into teams and sub-teams to produce deliverables as well as coordinate with one another. Doing so requires effective communication. Better communication results in better performance both on an individual and a team level. Additionally, it improves allocating and deploying resources, whether people, money, or time.

APPROACH

A project consists of six major processes: defining, planning, organizing, executing, monitoring and controlling, and closing.

Defining is creating the authority document for a project and the assigned project manager to commit resources for the project, performing stakeholder analysis, and defining roles and responsibilities. The principal deliverables for this process are the charter, the stakeholder matrix, business case, and project announcement.

The charter is a high-level document, no more than two or three pages signed by key stakeholders, such as a project sponsor and a customer. It defines, at a high level, the scope of a project and gives a project manager the authority to proceed. Contents often include:

- Assumptions
- Constraints
- Deliverables
- Goals
- Overall description
- Principal participants
- Responsibilities
- Risks
- Scope (in and out)
- Signatures

The stakeholder matrix records information about those individuals or organizations having an interest in the outcome of a project. The information contained in the matrix may include:

- Concerns
- Criteria for success
- Stakeholder name
- Type of support

The business case determines whether the project is a positive investment for an enterprise. It basically covers two topics:

- Intangible, e.g., customer satisfaction
- Tangible, e.g., return on investment (ROI)

The project announcement is a brief, one-page memo or email announcing the existence of a project, to include its goals. The project charter is sometimes attached.

Planning is defining in greater detail the scope of the project and, ultimately, what is known as the performance baseline. The principal deliverables for this process are the work breakdown structure (WBS), network diagram, time estimates, cost estimates, resource requirements, assignments, risk management (for the project), schedule, and performance baseline.

The work breakdown structure (WBS) is detailed listing of deliverables and activities required to complete a project; it requires taking a top-down approach by defining the major phases, deliverables, and activities to complete a project. It forces project managers and their team members to think hard about what to do to finish a project; establishes a solid groundwork to make realistic time and cost estimates; allows project managers to build accountability among project team members; and forces significant issues to arise early rather than later in a project rather than later. Ultimately, it defines the scope of a project.

The network diagram is a tool to display the interrelationships among activities that were identified in the work breakdown structure. Upon estimating the effort to complete each activity, the network diagram enables creating a schedule. The network diagram displays which activities occur sequentially while others are performed concurrently.

Time estimating is determining how long an activity will likely take to complete. There are several techniques, e.g., heuristics, three-point estimates. Cost estimating is determining how much an activity will cost to complete. Both time and cost estimating are performed similarly in respect to labor while different, of course, for nonlabor. Estimates can be made at different levels of the work breakdown structure.

Resource requirements estimating involves determining the types and number of labor and nonlabor resources necessary to complete a project. The quantity of resource requirements is based upon the time and costs estimates. For labor resources, other considerations may include education, experience, and level of expertise.

Risk management is performed, in this context, for a project and not to be confused with political risk management. It requires identifying potential threats and opportunities that may impact a political risk management project and the responses to address them. Risk management on a project is not a one-time affair; it requires attention throughout the life of a project.

Scheduling is determining when activities start and stop in a schedule for a project. To build a schedule requires using the work breakdown structure, time estimates, the network diagram, and resource requirements to calculate the start and stop dates for each activity and for the entire project. Additionally, the schedule provides the critical path or paths, meaning if any activities slides are on it the project end date will also do the same.

Once the scope, cost, and schedule are agreed upon by team members and the project manager and the executive sponsor, the performance measurement baseline becomes the criteria to determine how well a project is executed. Deviations from the performance measurement baseline may eventually indicate corrective action is necessary to get back, for instance, on schedule. More about this topic when discussing the executing and monitoring and control processes for managing a project.

Organizing is setting up the infrastructure for a project and establishing communications. The principal deliverables are procedures addressing topics like configuration management, change management, requirements management, budgeting, communications management, quality management, reporting, procurement management, scheduling, time and cost estimating, organizational structure, and staffing management. These procedures explain what and how to apply each topic. Below is a brief description of each procedural topic.

- Change management: detecting, analyzing, evaluating, and implementing changes to all baselines.
- Communications management: providing the right facts and data at the right time in the right format to the right person to make the right decisions and take the right actions.
- Configuration management: maintaining the baseline and tracking changes to deliverables created on a project.
- Cost management: allocating and managing funds for initiating, defining, planning, organizing, executing, monitoring, and controlling, and closing a project.
- Human resource management: identifying the resources required for a project, team organization, staffing management plan, and roles, responsibilities, and authorities.
- Procurement management: obtaining the appropriate products or services to complete a project.
- Quality management: determining the standards for quality on a project and ascertaining whether they are being met and, if not, take the necessary corrective action.
- Requirements management: determining and documenting the needs and wants of the internal or external customer which will be used to ascertain the scope for a project.
- Schedule management: determining the type of schedule (e.g., bar chart, milestone chart, or precedence diagram), the types of relationships among activities, and updating status.

Executing is implementing the project plan according to the performance baseline. The principal deliverables are managing activities, procuring resources, and making adjustments, e.g., corrective actions.

Managing activities includes:

- Adhering to processes
- Executing activities according to schedule with the applicable resources
- Making timely decisions and following up on them
- Setting priorities and following them
- Sticking to baseline plans
- Taking preventive or corrective actions

Procuring resources includes:

- Determining contract types
- Following up on decisions
- Negotiating and signing contracts with suppliers and vendors
- Soliciting bids
- Taking preventive and corrective actions

Monitoring and controlling is observing, measuring, and assessing the performance of a project. Controlling is taking preventive or corrective actions to achieve the goals of a project. The principal deliverables for monitoring and controlling are status collection and scope verification.

Monitoring includes:

- Assessing how well a project has progressed up to any given point in time for budget, schedule, and quality
- Collecting status
- Identifying variances to cost, schedule, and quality plans

Controlling includes:

- Determining the options for project performance improvement and selecting the best one
- Developing a plan to implement the option
- Implementing the plan to improve cost, schedule, and quality performance

In some cases, re-planning is necessary. It involves revising, in whole or part, project plans to meet project goals.

Closing are actions taken to complete all activities and tasks and informing stakeholders of the results. The principal deliverables for closing are validation of performance pertaining to schedule, cost, quality, e.g., satisfy requirements, financial closure, and contractual closure (if applicable).

Closing includes:

- Closing financial requirements
- Compiling and completing records
- Compiling statistics on cost, schedule, and quality performance
- Conducting post-implementation audit
- Obtaining final signatures
- Perform winding down activities, e.g., fulfilling remaining contractual obligations, addressing remaining requirements
- Preparing lessons learned
- Verifying completion criteria in compliance with other aspects of the project

Albeit not a process, leadership is a key ingredient for the success of a project. Leading a project involves motivating people to achieve its goals. Leading is not the same as managing although project managers must do both. Managing is about doing things right; leading is about doing the right things. The former is associated with doing the functions of managing, e.g., budgeting, planning. The latter is associated with issues like motivation, listening, and other "soft" topics. Someone once described the difference in a more down to earth difference. Managing is about perspiring; leading is about inspiring. Leading is required across all the processes of project management. In other words, leadership is at the center of every project process.

Projects also follow a project life cycle, consisting of phases that upon completion produce a product or deliver a service to a customer. The processes of project management are deployed to manage an entire project and each of the phases. A generic life cycle for a project might consist of these phases:

- Define, e.g., scope, requirements
- Design, e.g., functional components, architecture
- Develop, e.g., build
- Detect, e.g., testing
- Deploy, e.g., implement
- Sustain, e.g., upgrade

In some cases, especially if an enterprise is global and has numerous business units or subsidiaries, establishing a program is more effective. A program consists of multiple projects; completing projects, in turn, completes a program; in other words, it is the sum of the projects constituting it. A program has these fundamental characteristics which are at a higher level of abstraction than a project:

- Aligns its vison with that of the enterprise as well as provide vision and leadership to its projects
- Applies change management discipline
- Creates high level plans for projects to follow
- Facilitates problem resolution
- Focuses on managing relationships and conflict resolution among its projects
- Has a broader scope than projects
- Manages political aspects of stakeholder management, usually at an executive or senior management level
- Manages project managers
- Measures ROI, new capabilities, and benefit delivery beyond just one project
- Monitors projects and ongoing work using governance structures

A project, therefore, as opposed to a program, has these characteristics:

- Conducts detailed planning
- Focus on activity delivery
- Has a narrow vision and scope
- Manages specialties
- Measures success by schedule, budget, and quality performance at the activity level
- Monitors and controls activities and work
- Motivates using knowledge and skills
- Seeks to minimize change

Enterprises often have a population of projects which are part of what is known as a portfolio. It is a collection of projects and programs that are aligned with the vison, goals, and objects of a parent organization, such as the enterprise or a business unit. A portfolio has some of these characteristics:

FIGURE 4.4
Enterprise-wide Programs and Projects Hierarchy.

- Adds value to decision-making to executive of senior management
- Aligns programs' and projects' scopes with strategies of the enterprise as a whole
- Creates and maintains common processes among programs and projects
- Determines fate of programs and projects populating the portfolio
- Looks at aggregate performance using indicators
- Monitors changes in a broad environment, e.g., business environment
- Provides analysis and synthesis of the entire population of programs and projects

Ideally, all portfolios, programs, and projects align with the vision, goals, objectives, and strategies of the entire enterprise as shown in Figure 4.4. This relationship can be seen as an inverted pyramid, flowing from broad to specific, in the following order: vision, goals, objectives, strategies, operational plans, programs, and projects. This relationship can be at the corporate levels as well as at the business unit or subsidiary levels.

CHALLENGES

Deploying project or program management disciplines, tools, and techniques does present some challenges.

Keeping stakeholders engaged in a political risk management project. Stakeholders often have other responsibilities beside political risk management. They are frequently engaged in keeping some aspect of a strategic enterprise operational, even at the strategic level. They also face with irrelevant issues and concerns that may require immediate attention, drawing their attention temporarily away from political risk management. Even with the best plans of a project, external circumstances can draw some stakeholders from a project; these might include a downturn in economic performance and legal action against an enterprise.

Having the right people to attend meetings. Many stakeholders spend a large percentage of their time already attending meetings, especially as one moves up a hierarchy. These meetings often conflict with one another. If they cannot attend some meetings, stakeholders may send a representative. However, this person may lack the authority to make a decision or have expertise to contribute effectively.

Maintaining visibility of results. With everything going on in a global enterprise, maintaining visibility of a risk management project can be difficult. The competition among other high priority projects is often extreme, the equivalent of salmon moving upstream to spawn. The project receiving the requisite attention may reflect internal politics such as it does out of a business necessity. Political risk management projects especially face this situation unless a powerful executive, such as a member of the board of directors, becomes the sponsor.

Coming up with problems without developing solutions. On just about any project, problems arise. Most problems are usually handled internally to a project. However, in some cases, especially cross-functional projects, like political risk management ones, determining and implementing solutions requires time. Extremely complex problems involving many stakeholders, resulting in a financial and schedule impact to a project. Reviews and approvals by key stakeholders take time since the project is competing against other ones. The result is often slowing the momentum of the political risk management project or program.

Reporting with valid and reliable facts and data. Managing projects and reporting on them, as already discussed, requires having access to valid and reliable facts and data. In a typical project environment, such facts and data are not always available just by the inherent nature of a project. Technology projects often lend themselves to produce "hard" deliverables for the most part and, therefore, make progress reporting easier in comparison with projects with "soft" deliverables which frequently require judgment by key stakeholders about accuracy and completeness. The soft deliverables created on political risk management projects include decisions and identifying and communicating with key political actors in a country, across a region, and throughout the globe.

Keeping executive and senior management support for the political risk management project. The reality is that executives and senior managers in a global enterprise are constantly on the move from one position to another. Their transfers may be lateral, upward in the hierarchy, onward toward a special assignment. One of these executives or senior managers may be the sponsor for the political risk management project. Sometimes a new sponsor from the executive and senior ranks is assigned. Ideally, the new sponsor will be supportive but that may not always be the case.

Having sufficient resources. Very few enterprises, large or small, local or global, have a situation where money is no object. Resources are treated as finite and distributed among projects based upon priority. The ones with the highest priority, naturally, receive the largest budget, after that, the purse is reduced for other projects. A political risk management project will likely have a high priority status since it often has the enterprise's risk management executive or a member of the board of directors as its executive sponsor. However, as mentioned previously, executive and senior management sponsors can change and so can the priority of a project. Frequently, when the sponsor goes and the priority falls, the budget declines unless the new sponsor generates the same level of support, financial or in kind.

Providing protection from stakeholder saboteurs. Not all stakeholders will support a high visible project, such as a political risk management one. Some stakeholders will stand on the sidelines, at best feigning support. Other stakeholders may express support for a project but try to sabotage progress. Still others might level criticism right from the start; usually these are the ones a project manager does not have to worry about since they can identify and understand the issues and concerns. Stakeholders who feign support or remain on the side lines occasionally lobs grenades are the ones to worry about. They may use a misstep on a project as a way to pull the pin on the grenade.

FINAL THOUGHTS

Political risk management does not arise out of a void. It requires governance infrastructure to support its development and provide ongoing support. It also requires project or program management to make it a reality. Without governance and project or program management, political risk management will likely not last.

GETTING STARTED QUESTIONS

Questions	Yes	No

1. Is there an infrastructure or organization that currently exists which performs risk management? If so, what are its goals? How does it fit with the organization?

2. If a risk management infrastructure or organization exists, does it perform political risk management performed? If yes, how effective is it? If not, why?

3. Assuming political risk management is not performed, is it at least being considered?

4. If so, are the following being considered?
    a) Obtaining executive sponsorship?
    b) Identifying potential stakeholders?
    c) Establishing and maintain visibility about the maintenance of political risk management?
    d) Drafting a vision statement for political risk management function or organization?
    e) Preparing a business case?
    f) Using the vision statement to develop and document processes to turn political risk management into a reality?
    g) Hiring a competent team to conduct political risk management?
    h) Encouraging stakeholders to share their thoughts about the value of political risk management for the enterprise?
    i) Coordinating or integrating with other internal organizations that may touchpoints with the political risk management organization or process?
    j) Identifying a portfolio of global investments, projects, and programs that may be affected by political risks and events?
    k) Adopting or developing a framework to perform political risk management?

5. For defining a political risk management project or program, have you considered the following?
    a) Drafting a charter? And, if so, has it been approved by key stakeholders?
    b) Preparing a business case for the project or program?
    c) Having an executive sponsor prepare and send a project or program announcement to stakeholders?

6. For planning a political risk management project or program, have you and your core team considered the following?
    a) Developing a work breakdown structure?
    b) Creating a network diagram?
    c) Estimating the time, cost, and resource requirements?
    d) Performing risk management for the project or program itself?
    e) Developing a schedule?

Questions	Yes	No

7. or organizing a political risk management project or program, have you developed and implemented procedures on the following topics?
   a) Configuration management?
   b) Change management?
   c) Requirements management?
   d) Communications management?
   e) Quality management?
   f) Procurement management?
   g) Schedule management?
   h) Human resource management?
   i) Cost management?

8. For executing a political risk management project or program, have you considered the following?
   a) Executing activities according to the schedule?
   b) Adhering to baselines?
   c) Setting priorities and following up on them?
   d) Making timely decisions and following up on them?
   e) Taking preventive or corrective actions?
   f) Adhering to processes?
   g) Procuring resources?
   h) Making adjustments?

9. For monitoring and controlling a political risk management project or program, have you considered the following?
   a) For monitoring:
      1) Collecting status?
      2) Identifying variances to cost, schedule, and quality plans?
      3) Assessing how well a project or program has progressed from a budget, schedule, and quality perspective?
   b) For controlling:
      1) Determining the options for project or program performance improvement and selecting the best one?
      2) Developing a plan to implement the option selected?
      3) Implementing the plan to improve cost, schedule, and quality performance?
      4) Following up on the effectiveness of the implemented option?

10. For closing, have you considered the following?
    a) Compiling statistics on cost, schedule, and quality performance?
    b) Preparing lessons learned?
    c) Performing winding down activities?
    d) Compiling and completing records?
    e) Choosing financial requirements?
    f) Verifying completion criteria?
    g) Conducting a post-implementation review?
    h) Obtaining final signatures?

11. Have you determined whether to plan and deploy a risk management project or program? If a program, what additional processes should be implemented and to what degree are the ones described previously to be implemented down to a project manager?

NOTE

1. Condoleezza Rice and Amy B. Zegart, *Political Risk* (New York: Twelve, 2018), 11.

5

Identify Enterprise Strategic Goals

One of the first actions to take when performing political risk management is to identify the strategic goals for an enterprise as they pertain to a global supply chain and determine if they can be impacted by political risks. These goals should pertain to the entire enterprise, not just to a specific department.

The ultimate purpose is to translate the goals, which are supported with objectives, and strategies into realistic behaviors and actions and then be able to track performance against them. The goals and strategies apply to the ones associated directly or indirectly with political risk management. A goal is a broad aspiration that is difficult to define but has some inherent meaning but may be interpreted differently. An example of a goal might be becoming a premier systems integrator. An objective is specific, its meaning clear, and lends itself to less interpretation. An example of an objective is to reduce delivery times from offshore suppliers by fifty percent. An example of a strategy is to transition to a just-in-time delivery. Political risks that could impact the goal, objective, and strategy might be civil disturbances in the country of a major supplier, resulting in missed shipments.

That is why it is important to view an enterprise as an integrated entity subject to internal or external threats and opportunities affecting it holistically.

For example, a goal to achieve customer satisfaction is broad, has an inherent meaning, but is interpreted differently; everyone has a sense of what customer satisfaction means but disagree over its definition.

An example, ninety-five percent of customers must give a five-star rating in their feedback.

One way to understand the importance of goals for performing political risk management is to keep the following simple, conceptual equation in mind:

$$(\text{Goals}) + (\text{Risks} - \text{Management Activities}) = \text{Exposure}$$

This formula has been around for quite a few years and is particularly applies to political risk management.

The goals reflect the ones at the enterprise level, specifically ones related to a global supply chain. An example of a goal related to a global supply chain is becoming a premier systems integrator.

The risks are primarily political threats (or in some cases opportunities) impacting a global supply chain. An example of a political threat to a global supply chain are bureaucratic delays by host governments in approving product shipments to a warehouse in the home country.

Management activities are determining in advance the strategic responses and the contingencies (or tactical actions) are deployed to deal with political threats (or opportunities). An example of a strategic response is mitigation. An example of a management activity is to mitigate the threat by having additional products manufactured in another country.

Exposure is the degree of vulnerability an enterprise faces based upon the effectiveness of the management activities. An example of an exposure is loss of customer expectations in the home country.

KEY POINTS

Keep the following points in mind when identifying strategic goals.

Obtain access to the most current strategic goals. While this might seem like common sense, the reality is that the business environment constantly changes and so does an enterprise's strategic goals in a large enterprise, different versions of a strategic plan may float around, especially if strategic plans are not readily available which is frequently the case since they often containing proprietary information. A good place to start is to review the annual report to gain clues about an enterprise's strategic goals.

Recognize the most current strategic goals may reflect the "official" ones but infighting among executive and senior management ranks may reflect the "real" ones. Corporate mergers often result, for example, in bitter infighting over what path an enterprise should pursue in the future. Simple infighting over who bought whom, despite words of cooperation and teaming, add difficulty in determining the actual strategic goals. That is why it is important to carefully select the right stakeholders to obtain the most reliable documents describing an enterprise's strategic goals.

Remember that strategic goals and objectives are sometimes indistinguishable from one another; they may be treated as the same. Goals are often too broad to have specificity, resulting in subjective interpretation; objectives give specificity to goals and reduce the room for interpretation. Usually for large enterprises, this is not a problem since they are likely to have a strategic planning office; however, some companies on a smaller level may not have the resources even to hire a strategic planner. Sometimes, goals follow objectives. The point key is to understand how strategic goals differ and how they relate to one another.

Understand the differences between strategies and goals. Strategies move an enterprise from a current state to a future one; the goals are the targets. Goals, objectives, and strategies should work together to provide a statement of a desired direction and outcome. Strategic goals and the strategies should be mutually supportive, linked in a way so that if any of the three change then the others may need to change.

BENEFITS

Several benefits are attributed to identifying strategic goals.

Provides the basis to determine the direction of political risk management sessions. Knowing the strategic goals can reduce to the urge to address the entire business universe and take a shotgun approach and cover everything.

Helps to identify the scope of risk management. With direction and focus, as agreed upon by executive and senior management, political risk management activities can occur more efficiently and effectively. For example, a defined scope makes it easier to collect more relevant and precise facts and data when conducting primary and secondary research. It will also reduce the facts and data to collect, thereby expediting the time and effort to perform political risk management.

Provides a common vision among key stakeholders. Executive and senior management will know which strategic goals matter from the perspective of political risk management. However, other stakeholders may not have that same vision, either being focused more on daily activities or simply unaware of the relevant strategic goals Stakeholders can conduct political risk management more efficiently and effectively by focusing on

pertinent strategic goals; they keep the goals in the forefront help to identify pertinent risks as well as have a better understanding of the impacts
on an enterprise.

Keeps political risk management relevant by demonstrating its value.
Stakeholders can interpret enterprise-wide political risks through the lens
of the strategic goals, thereby making it easier to ascertain the impacts of
threats and opportunities to an entire enterprise and its global supply
chain. In other words, the importance of the relationship between the
strategic goals and global supply chains becomes clearer.

Narrows the reach for facts and data. Stakeholders will better know who
to contact and other sources to pursue. Stakeholders can easily find themselves going astray when pursuing of facts and data by interviewing the
wrong people. Strategic goals applying to global supply chains serve as
guides to pinpoint the relevant data sources.

APPROACH

One would think that a sizable enterprise would have plenty of sources
regarding strategic goals. In some enterprises, however, some sources may
be difficult to locate. Strategic goals may be considered proprietary and
may be unavailable to the general employee involved with political risk
management. Even if strategic goals are available, they may be dated, modified, contradictory, or incomplete. Also, enterprise goals may complement
one another and may likely be linked, adding to the complexity of determining relevant facts and data. Some common sources are discussed below.

A mission statement often contains some high aspirational goal or statements. It tends to be visionary and long-term but serve as a guide to find
other sources within the enterprise.

Most large enterprises, and especially global ones, create a vision statement. This vision statement is at a high level of abstraction but is useful to
develop strategies and strategic goals. This explosion into greater detail is
done at the parent company level. Below the parent company are operations, mainly consisting of business units and subsidiaries which at this
level the vision, strategic goals, and strategies are, in theory, turned into
reality, as shown in Figure 5.1. For example, executive and senior management prepares the vision statement which is cascaded down from the
enterprise to the business unit or subsidiary levels. Each business unit or
subsidiary aligns with the vision at the enterprise level.

FIGURE 5.1
Cascading Enterprise-wide Vision throughout an Enterprise.

Ideally, this broad to specific, top-down view should be the norm but realistically this arrangement is harder to achieve. Cultural differences within business units; the degree of autonomy; internal politics; and many other factors interfere with realizing the ideal. The variance between the ideal and reality becomes wider as an enterprise increases in size and its global reach increases. Both at the parent company and at the business unit levels and subsidiary levels formed to achieve the vision, goals, objectives, and strategies for the overall enterprise are adapted within each business unit or subsidiary. Strategic plans provide considerable information, which probably includes references to a vision statement; key performance indicators, such as financial and nonfinancial objectives; strengths; weaknesses; high-level risks; and global marketing strategy (if applicable). It can also provide facts and data about any other issues that may relate to political risks. Most importantly, it provides a synergistic perspective of how an enterprise's components work together to achieve goals.

Management by objectives (MBOs) which are based upon cascading goals. Ideally MBOs reflect a top-down portrayal of an enterprise's goals.

Operational plans should reference strategic goals and provide the details on how to achieve them; depending on the size of an enterprise, these plans may be combined in the strategic plan.

The financial statement of the company which often reflects (thanks to Sarbanes-Oxley) any risks having potentially a material impact to a public enterprise. Some of these risks may be political.

A matrix, such as the one shown in Figure 5.2, is a way to display the relationship between strategic goals and an enterprise's supply chain. The matrix is divided into quadrants. The cells reflect the intersection between the priority of strategic goals and the impact to a global supply chain. The goal is then recorded in the appropriate cell. For example, a goal might be becoming a systems integrator and its relevancy is high. The goal is then recorded in the upper right corner.

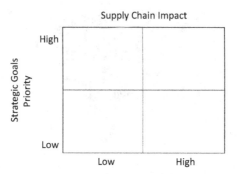

FIGURE 5.2
Matrix Showing Relationship between Goals and Supply Chain Impact.

CHALLENGES

Two main challenges present themselves when identifying strategic goals.

One is that executive and senior management may be split over the strategic goals, thereby making it difficult to narrow the focus of political risk management. As mentioned earlier, this often occurs after a merger and an internal political split exists among the executive and senior management ranks. Such circumstances result in indecision, making it tough to identify strategic goals that relate to political risk management.

The other challenge is restricted access to documents or information identifying the strategic goals. Some information may be considered highly proprietary. Such restrictions can become cumbersome when a need exists to share information pertaining strategic goals with subject matter experts who may not have executive or senior management status but have valuable insight and expertise may not be able to participate fully. In some cases, this situation may be surmountable by having a person sign a nondisclosure agreement.

FINAL THOUGHTS

An old saying goes that if you do not know what you are shooting at, then everything looks like a target. The same philosophy goes with political risk management. By knowing the strategic goals of an enterprise and determining which ones apply to the global supply chain, stakeholders can better focus their time and energies on relevant political risks.

GETTING STARTED QUESTIONS

Questions	Yes	No

1. Have you identified the strategic goals of the enterprise?
2. Have you determined how the strategic goals apply to the global supply chain?
3. Did you get access to the following sources of information to identify strategic goals?
   a) Mission statement?
   b) Strategic plan?
   c) Operational plans?
   d) Financial statement?
4. Do you have the following challenges concerning the strategic goals?
   a) Executive and senior management split over what the strategic goals are?
   b) If conflict exists over the strategic goals, have you decided which ones to use?
   c) Restricted access to documents and information?
5. Have you identified the potential stakeholders in the enterprise affected by or have an interest in political risk management?
   a) Board of directors?
   b) Chief executive officer?
   c) Chief financial officer?
   d) Vice President of Internal Audit?
   e) Chief Risk Officer?
   f) Business unit/subsidiary executive and senior management?
   g) Subject matter experts?
   h) Others?
6. When identifying the strategic goals, have you considered the following points?
   a) Accessing the most current strategic goals?
   b) Determining which strategic goals are the official or the real ones?
   c) Understanding the strategies to achieve the strategic goals?
7. When identifying strategic goals, did you consider the following?
   a) Conducting interviews with key stakeholders?
   b) Using the Delphi technique?
   c) Conducting a business impact analysis?
8. Have you determined whether you face any of the following challenges and, if so, determining how to deal with them?
   a) Time availability of stakeholders?
   b) Internal political differences?
   c) Competing with daily operational priorities?
   d) Scope misinterpretation?
   e) Changing stakeholders?
9. Have you prepared a stakeholder listing (also known as a stakeholder register), not for the project or program but for political risk management?

6

Identify Stakeholders for Political Risk Management

A stakeholder is a person or organization having a direct or indirect interest in the outcome of a process or project. Using the goals, political risk management processes will provide an idea of whom to contact to capture facts and data, concerns, potential risks, etc. Political risk management involves many stakeholders at the strategic level of the enterprise or senior executive levels of a business unit or subsidiary.

The Board of Directors is, of course, the highest level of stakeholders, usually consisting of the chairman, chief executive officer, chief financial officer, significant shareholders, senior vice presidents from various areas, and presidents of operating divisions. The Board determines, among other things, the overall strategic direction of an enterprise. Most enterprises have an audit or risk committee which is responsible to ensure enterprise risk management occurs and, in turn, reports its findings to the board.

Actual political risk management is often conducted by a chief risk officer (if one exists) or by internal audit. If internal audit collects and compiles the facts and data, it presents the results to an audit committee for review and analysis before presenting it to the Board. Internal auditors may collect and compile facts and data from public relations, government affairs, legal, finance, consultants, vendors, staff, suppliers, senior vice presidents, operational management, and subject matter experts. The facts and data are compiled and presented to the audit committee prior to the delivery to the board. If not approved, internal audit continues to refine its facts and data to present one more time to the audit committee, if necessary. Once accepted by the audit committee, internal audit or a senior management officer presents the pitch or paper to the Board for review and approval. If accepted, the political risk management results are then used in the Board's decision-making.

The process essentially repeats if a risk management officer and his or her organization reports to a risk committee of the board of directors for a global enterprise.

KEY POINTS

Keep the following points in mind when identifying stakeholders.

A stakeholder today may not be one tomorrow. Business conditions constantly change for a global enterprise; organizational restructuring and movement of key executives and senior managers to different positions (sometimes out of disfavor; others for greater opportunities) is constant. When a stakeholder changes, the new one may not share the same level of interest, more or less, in political risk management.

Stakeholders are not always apparent, especially in a global enterprise. For example, a special project, such as one implementing political risk management, may continue efficiently and effectively for a while. Then, seemingly out of nowhere, a stakeholder, such as an executive or senior manager, appears, demanding why he or she was not consulted from the beginning. The project may have to be suspended, halted, or require re-planning to account for the stakeholder's interests.

A stakeholder's interest may change over time. For example, some stakeholders may be highly enthusiastic over a political risk management in the beginning. Over time, however, their support may begin to wane. This declining enthusiasm can hinder project performance or increase the potential for failure in regards for developing or deploying political risk management. Whatever the reason, keep in mind that most stakeholder interests should never be taken for granted.

Not all stakeholders are believable when expressing their commitment. For example, some stakeholders may express support for political risk management but behind the scenes try to interfere with its chance for success. They may slowly reduce headcount to support a project or start complaining about how political risk management, for example, is increasing their overhead costs.

If strategic goals of an enterprise change, so may stakeholders. Changing strategic goals and objectives may require organizational restructuring as well as moving around executives and senior management into different positions. As a result, for example, different stakeholders with varying interests will have to be consulted to understand their needs and wants regarding political risk management.

Not all stakeholders are equal in terms of power and influence. In a large global enterprise, some stakeholders may be in greater positions of authority and responsibility which frequently means acquiring more power and influence. At least that is how it appears formally; in some cases, however, some stakeholders may not have formal positions of authority and responsibility but have considerable informal power and influence by virtue of their connections. Overlooking such positions can jeopardize the success of any political risk management processes.

BENEFITS

Identifying stakeholders offers several benefits.

Provides an opportunity to obtain buy-in from stakeholders on the processes and results of political risk management. When buy-in occurs, it reduces the probability of refusal to accept the results but, just as importantly, offers them the opportunity to share facts and data of value to other stakeholders.

Helps to ease determining priorities regarding processes and risks. Stakeholders providing the input to political risk management know more about their operations than the people conducting the interviews. Their knowledge and experience can provide insight on what risks could occur; their priority relative to one another; and impacts to their areas of responsibilities and the entire enterprise.

Enables stakeholders, especially key ones, to take a holistic, multi-disciplinary perspective. Discussing risks at the strategic level requires seeing an enterprise from many different angles. Executive and senior management often know how their areas of responsibility affect an entire enterprise as well as its other organizational units; they may also have a good idea how their operations impact other areas beyond the enterprise, e.g., government or another enterprise. Key strategic stakeholders play an important role to ensure that the big picture perspective remains the focus of political risk management.

Allows executive and senior management stakeholders to capture scenarios or risk events that no one else had considered. The big picture perspective provides unique insights resulting from their broader responsibilities; stakeholders in the lower levels of the hierarchy cannot or do not have the experience. By virtue of their position, executive and senior managers, often move from one organization to another which augments their knowledge and experience concerning their enterprise. As a result, they can see how the different organizations within an enterprise affect one another. This exposure increases perspective and, therefore, helps to identify risks and their relationships to one another.

Enables determining a person's or organization's risk attitude and risk tolerance. Risk attitude is a person's or organization's degree of perception about uncertainty; risk tolerance is a person's or organization's degree of willingness to withstand uncertainty. By knowing stakeholders' risk attitude and tolerance, determining their willingness to take on risk and to what degree helps in determining the extent of risk analysis and response.

A common way to depict the risk profile of stakeholders is to create a 4 x 4 chart shown in Diagram Figure 6.1. The chart helps working with stakeholders based upon their perceptions and feelings about risk taking; not everyone or organization within a global enterprise has the same perceptions and feelings about risk, especially about political risk. Each quadrant depicts, for each stakeholder, risk tolerance and risk appetite. The vertical, or Y-axis, reflects the degree of risk tolerance for a stakeholder. The horizontal, or X-axis, reflects the risk appetite for a stakeholder. Each stakeholder, based upon the combination of risk tolerance and risk appetite, falls into one of the quadrants. For example, one stakeholder has a low risk tolerance and a low risk appetite so its name goes into the lower left quadrant and another has a high risk tolerance and a high risk appetite,

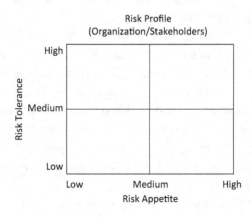

FIGURE 6.1
Chart Displaying Risk Profile of Stakeholders.

thereby going into the upper right quadrant. Each axis has continuum reflecting an assessment of the degree of magnitude, such as low, medium, or high, or numeric, such as 1 through 10.

APPROACH

Here are some ways to start identifying stakeholders.

One approach is to conduct interviews with key stakeholders. An interview usually lasts no more than one hour but sometimes two depending on the time available and importance of the interviewee. A prepared set of questions are asked, some being dichotomous choice questions and others open-ended. The idea is to encourage stakeholders to share facts and data regarding their thoughts about political risks that may occur under their purview also elsewhere in an enterprise. A key, but often overlooked, question to ask is "what keeps you up at night?" Naturally, the facts and data are held confidential as to the source and documented.

Another common approach is the Delphi technique. It requires sending a questionnaire or survey to key stakeholders, asking them a series of questions or ratings on political topics, issues, or risks or a combination of all three. The questionnaire or survey is repeatedly sent to the stakeholders until reaching a consensus. The Delphi technique works well if stakeholders lack the time to meet or cannot participate in an interview.

A third approach, used in business continuity, is the business impact analysis (BIA). This approach requires analyzing all operations within an organization to identify critical business processes as well as the impacts of potential risks, especially threats. The BIA can occur at the strategic and operational levels. During the sessions, which again should not exceed two hours, the interviewer discusses any political topics, issues, or risks. Of course, parts of the facts and data from the BIA may have to be kept confidential.

CHALLENGES

Identifying stakeholders and obtaining their involvement is easier to talk about than making it happen. Here are some common challenges.

Limited time availability of stakeholders, especially executive and senior management. Their operational responsibilities alone consume their schedules granting them little time to participate in political risk management. For example, this time constraint also hinders assembling at a mutually convenient time to identify and assess risks.

Internal political differences may result in infighting, making it difficult to get stakeholders to willingly participate jointly with others. For example, after a merger, certain stakeholders might not be willing to share facts and data due to internal political infighting. Even under a one-on-one session, a stakeholder may reluctantly to share information for fear of what is shared is advantageous to another stakeholder. The quality of the facts and data shared, if at all, may be unreliable.

Daily operational priorities may pose a challenge. Certain key stakeholders may be too occupied with operational concerns and may lack the time to participate, even for an hour. Key executives often have this problem; frequently, a replacement is provided who sometimes lacks the knowledge and authority to make decisions, for example, on a political risk management project.

Scope misinterpretation. If the scope of political risk management is unclear, such as vague or unknown goals, identifying stakeholders may prove too challenging to perform. Even if stakeholders become involved, uncertainty over scope can cause conflict as well as a slide in a timeline to complete a political risk management project.

Finally, rotating stakeholders. A stakeholder may circulate from one organization to another, get fired, or depart the enterprise. A replacement may not be readily available which can result in a loss of knowledge and experience deemed valuable to an enterprise risk management project.

The eventual deliverable from identifying stakeholders is what is called a stakeholder listing or register. For each stakeholder, this information is recorded: name, organization, position, risks identified, potential responses to those risks, their risk tolerance, risk attitude, and any other pertinent facts and data. This listing is updated throughout political risk management because stakeholders come and go or may no longer have a stake in the outcome.

FINAL THOUGHTS

Knowing the stakeholders having a vested interest in political risk management is important. Obtaining their support, participation, and commitment can significantly overcome resistance to change as well as well as further developing, deploying, and maintaining political risk management processes.

GETTING STARTED QUESTIONS

Questions	Yes	No
1. When identifying stakeholders for political risk management, have you considered the following?		
a) Determine who on the Board of Directors could serve as the executive sponsor for political risk management?		
b) Determine who is the chief risk management officer or risk management process owner for the enterprise?		
c) Identify other potential stakeholders in the chain of command for the enterprise?		
d) Recognize that stakeholder interest in political risk management may change over time?		
e) Maintain a healthy skepticism regarding a stakeholder's express commitment to political risk management?		
f) Understand that strategic goals as well as organizational changes may require reassessing the list of stakeholders or their degree of commitment to political risk management?		
g) Recognize that stakeholders vary in terms of their power and influence?		
2. Are you taking the following actions?		
a) Interviewing potential stakeholders regarding their thoughts, insights, concerns, and issues concerning political risk management being adopted in the enterprise?		
b) Using the Delphi technique to ask a series of questions or ratings on political risk management topics, issues, threats, or opportunities?		
c) Conduct a business impact analysis to gain information and insight on how political risk management may impact critical business processes?		
3. Are you experiencing any of the following challenges and, if so, determining how to deal with them?		
a) Time availability of stakeholders?		
b) Internal political differences among stakeholders?		
c) Daily operational priorities conflicting with political risk management efforts in the future?		
d) Scope definition of what political risk management might be in the enterprise?		
e) Stakeholders changing positions or departing the enterprise?		

7

Prepare a Political Risk Management Plan

Stakeholders need to follow agreed upon political risk management processes. Failure to do so can result in inefficient and ineffective performance of political risk management. These processes should also be known to all stakeholders participating in political risk management. The key for doing so is the political risk management plan.

KEY POINTS

Keep the following points in mind when preparing a political risk management plan.

Tap as many sources as possible when drafting a political risk management plan. The document describes the processes to manage political risk in an enterprise. Many political risk management processes are similarly to risk management in general and may simply need tailoring for inclusion in the political risk management plan. For example, one source might be the risk management processes of a parent organization; the contents are tweaked to address political risk. Other sources might include adapting enterprise risk management to the specific needs of managing political risks, such as described in this book.

Ensure that all key stakeholders have an updated copy of the political risk management plan in their possession or at least have access to it. They should all be using a copy with the exact contents; otherwise, confusion may arise when executing political risk management processes.

Obtain input from key stakeholders when drafting or updating a risk management plan. By providing an opportunity for input, it can help off-set the criticism of having a separate set of processes for political risk management, especially if conflicting with risk management processes of the parent risk management organization. It also generates more ownership and commitment in support of political risk management. In some cases, updating the risk management plan of the parent organization to reflect the processes of political risk management may suffice and likely require less input from stakeholders.

Keep the political risk management plan under configuration management. Once key stakeholders have approved the plan, an approval process should be in place to allow for managing changes. Upon receiving the requisite approvals, a political risk management plan should be distributed or accessible to all relevant stakeholders.

BENEFITS

The risk management plan provides several benefits.

Serves as a communications tool. If stakeholders need to clarify a political risk management topic, they can refer to the document. For example, if they want to know the definition of a term used in the context of political risk management, they can refer to the document. Or, if they need to know what reports to prepare, they can refer to the plan. Just the act of preparing and reviewing the document can facilitate good discussion.

Provides the basis to coordinate effectively among stakeholders. If a question arises over general roles, responsibilities, and authorities, such as with risk owners, for example, stakeholders can refer to the plan.

Provides a common, consistent approach. Upon granting approval to the plan, key stakeholders have given their agreement or consensus to follow the procedures, tools, and techniques described for political risk management processes. For example, they may have agreed to use the Crawford slip method to identify risks and then reflect them in a risk breakdown structure.

APPROACH

The most common approach is to prepare a "straw horse" by someone on the team and submit the document for review, nowadays using electronic review. Electronic review reduces time and captures changes. If conducting a serial electronic review (that is, the draft goes from one reviewer to the next) that may increase the flow time to complete the review but is easier to see the trail of changes. If doing a concurrent electronic review (that is, people receive a copy of the document at the same time) that reduces the flow time but then requires more effort to resolve differences. Naturally, with reviews by groups, several drafts will likely be produced before obtaining final approval. The approach taken depends on the availability of time and the effort desired to expend on the document. In the end, the goal is to obtain approval from all stakeholders. Once approved by key stakeholders, the document is under configuration management.

Configuration management is often overlooked but is important. A risk management document provides direction and information on conducting enterprise risk management for a specific project. All stakeholders need to have confidence that they are employing the same processes as described in the plan.

The political risk management plan generally contains at a minimum the following content.

Reference to the governing policy on risk management for the enterprise. A policy is a high-level statement of the high-level goals and principles that all employees must adhere to when performing political risk management.

Executive summary. The plan provides an overview of the document; sometimes it includes background information.

Background. A plan contains information, sometimes data, that describes why the political risk management is being implemented in the first place. Sometimes the scope is included in the background along with any other pertinent information, such as assumptions.

Scope. The plan describes the parameters for political risk management. The scope contains a description of what is and, just as importantly, not in scope.

Goals. Goals may sometimes be covered in the background or scope and pertain to political risk management.

Critical success factors. These factors address those assets or activities necessary to achieve the goals of political risk management.

Descriptions of each political risk management process, e.g., identify political risks. These descriptions include tools and techniques. Each description might include any unique considerations specific to political risk management, such as different thresholds and metrics regarding performance and the uncovering of political risks needing attention right away, e.g., a risk with a material impact.

Risk Breakdown Structure or Listing. The structure may simply describe whether one or the other or both are used. It may also list categories of risks and modeling techniques.

Organization's risk attitude and tolerance. This description may contain a review of the history as well as current risk attitudes and tolerances. Circumstances facing the enterprise may have changed over time; risk attitudes and tolerances may have changed, too.

Roles, responsibilities, and authorities are also described in the risk management plan. It describes, again, at a high level. The goal is to ensure that stakeholders understand what areas they represent and whether they can participate in decision-making.

Data and information requirements. A plan describes what facts and data are required for the success of political risk management. It describes who is responsible to provide which facts and data as well as the protection requirements for specific content.

Meetings. These meetings can occur weekly, bi-weekly, monthly, or quarterly (or a combination thereof). Each description of a meeting provides the purpose and a high-level agenda. These descriptions are high-level descriptions; more detailed information is often contained in a communications management plan.

Templates of forms and reports used. Reports may be weekly, bi-weekly, or monthly (or combination thereof) and provides details on who receives them.

Supporting references. A plan includes just about any related document that can assist in performing political risk management, such as internal handbooks and publications by professional societies.

Approvals. The plan includes the signature blocks for key stakeholders.

Glossary. A plan contains agreed upon definitions of jargon related to political risk management. It may also contain definitions of terminology that are industry specific or used in the enterprise. It may also contain a list of abbreviations.

CHALLENGES

The risk management plan presents several challenges.

Ensuring stakeholders approve the risk management plan on time. Even in the electronic world, obtaining approval may be difficult. Key stakeholders may find it difficult to take time in their busy schedule to review the plan. Or the differences among the stakeholders may be divisive either because of internal politics, real differences, or hidden agendas, making approval seem impossible. Whatever the reason, sometimes discussions over the risk management plan can, but not always, delay the start of political risk management. During meetings, visibility should include the status of the plan as it proceeds through the approvals.

Keeping the plan updated and distributed. As with the case with many plans, documents are produced and then nobody updates them. Soon enough, the documents become obsolete. A stakeholder on the team should have responsibility to keep the political risk management plan current.

Having people to follow the plan. Some stakeholders may simply ignore the plan even after approval. They may decide to want to take a different approach. If that occurs, the best approach is to present any deviations to the plan before the team for review and approval.

FINAL THOUGHTS

The political risk management plan must accurately reflect the processes being implemented. It must also be accessible and understandable to stakeholders to apply the contents described within it. Just as importantly, it must describe a consistent approach for all subsequent processes.

GETTING STARTED QUESTIONS

Questions	Yes	No
1. Have you decided to prepare a risk management plan (not to be confused with one for managing a project or program)?		
2. Does the political risk management plan cover these topics?		
a) Reference the governing policy on risk management for the enterprise?		
b) Scope?		
c) Glossary?		
d) Critical success factors?		
e) Background information?		
f) Reference to enterprise strategic goals?		
g) Supporting references?		
h) Reference to risk management goals?		
i) Description of each political risk management process?		
j) Templates of relevant forms and reports?		
k) Roles, responsibilities, and authorities?		
l) Description of enterprise's risk attitude and tolerance?		
m) Risk breakdown structure for the enterprise?		
n) Executive summary?		
o) Data and information requirements?		
3. Did you develop a straw horse of the risk management plan?		
4. Have you decided which stakeholders should review the political risk management plan?		
5. Have you decided which stakeholders should approve the political risk management plan?		
6. Are you experiencing any of these challenges and, if so, determining how to deal with them?		
p) Ensuring the stakeholders approve the plan on time?		
q) Keeping the plan updated and distributed?		
r) Having people follow the political risk management plan when implemented?		

8

Identify Political Risks

Recognizing the risks that may confront an enterprise and its global supply chain is the obviously important. The result of this process is a risk listing that provides the foundation to perform all subsequent political risk management processes. It provides the basis for performing risk assessments; determining risk responses; and performing monitoring and controlling risks; responding to risks; and reporting on risks. The only exception is maintaining risk processes.

KEY POINTS

Keep the following thoughts in mind when identifying political risks.

Take a holistic perspective. Keep looking at enterprise as a system consisting of interdependent, integrated components seeking to reach goals. This perspective makes it easier to see how risks impact an enterprise and its global supply chain, not just its individual components. Some political risks, of course, impact a subcomponent of an enterprise which can impact the overall performance of an enterprise and its global supply chain but this situation is infrequent. Political risks often have an impact on an entire enterprise.

Identify specific conditions or events that could potentially impact an enterprise's global supply chain. While one's perspective is broad, each identified risk should be specific enough to enable a meaningful assessment and determine an effective response. It is okay to come up with an initial list of generic political risks to use them as a starting point. The list can be tailored so they relate to the actual business environment. Ideally, the best way to generate a specific list of risks is create a risk statement for each one, such as "If Risk A occurs it can cause noncompliance with government regulations." Remember, a risk has a condition, and a consequence. Remember, too, that a risk can have multiple causes or consequences or both.

Stakeholder participation is critical when developing a risk listing. Participation generates buy-in of the results; serves as a way to generate communications; provides many different insights and perspectives; and generates many risks. Sometimes, to obtain participation, it may be necessary to develop a straw horse listing of risks; stakeholders can then modify it, serving as a way to encourage participation. The straw horse lays the groundwork to assemble all stakeholders together to refine the listing.

The risk listing, also known as a risk register, is a living artifact. The environment of an enterprise and its supply chain changes, necessitating some risks being modified, added, or dropped as they relate to the global supply chain. Revisiting the risk listing should occur regularly so it remains relevant when conducting political risk management.

To generate a risk listing, think in terms of exposure to an enterprise. What are the risks that could keep stakeholders up at night? What are the events that expose the risks, what are their causes, and potential impacts? The impacts during identifying risks are only preliminary at this point and will be conducted in greater depth during political risk assessment. The main emphasis right now is on generating a useful list of risks for subsequent political risk management processes.

Remember that risks can be negative or positive. Negative risks are threats and positive risks are opportunities. Making a list of both negative and positive risks is important. Eventually, the goals are to minimize the impacts of threats and to maximize the impacts of opportunities when assessing political risks.

Group political risks into categories but do so only after the risk listing is exhaustive. Grouping risks into categories makes it easier to manage them when performing all processes of political risk management. Just as importantly, grouping of risks will indicate what types of risks will have the most impacts on an enterprise and its global supply chain. This categorization of risks is really based upon the preferences of stakeholders. For example, here are different ways to group risks into related categories:

- Acceptable vs. unacceptable
- Internal vs. external
- Manageable vs. unmanageable
- Short-term vs. long-term

A common way to look at political risks is according to some rudimentary hierarchy. For example, risks can be viewed as international, regional, and operational. Another example is to view political risks as international, macro, and micro. Regardless, political risks do not often fit neatly into a hierarchy. Political unrest at a local level can propagate to a regional or international level. Just keep in mind whatever viewpoint taken it serves as a conceptual framework to look at risks.

The categories can be broken into subcategories, such as:

- Business
- Legal or compliance
- Socio-political
- Subject matter
- Technical

All political risks are rarely identified at this point. Some of the ones not appearing are called unknown unknowns (also called unk unks) which are unidentifiable ones that have an undetermined probability or likelihood of occurrence. Some of these risks will later pop on or fall off the list due to changing circumstances. The most terrifying ones are the black swans which technically are issues (a realized risk) because they are events that happen seemingly out of nowhere, are explainable after the fact, and have a severe, even catastrophic impact. Keep in mind that once a risk becomes a reality, it is no longer a risk but an issue that requires implementing a risk response. Naturally, unk unks and black swans have no predetermined response, being unanticipated. Keep in mind, political risk management involves considerable uncertainty, making it a candidate for many unknowns and black swans.

Some political risks do not exist independent of other risks. A risk may depend on the existence of another risk or risks for it to occur. If Risk B arises and its response is implemented, for example, then Risk C may occur. The latter are known as secondary risks. Other risks may be residual risks which is part of a risk that remains after implementing a less than totally effective response. In other words, the response is incomplete. These relationships can become quite complex when identifying risks. Complexity increases when identifying and unraveling the dependencies among risks.

Political risks may arise due to a unique set of circumstances. Some risks are time-based, e.g., occur early or later. Other risks depend on the situation, e.g., extremely unstable economic environment. Still others depend on how well an enterprise's global supply chain is meeting its goals. The key point to remember is that some risks will occur only under unique circumstances and, if the risk statements are specific enough, enable recognizing the unique circumstances should be nonproblematic.

An interesting unique threat is known as obsolescing bargain. An enterprise has an investment in a host country. As a project or other investment becomes successful, the government seeks to improve terms on what the original agreement stipulated. In the beginning of an agreement, an enterprise has the bargaining power; however, later the relationship turns in favor of the host country since the initial risk and uncertainty has declined or shifted. Naturally, this circumstance can lead to an unstable relationship between the enterprise and host country's government.[1]

Another interesting trend is the evolution of expropriation which is a host government seizing a foreign investment. For the most part, outright expropriation has evolved to creeping expropriation which a host government gradually turns a foreign investment into a loss for an enterprise by applying punitive measure and taxes on an enterprise.[2]

Political risk management generally impacts fives areas: compliance with laws, regulations, and internal policies and procedures; authorities and responsibilities; reporting; efficiency and effectiveness; and safeguarding of assets. The idea is to have a prepared response if a risk occurs. Having a robust risk listing is the first process to provide reasonable assurance that an enterprise's goals related to its global supply chain will be met and has laid the groundwork to respond accordingly.

Identify the sources of information as early as possible. Be careful, however, not to allow the choice of resources be influenced by a stakeholder's preference or biases and becoming the result of cherry picking. Stakeholders must have access to as many resources as possible to generate a useful risk listing. A common danger during working sessions is to generate a list of risks using stakeholders from one field, such as finance or information systems, to dominate the development of a risk listing. Cognitive bias can reduce the value of a risk listing which can have a cascading impact on the quality of results in subsequent political risk management processes.

The nature of a business that an enterprise finds itself will experience certain inherent risks. For example, state-of-the-art information technology has some inherent risks, such as a new system crashing at peak usage hours. Or a new vaccine having unforeseen negative physical consequences. Starting a new supply chain in a less developed country has some inherent political risks. Inherent risks are more easily identifiable if a history exists for an enterprise in a specific industry, such as expropriation in an extractive industry.

Ila Manuj and John Mentzer in the *International Journal of Physical Distribution and Logistics Management* identifies four categories of global supply chain risks: supply, operational, demand, and security.[3]

Supply risks pertain to inbound supplies coming into a global enterprise which can impact an enterprise's ability to meet customer requirements. Operational risks affect the internal performance of an enterprise to produce goods and provide services which can ultimately affect its profitability. Demand risks relate to outbound flows to satisfy customer requirements. Security risks pertain to ones concerning personnel, information systems, and other functional responsibilities of an enterprise.

These categories of risks simply reflect one way of carving up a global supply chain. Unfortunately, they typically reflect a narrow economic perspective. The reality is that there is another category of risks that are ignored – political risks. In fact, one could argue that a political risk can be a primary risk and causes the other risks to become secondary risks. By the same token, one of the four risks can be the primary risk and a political risk to become a secondary one. Manuj and Mentzer mention the "interconnectedness" among the four risks but the same occurs with political risks with them. The point is that political risk is not an isolated phenomenon from economics.

BENEFITS

Identifying political risks offers several benefits.

Encourages early communications among key stakeholders since it requires exchanging information and ideas. People start asking questions of others, especially about areas of responsibility and soon recognize that their organization has certain touchpoints with other ones as well as recognize they may need to work together more often, especially if one or more political risks become an issue.

Minimizes surprises. Stakeholders will know that certain political risks and their corresponding events may arise, thereby enabling them to prepare themselves. In other words, they can avoid reacting and begin proacting. The same goes for opportunities, not just threats. If the stakeholders realize that an opportunity could arise then they can more quickly seize it.

Offers stakeholders a sense of control. Albeit uncertainty will never be eliminated, stakeholders having at least the "feeling" that they know what to expect and can prepare themselves to deal with what confronts them.

Provides the building blocks to complete subsequent processes of political risk management. The risk register provides additional focus on the political impact on an enterprise's global supply chain. As the review of the risk register continues, some political risks may be deleted, changed, or added by stakeholders; they will consequently have a better understanding of the impact of political risks on an enterprise's global supply chain.

Brings out to the forefront threats before they become an issue. Stakeholders can bring up risks early so that an enterprise can develop appropriate responses. It is easier to deal with a risk if identified earlier than to wait for the last minute when it becomes an issue. Preparation is key; it grants time to deploy responses.

APPROACH

Many approaches exist for identifying risks. The final deliverable of any of these approaches, of course, is the risk register.

Brainstorming is one approach and is perhaps the best known one. It is a facilitated group session that encourages free generation of ideas, in this case political risks. All judgment is suspended as the risks are simply jotted on a white or black board. This approach enables generating many risks over a short time without judgment. It can be done in one of two ways as a group. One way is to have one risk generated by one person and then another one, each taking turns (called structured brainstorming) or ideas can be generated by the group all at once (called unstructured brainstorming). Either way, the emphasis is on quantity over quality. No judgment of risks occurs until the list is considered complete. Then the list of risks is reduced either by elimination, combination, or rephrasing. The person before the group acts as a facilitator and makes every effort to avoid influencing the output of either individuals or the group.

The Crawford slip method is a variant of brainstorming that, with the aid of a facilitator, defines an upfront topic or question. Individuals then record thoughts, in this case political risks, on slips, which the facilitator compiles, groups, and summarizes. The results are then communicated to the group. This method helps to alleviate peer pressure which can often skew results.

The nominal group technique, another variant of brainstorming, is an approach whereby each person writes their issues, ideas, risks, etc. on cards in a short time. The facilitator collects the cards, conducts discussions, takes a vote, and tabulates the results. This technique is often used to resolve disputes using an agreed upon voting system.

The Delphi technique is another popular approach that was developed by the RAND Corp. The technique is used to achieve the consensus of independent experts by submitting a questionnaire to them multiple times; each time the results are compiled and resubmitted until consensus is achieved. Like the Crawford slip method, this approach helps to relieve stakeholders from peer pressure but the technique is time consuming.

Benchmarking is a technique used to capture the performance of a process being executed one or more organizations. It is an excellent way to judge how well the political risk management process functions vis-à-vis another enterprise's in terms of efficiency and effectiveness. It is also a good way to determine if similar enterprises face the same risks and how well they responded.

Checklists of risks, of course, can be handy to generate a risk listing. The caveat with checklists is that the risks will likely require tailoring to the requirements of the enterprise and its global supply chain. Some risks may need to be reworded, dropped, or added.

Lessons learned from other political risk management endeavors are an excellent source to identify risks. They serve as a great reservoir of information on what went well, what did not, and what improvements were made. Previous risk management endeavors can provide a good supply of lessons learned, regarding enterprise risks and responses.

Interviews are useful to collect political risks and other related information. These can be one-on-one or group interviews, with the former often the quickest but also less objective; however, the latter can inhibit some stakeholder from speaking honestly. All interviews should be planned in advanced, especially regarding what facts and data to acquire from the interviewee and how their responses are compiled.

SWOT analysis is another useful technique to collect political risks. SWOT stands for Strengths, Weaknesses, Opportunities, and Threats. Knowing all four helps to generate a list of risks. Obviously, opportunities and threats are risks, so the distinction is made in SWOT analysis.

Weaknesses can lead to threats while strengths can help alleviate the impact of their counterparts. SWOT analysis can be used with other techniques.

Force field analysis is a somewhat related technique to SWOT. It is a technique that assumes that for every action, one or more counteractions (constraining and restraining forces) exist. If corresponding counteraction exists, it may indicate a risk. Scoring can also be applied that might identify a political risk.

Robert McKellar in *A Short Guide to Political Risk* developed a useful categorization of political risks. The two primary categories are essentially ones that have been present for some time and will continue in the future. There are also ones that occur now and likely not appear in the future.

Some of the risks that are continuous include:

- Domestic unrest
- Ethical criticism
- International terrain
- Political criminality
- Terrorism

Some of the risks that appear in the current or immediate future include:

- Failed and failing states
- Global asymmetrical terror
- Political Islam[4]

Categorization can be managed by using techniques like brainstorming, Crawford slip method, and affinitization.

Many sources of political risk exist. To assess political risks effectively a good deal of the situational awareness is needed by stakeholders. This awareness should look for unstable conditions, not just political but also economic and social ones. As discussed earlier, economic and sociological circumstances can result in political instability. Government, economy, and society can, for example, cause political risks to arise. Political risks may manifest themselves through instability, conflict, inaction, etc. within its public and private entities, such as government, political parties, military, and national banks. The failure to not have solid situational awareness can result in a miscalculation when determining risk responses and their execution.

Regardless of the technique used during political risk management, it is important to keep these thoughts in mind. For group sessions, use a facilitator and a scribe. Both will allow stakeholders to focus on generating risks. Usually, finding someone to perform these roles is not a problem when executive and senior managers are involved. Also, develop an agenda; keep time to a minimum; and have the right stakeholders in attendance. For one-on-one meetings, again keep time to a minimum and honor requests for certain facts and data to be held confidential. Keep in mind, too, that many of the approaches and techniques are not mutually exclusive. Mixing and matching of approaches and techniques when performing political risk management are fine; however, be sure in the end that the results are compiled in a manner that is logical and consistent with one another. Remember, the aim of identifying risks is a reliable risk listing.

One way to display the final risk listing is either in outline or tree format, shown in Figure 8.1, which reflects the grouping of related risks according to some criteria. "Affinitization" is the technique used for grouping. It is logically grouping many items, in this case political risks, having similar characteristics. It helps to reduce complexity and serves as a good communications tool. As a side note, if a grouping appears larger than other ones, it may indicate that a serious vulnerability exists.

A political risk listing, also known as a political risk register, is a table recording all the characteristics of each political risk identified, assessed,

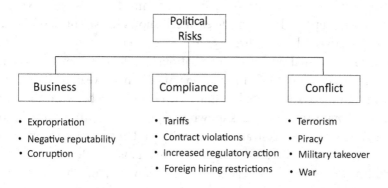

FIGURE 8.1
Tree Format Showing "Affinitization" of Political Risks.

and managed when conducting political risk management. The listing, shown in Figure 8.2 has these contents:

- Risk number (a unique identifier for each risk)
- Risk title (a short description)
- Risk description (one or two sentences describing each risk)
- Risk category (mainly political but sometimes economic and sociological)
- Probability (or likelihood)
- Vulnerability (or severity)
- Impact
- Risk score (probability x vulnerability x impact)
- Priority
- Risk response(s)
- Tactical action(s)
- Risk Owner
- Additional comments

The political risk listing can be created using a spreadsheet program. It is updated continuously, from the processes identify political risks through perform political risk reporting.

One of the best ways to show the relationships between a global supply chain and the political threats is to create a matrix. An example of the matrix is shown in Figure 8.3. The purpose of the matrix is to show which threats impact the global supply chain.

At the top of the matrix is a list of the political threats that could affect a global supply chain. Along the left is a column (or Y-axis) showing the assets of the supply chain. Inside each cell shows the strength of the relationship between both a threat and the pertinent strategic goals, which might be weak, medium, or strong relationship. Below the matrix includes a legend, for example, defining a strong, medium, or weak relationship.

A similar matrix is created to show the relationship between the supply chain and opportunities and is shown in Figure 8.4. Again, each cell shows the relationship between an opportunity and the supply chain, which might be a weak, medium, or strong relationship. Below the matrix includes, for example, a legend defining a weak, medium, or strong relationship.

Both matrices can be created using a spreadsheet program.

Risk Number	Risk Description	Risk Category	Probability	Vulnerability (Severity)	Impact	Risk Score	Risk Response	Tactical Actions	Risk Owner	Comments

FIGURE 8.2
Political Risk Listing.

Threats -> Assets	Foreign hiring restriction	Tariffs	Military takeover	Contract violations	Terrorism	Piracy	Increased regulatory actions	Bureaucratic delays	Territorial conflict	Expropriation
Inventory										
Suppliers										
Manufacturers										
Materials										
Transportation										
Warehouses/Distribution centers										
Customers										

FIGURE 8.3

Matrix Showing Relationship of Supply Chain Assets and Threats.

Assets	Opportunity	Opportunity	Opportunity	Opportunity
Inventory				
Suppliers				
Manufacturers				
Materials				
Transportation				
Warehouses / Distribution Centers				
Customers				

Legend (Impact)
Strong
Medium
Low

FIGURE 8.4
Relationship between Assets of a Supply Chain and Opportunities.

One of the best ways to capture and show which stakeholders have an interest in or being impacted by a political risk is to create a matrix. An example of such a matrix is shown in Figure 8.5. The purpose of the matrix is to identify which stakeholders have an interest in a specific threat.

At the top of the matrix is a list of stakeholders that potentially could be affected by a risk. Along the left (or Y-axis) is a column showing the political risks. Inside each cell reflects the strength of the relationship between

Risks	Stakeholder	Stakeholder	Stakeholder	Stakeholder
Foreign Hiring Restrictions				
Tariffs				
Military Takeover				
Contract Violations				
Terrorism				
Piracy				
Increased Regulatory Actions				
Bureaucratic Delays				
Territorial Conflict				
Expropriation				

Legend (Impact)
Strong
Medium
Low

FIGURE 8.5
Matrix Showing Stakeholders Impacted by Risks.

both a risk and the pertinent stakeholder, for example, which is a weak, medium, or strong relationship. Below the matrix includes a legend defining a weak, medium, or strong relationship.

The matrix can be created using a spreadsheet program. It is updated continuously, from the processes identify stakeholders through perform political risk reporting. Another option is to create a separate matrix for threats and another for opportunities.

CHALLENGES

Several challenges are attributed to identify political risks.

Reconciling differences among stakeholders regarding risk appetite and tolerance. This difference can have a substantial impact on which political risks are identified and which ones are omitted. All political risks should focus on the strategic goals related to a global supply chain to deal with differences over risk appetite and tolerance. Otherwise, these differences can widen which could prove quite challenging when seeking consensus among stakeholders. Techniques like brainstorming and the Crawford slip technique can help keep focus on strategic goals while at the same time bridge differences over risk appetite and tolerance.

A lack of understanding between a risk and an issue. As previously mentioned, a risk is something that potentially can happen in the future; an issue is a risk that has occurred. Many people, not familiar with the distinction, get confused over the differences. The best approach is to begin any session, individual or group, with a definition of both. If a threat has not occurred, it is a risk. If it has occurred, it is no longer a risk but an issue and requires a risk response.

Difficulty thinking too far into the future. The further out in the future one must think about risks the more abstract the thinking becomes. Despite all the discussions and the availability of information some stakeholders find it difficult to identify any risks that go beyond a year or more. Generally, this probably rarely surfaces if the political risk management scope involves anticipating what is happening within a year; it becomes more challenging if identifying political risks beyond a year. A common way to address this challenge is to identify risks that may arise within one year. Then other review the risk listing periodically.

Lack of facts and data. Even in the world of cloud computing, it may be difficult to acquire access to all the requisite facts and data to determine political risks. Facts and data may be buried in electronic or physical silos across an enterprise. Some facts and data may be considered so proprietary that only the highest positions of enterprise have access. Regardless, the lack or unavailability of facts and data can have an impact on the results of political risk management. This problem is probably insignificant for very executive and senior management since they will likely have access to very sensitive content; this situation may not be the case for other stakeholders who are lower in the hierarchy but participate in political risk management. Nevertheless, even executives and senior managers can face this challenge from time to time. A good practice is for the person responsible for coordinating political risk management measures is to ensure that most of the facts and data are accessible or available to the participants.

Unfamiliarity with political risk management. Not everyone may have experience or knowledge about political risk management. They may be new to an enterprise, may have recently been promoted to a senior position, or never learned it elsewhere. This challenge can slow the flow time to develop and deploy political risk management as these people take time to get up to speed. A brief introductory training on political risk management may suffice for these stakeholders.

Some stakeholders might not raise a political risk to a global supply chain out of fear, perhaps because they feel it reflects badly on them or their organization. Since political risk management involves the participation of executive and senior management the last image that they often want to portray is a lack of control. They may have no problem during one-on-one interviews revealing risks of another executive's organization but they will likely be reluctant to reveal ones concerning their own. Most executives and senior managers tend to be highly competitive and will present their organization positively. Consequently, this situation may become a serious challenge when developing a comprehensive risk listing. A good facilitator can play a significant role in overcoming this challenge with preparation.

Peer pressure among stakeholders can pose a significant challenge. Some of them may not want to raise a risk for consideration because it might be politically sensitive. While many are competitive, executives and senior managers also recognize they are part of an elite group. They may decide to forego mentioning a political risk if it could result in ostracism. This situation often arises when little trust exists within senior leadership, such as after a merger. The pressure is to get along to move along, at least for the moment. Consequently, a risk listing may be incomplete. Having a diversified team when identifying risks can help overcome this challenge.

Lack of transparency is a challenge and may be tied closely to the last two challenges. Stakeholders may be reluctant to speak or share facts and data. If they do, the words are carefully phrased to avoid offending anyone or they may provide incomplete facts and data that raises more questions than answers. Despite the competitive nature among executive and senior managers, they often "read the tea leaves" which can, not always, restrain their insights based upon internal political considerations. This challenge is difficult to overcome since the tone starts at the top. However, employing the Crawford slip method or the Delphi approach can help deal with this challenge.

Cognitive bias is a common challenge. Prejudices affect one's perception of the world, whether intentional or not. Often, bias is reflected in the assumptions which, in turn, affects what is considered "truths" to some individuals. From a risk management perspective, it can mean filtering between what are the political risks and what ones are not. Cognitive bias affecting identifying risks impacts decisions when responding to risks. The consequences can be severe if a risk that should have been identified and is not, such as one affecting a global supply chain.

Dominant personalities. Certain personalities can pressure people, whether implicitly or directly, to alter the judgment of others. They often, by virtue of their personality, run over participants to gain their own way or "win." Unsurprisingly, some risks may be ignored to avoid tangling with such personalities; some of these risks may be severe but others may not speak. Again, techniques such as the Crawford slip method can help to deal with this challenge.

An integrative perspective is ignored or overlooked. This challenge often reflects silo thinking, possibly because participants lack the breadth of experience or knowledge to see how an entire enterprise works together to achieve its strategic goals or they do not seek to integrate with other organizations or disciplines. This challenge may interrupt into conflict when identifying risks if the teaming among executive and senior management is not present. Having a good facilitator can go a long way in helping everyone take an integrative perspective by highlighting opportunities for integration when identifying risks.

Lack of organizational commitment. Many executives and senior managers will express their favor of political risk management but as time passes their commitment declines. The reality is that political risk management takes time and effort, particularly in the beginning. Some will have declining commitment for many reasons, e.g., conflict with other commitments. The impact of this challenge can be overcome by having the board of directors embracing the importance of political risk management and making it a performance objective for executive and senior managers by tying participation to their compensation.

Most of the challenges happen in about all of the subsequent processes of political risk management. If these challenges are not addressed early, the intensity of the impact will increase. Stakeholders will lose their commitment if they believe that political risk management lacks value to themselves and to the enterprise.

FINAL THOUGHTS

An enterprise needs to know about as many threats and opportunities that could impact its global supply chain. Political risks are an important subset of those risks. However, just knowing the political risks is not enough. Not all risks are equal; some are more important than others. The next process, assess political risks, helps to determine which risks are more important relative to each other and to determine the impacts to a global supply chain.

GETTING STARTED QUESTIONS

Questions	Yes	No

1. When identifying risks are you considering the following?
   a) Taking a holistic approach?
   b) Identifying specific events or conditions that could potentially impact the enterprise?
   c) Obtaining stakeholder participation?
   d) Treating the risk listing (also known as risk register) as a losing artifact?
   e) Thinking in terms of exposure to the enterprise?
   f) Recognizing that risks can be negative (also known as threats) or positive (also known as opportunities)?
   g) Grouping risks into categories?
   h) Recognizing that not all risks are independently of each other?
   i) Understanding that risks may arise due to a unique set of circumstances?

Questions	Yes	No

2. Recognizing political risk management impacts in these five areas?
   a) Compliance with laws, regulations, and internal policies and procedures?
   b) Authorities and responsibilities?
   c) Reporting?
   d) Efficiency and effectiveness?
   e) Safeguarding of assets?

3. Identifying the sources of facts and data as early as possible?

4. Understanding that the nature of the business has inherent risks?

5. Have you decided which of the following approaches you will use to identify risks?
   a) Brainstorming?
   b) Crawford slip method?
   c) Nominal group technique?
   d) Benchmarking?
   e) Checklists?
   f) Lessons learned reviews?
   g) Interviewing?
   h) SWOT analysis?
   i) Force field analysis?

6. Have you "affinitized" the list of risks?

7. Did you decide to display risks in one of the following formats:
   a) Tree?
   b) Outline?

8. Have you faced any of the following challenges and, if so, determining how to deal with them?
   a) Reconciling differences among stakeholders regarding risk appetite and tolerance?
   b) Lacking understanding between a risk and an issue?
   c) Finding it difficult for some stakeholders not thinking too far in the future?
   d) Lacking sufficient facts and data?
   e) Being unfamiliar with political risk management?
   f) Dealing with fear on the part of certain stakeholders?
   g) Lacking transparency on the part of certain stakeholders?
   h) Handling cognitive bias?
   i) Managing dominant personalities?
   j) Encouraging some stakeholders to take an integrative perspective?
   k) Obtaining organizational commitment?

NOTES

1. Theodore H. Moran in "The Changing Nature of Political Risk, in *Managing International Political Risk*, ed. Theodore H. Moran (Oxford: Blackwell Publishers, 1998), 9–10.
2. Daniel Wagner, *Managing Country Risk* (Boca Raton: CRC Press, 2012), 252.
3. Ila Manuj and John Mentzer, "Global Supply Chain Risk Management," *International Journal of Physical Distribution and Logistics*, vol. 3, (2008), 197–198.
4. Robert McKellar, *A Short Guide to Political Risk* (Burlington, VT: Gower Publishing Limited, 2010), 11–52.

9

Assess Political Risks

After identifying political risks, the next process is to assess them. The goal of assessing political risks is to determine the relative importance of each risk and focus time and effort accordingly. It accomplishes that by determining for each political risk the probability or likelihood, impact, and the priority each relative among all risks. This process shifts the focus from what to measure to how to measure.

KEY POINTS

Keep the following thoughts in mind when assessing political risks.

Continue to have a balanced team during the risk assessment, preferably using the same stakeholders who participated when identifying political risks. Balancing means having executive and senior management from pertinent functional areas, disciplines, and business units. Not only does it help ensure consistency in thinking, but it also prevents unintended biases affecting the outcome of this process.

Maintain situational awareness which is essential when conducting political risk management. It requires knowing the who, what, when, where, why, and how of a political circumstance. Just as importantly is understanding through facts and data the relationships among the who, what, when, where, why, and how.

Situational awareness is important when assessing political risks. It helps in determining likelihood, impact, and priority of each risk and, in turn, determine the appropriate strategic response and the accompanying tactical actions.

Just as in identifying political risks, use multiple sources of facts and data. Using multiple sources of facts and data serves as a means to cross-check their reliability and validity. Reliability addresses the issue of variation in facts and data; ideally, the less the variation, the more reliable the facts and data. Validity is whether what is measured is supposed to be measured. Having reliable and valid facts and data when assessing risks helps to build confidence in results.

Sometimes a tradeoff exists between quantity versus quality of facts and data. Too much time can be spent collecting facts and data, reaching a point that additional effort provides little payback. Also, too many facts and data may prove unwieldy to assess risks, requiring too much effort to review and organize the content. What is important is having the right amount of facts and data that meets specific needs to perform a political risk assessment. The compulsion to collect endless facts and data often reflects the insecurity of some stakeholders. It is important, therefore, to know what specific facts and data requirements to fulfill and ensure validity and reliability. Many political risk assessments drag on needlessly because some people on the team constantly want a little more facts and data which, ironically, can result in further insecurity.

No matter how hard one tries, uncertainty will remain even after performing the best possible political risk assessment. The goal is to try to obtain some idea about the degree of uncertainty to derive probability and impact. Uncertainty will never be eliminated; however, it is possible to ascertain some idea about what degree of uncertainty is tolerable for each risk. Of course, for unknown risks or black swans the uncertainty is indeterminable. All one can do is strive to formulate parameters on uncertainty for known risks.

Provides the basis for better political reporting. The combination of a risk listing and the corresponding probability or likelihood and impact of each risk provides a solid basis for reporting. Not only will management know what risks may occur but also their potential probability or likelihood, and impacts. If any risks do occur, they can proceed with reasonable confidence.

Lays the groundwork to develop responses to risks. If a risk becomes an issue, executive and senior leadership can prepare to respond accordingly. Or, having recognized that a risk will likely occur, act ahead of time to reduce or eliminate the impact. In other words, assessing risks lays the groundwork to prepare for what may impact a global enterprise and its supply chain.

Limits the influence of subjectivity. No matter how hard stakeholders try, cognitive bias will influence results. Cognitive biases surface in the assumptions and the facts and data chosen used to perform political risk assessment. That is why it is important to have a balanced team of stakeholders to question and raise issues about assumptions and the reliability and validity of facts and data. The tools and techniques available to assess risks will also help to control the influence of cognitive biases. In the end, however, judgments will have to be made about the probability or likelihood and impacts of risks when realized, in which some subjectivity enters the process.

View a political risk based upon its impact to business performance of an enterprise and its global supply chain. For example, civil unrest in a host country building a key component has an impact operationally.

Some political impacts to global supply chains due to civil unrest are:

- Angry investors
- Border crossing impediments
- Customer dissatisfaction
- Disruption of supply chain optimization
- Lead times extended or missed
- Loss of competitiveness
- Loss of reputation
- Missed shipments
- Poor coordination throughout a supply chain
- Strained relationships with vendors and suppliers
- Theft

The point here is that political risks can impact the efficiency and effectiveness of a global supply chain. The goal is to minimize the negative impacts and maximize the positive ones. By knowing such impacts an enterprise can assess the business impact of a political risk and eventually develop and deploy strategic responses and tactical actions.

Set priorities. Not all threats and opportunities are equal. Assessing risks provides systematic ways to determine which political risks have a higher priority than others when determining the combination of probability or likelihood, and impact. A risk management plan should provide guidelines on using tools and techniques to assess risks. Some risks may be deemed urgent, meaning they require immediate attention; others addressed on an as-needed basis; and still others may be placed on a watchlist. The risk management plan should provide the criteria for making such a judgment.

The risk assessment results should be recorded in the risk register. The risk register should have the name of each risk and its corresponding probability or likelihood; its impact to an enterprise and its supply chain; any assumptions made; its priority; and any additional pertinent data, information, and comments. Usually, the risk listing is ordered by priority based upon a calculation.

Be aware of the risk appetite and tolerance of an enterprise and key stakeholders. Risk appetite and tolerance will influence the results of a political risk assessment, usually by skewing output. For example, stakeholders may exaggerate the probability or likelihood (e.g., low or high) and the impact (e.g., low or high). Ideally, the tools and techniques in the political risk management plan will offset the influences of exaggerated risk appetites and tolerances.

Both internal and external risks to strategic goals. A totally internal focus leaves an enterprise vulnerable to external threats, even if not directly applicable; for example, the probability or likelihood of a political risk may be low, but the impact high. At a minimum, such a risk should be on a watchlist so that an enterprise does not get broadsided. The same thinking goes for opportunities. At a minimum, too, an opportunity should be placed on a watchlist. An enterprise may not have control over an external risk, but if one arises it is prepared to implement a response or at least understand its effects upon occurrence.

Be systemic and systematic when assessing risks. Being systemic helps to see how the enterprise operates. It becomes easier to see how a political risk can affect the business performance of a global enterprise, especially its supply chain from the perspective of achieving its strategic goals. It will also help to assess how a political risk links with other risks; often, one risk has a cascading effect on other risks or may cause another risk to surface, called a secondary risk.

Being systematic enables to perform political risk assessment consistently to avoid the perception that results appear akin to "mixing apples with oranges." It will also make it easier for stakeholders to coordinate and communicate with one another more efficiently and effectively when assessing risks. A risk management plan should describe the adopted systematic approach.

Document the assumptions for each risk regarding its probability or likelihood, impact, and prioritization. By doing so, stakeholders will understand how the results were derived, especially as new stakeholders come aboard. Stakeholders can also, during periodic reviews of the risks, revisit the assumptions which, in turn, may cause a revision to political risk assessment results; some risks may have a lower or higher probability or likelihood, impact, or priority.

Recognize that risk assessment results will be imperfect for the first time. As circumstances change, whether in the environment or among the stakeholders, expect assessing risks to be an iterative process. Assessing risks reflects a point in time and will likely need changing even after everyone agrees to the results. That is why it is important to keep revisiting risk assessment results and to maintain visibility, such as at the board of directors or the audit or risk committee levels.

BENEFITS

Many benefits are attributed to assessing political risks.

Builds confidence among stakeholders despite the presence of uncertainty. Stakeholders will know the priorities and what to look for in case a threat or opportunity arises. Having the knowledge of the probability or likelihood, and impact of a risk, also adds to their own confidence level as well as in the results of a political risk assessment.

Provides an organized, systematic way to determine priority, probability or likelihood, impact, and priority for all known risks facing a global enterprise and its supply chain. Without a structured approach, the results from assessing political risks merely reflects internal politics, cognitive bias, strong personalities, or other influences. A structured, systematic approach helps to reign in negative influences.

Enables efficiently and effectively use of effort and capital to manage risks. Knowledge of priority, which is the product of probability, or likelihood, and impact, allows a more focused attention on risks having a greater impact to a global enterprise and its supply chain. In other words, it means not throwing good effort and money in a way that treats all risks the same. In addition, if a risk is no longer a high or even medium priority effort and capital can shift to risks deserving greater attention.

Furthers communication among stakeholders, more so than identifying risks. When assessing risks, stakeholders begin to share questions and knowledge about topics like probability, or likelihood, impact, and priority. Disagreements may arise (which is good during political risk assessment) as well as exchange of facts and data. Ideally, discussions do not become acrimonious and a consensus, maybe even an agreement, is reached.

Encourages a big picture perspective. Performing political risk assessment effectively requires removing the silo hat and putting on an enterprise one. That does not mean one disregards their areas of responsibility. Rather, it means considering how the risks impact their areas of responsibility from the context of an entire enterprise and its supply chain. That is where taking a systemic perspective can help ascertain the overall impact on a global enterprise and its supply chain.

Enables pro-action, not reaction, when an anticipated risk becomes an issue. Executive and senior management can remain alert for when a high priority risk becomes an issue. They will know its impact and priority. They may also realize its impact to an enterprise and its supply chain if it creates a secondary risk (that is, another risk is created as a result of an original risk) or a residual risk (the remainder of a risk because a response is not totally effective). Basically, it requires stakeholders to have their radar, so speak, operating.

Provides a solid basis to provide political risk responses. This point is tied to the last one. As mentioned earlier, a risk's priority has a direct relationship with its probability or likelihood, and its impact on the strategic goals of an enterprise and its supply chain. Based upon the results, stakeholders can develop appropriate responses to a risk that, hopefully, can be applied efficiently and effectively. Determining a risk response depends on the priority; a response ideally should not be overkill for a risk with a low priority.

Provides a learning experience to stakeholders. Discussions and sharing of facts and data provide a learning experience, but so does applying a systematic approach when performing this process. Taking a systematic approach adds discipline to help challenge biases, inaccurate assumptions, or extreme risk attitudes and tolerances. All participants following the same approach which should be described in the risk management plan.

Enhances the ability of an enterprise to adapt to changing circumstances. With greater awareness and confidence stakeholders will know the impact, whether qualitatively or quantitatively. They can make adjustments to deal with a risk event or condition.

APPROACH

Two basic approaches are applied during political risk assessment. These are: qualitative risk analysis and quantitative risk analysis. Both can be used together.

Qualitative risk assessment is considered the easiest and least time consuming of the two approaches, but it is considered the least reliable because it involves more subjectivity than quantitative risk assessment. When performing qualitative risk assessment, people create or use a scale to determine the likelihood and impact of a risk. Quantitative risk assessment requires more time and expertise and relies on probability to determine if a risk will occur and uses probability to determine, usually, financial impact.

Keep the following insights in mind about the two main approaches, to include their commonalities and differences.

One, qualitative and quantitative approaches use an estimate of the occurrence of a risk to account for uncertainty. The difference is that qualitative risk analysis uses an ordinal scale (for example, low, medium, high) while the quantitative one uses a cardinal scale (from 0 to 1).

Two, both approaches determine the priority of a risk. Qualitative risk analysis uses an agreed upon scale to determine the likelihood and impact of a risk on an enterprise and its global supply chain. Quantitative uses numeric calculations to determine the impact of a risk.

Three, qualitative and quantitative approaches can be used for both a threat or an opportunity to determine the impact on an enterprise and its global supply chain. The latter assesses an impact from a financial perspective.

Four, the results for both approaches are recorded in the political risk listing. Often, a color code scheme is used to reflect the rating for each political risk, e.g., red for high priority, along with the probability or likelihood and impact.

Five, both approaches rely on a risk management plan to describe how either or both approaches will be employed. The plan also includes the definitions of scales for probability or likelihood, impact, and priority.

Six, qualitative and quantitative approaches are reviewed continuously and performed iteratively. The reason is that an enterprise's environment is dynamic and will affect a political risk's probability or likelihood of occurrence, its impact, and, ultimately, its priority.

Seven, both approaches applied under the purview of the strategic goals related to a global supply chain. Whether using the qualitative or quantitative approaches, the focus is on risks that could potentially affect an enterprise and its global supply chain.

Eight, qualitative and quantitative approaches involve assumptions which must be recorded and, just as importantly, revisited regularly. Ultimately, professional judgments regarding risks, their impacts, and their priority rely on assumptions, regardless of approach. A change in assumptions can have a substantial impact on the results of a political risk assessment.

Nine, both lay the groundwork for better reporting. Whether on a weekly, quarterly, semiannual, or annual basis, both approaches provide meaningful, tangible information about risks potentially impacting an enterprise and its global supply chain.

Ten, qualitative and quantitative approaches use various methods to solicit input from stakeholders. These were mentioned earlier, such as brainstorming, Delphi technique, and the Crawford slip technique.

Both approaches, when used together, can provide an integrated assessment of multiple political risks. The probability, or likelihood, and impact of some risks used in the qualitative risk analysis can be translated into a quantitative impact to the supply chain of an enterprise.

A convenient way to track political risks and their corresponding trigger events is to list them in a matrix, shown in Figure 9.1. The purpose of the matrix is to identify which trigger events reflecting the occurrence of a risk. The vertical column (Y-axis) lists the risks. The top of the matrix lists

Political Risks	Trigger Event	Trigger Event	Trigger Event	Trigger Event
Foreign Hiring Restrictions				
Tariffs				
Military Takeover				
Contract Violations				
Terrorism				
Piracy				
Increased Regulatory Actions				
Bureaucratic Delays				
Territorial Conflict				
Expropriation				

FIGURE 9.1
Matrix Showing Relationships between Political Risks and Trigger Events.

of trigger events. In each cell that intersects between a political risk and a trigger event, record the desired strategic response to manage the applicable risk. The matrix can be updated throughout all the political risk management processes, from the processes identify political risks to perform political risk reporting. The matrix can be developed for threats or opportunities or combined into one matrix.

Ila Manuj and John Mentzer noted that a global supply chain has some other unique characteristics that go beyond loss and probability or likelihood of occurrence. One of the characteristics is speed, whereby a risk event occurs and requires looking at the rate of the loss happening and the quickness in discovering the risk. The other characteristic is frequency which is how often similar risks occur. These two additional characteristics can result in a substantial loss to an enterprise or a series of small ones that cumulatively result in a bigger one.[1]

Qualitative Risk Analysis

Qualitative risk analysis is considered easier than quantitative risk analysis, mainly due to the mathematics involved with the latter. Stakeholders can apply it much more quickly because the learning curve takes less time and the complexity; the downside, however, is that it is substantially more subjective. Nevertheless, this shortcoming can be ameliorated if a balanced stakeholder team is doing the qualitative analysis and the scales are defined in the political risk management plan.

This approach also requires several sources of facts and data to produce reliable results. Some more common sources include judgments by interviewees, such as experts; historical facts and data; and documents, such as reports about risks facing an enterprise and its global supply chain. The facts and data are then reviewed by the stakeholders; compiled; and used to determine likelihood, impact, and priority of risks.

A major challenge with qualitative risk assessment is when complex linkages exist among political risks. This challenge intensifies when multiple causes affect multiple political risks. Some political risks may be secondary ones, too. The relationships among political risks can be reflected in a matrix or table as a supplement to a risk listing. It could also be incorporated in the risk listing. Complex relationships can be identified using sensitivity analysis (modeling showing the impact of a risk on other risks); scenario analysis (modeling showing the impact of all risks on other risks); and decision trees or other mapping devices showing the relationships.

In qualitative risk management, the basic format to show the relationship among political risks via likelihood, impact, and priority is in the form of a 5 × 5 chart. The vertical axis reflects the likelihood scale while the horizontal axis the impact. The position of the political risk in the matrix reflects its priority which is the product of likelihood times impact. The product is known as the risk rating. The scale, of course, is defined in the political risk management plan. The matrix can use a variety of symbols to show information about each risk, such as whether its priority is increasing or decreasing, who the risk owner is, and any other pertinent information.

One of the most common ways to display the relationship between probability or likelihood and impact of a political risk is to create a 5 by 5 chart, shown in Figure 9.2. The chart displays the relationship between likelihood or probability and severity or impact from a visual perspective. The vertical side of the chart (Y-axis) reflects the probability or likelihood of a political risk. The horizontal side (X-axis) reflects the degree of impact of a political risk. Both the probability or likelihood and the impact are reflected in whole numbers, from 1 to 5. Each cell reflects the relationship between probability or likelihood and impact for each political risk. Each risk is represented by unique designator to indicate its position in the chart. The 5 by 5 chart itself can be broken into three categories of impact, such as high, medium, or low, usually with each one having its own color;

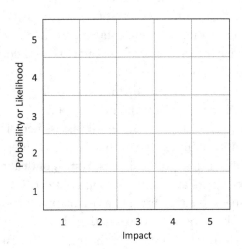

FIGURE 9.2
5 × 5 Charts.

for example, red for high priority cells; yellow for medium priority; and green for low priority.

The chart can also be used for opportunities with each one having a unique designator. The chart is updated continuously, from assess political risks through perform political risk reporting. The chart is mainly used for qualitative risk analysis; however, some risks shown in the chart may serve as the basis to perform quantitative risk analysis.

Another technique that can be used to determine priority using qualitative risk analysis is the forced choice method. This one requires choosing between two political threats by asking the fundamental question for each comparison: "Which threat is of a higher priority?" Each participant in a team session has one vote, which they can split. At the conclusion of a session, the scores are accumulated for each political risk and then ordered from highest to lowest score.

Using Figure 9.3, here is how to apply the technique. Using strategic goals as they relate to a global supply chain (whether for an enterprise or business unit, or subsidiary), a team assembles; develops or receives a list of risks; and then, using a form usually created in a spreadsheet, is filled in on the vertical column (Y-axis) with the risks. Across from each row is the same risk. Then, as the team works its way down the diagram, the team comes to a consensus on how to split their vote vis-à-vis other risks.

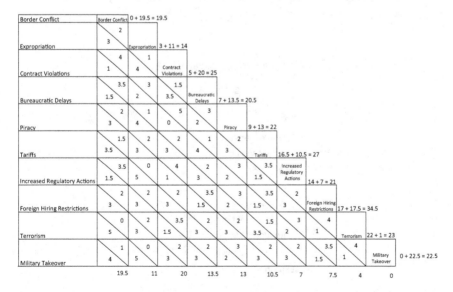

FIGURE 9.3
Forced Choice Method Applied to Threats.

Having split the votes, the next step is to tally them in each vertical column for the risk listed at the top; the tally comes from the numbers in the upper split for each cell in the applicable vertical column. Next, for each risk located on a horizontal row, a tally is taken of the numbers shown in the lower portion of the applicable split cells. Then, for each risk, a sum is calculated using the cumulative value in the vertical column and the cumulative value in the horizontal column.

The sum is used to determine the priority of a risk relative to one another. A matrix is then developed like the one shown in Figure 9.4.

Here are some good practices to follow when applying this technique. First, assign a scribe to record the discussions; he or she can participate in the deliberations, if necessary. Two, after completing Figure 9.3, revisit it with the team and seek consensus on the voting results. Then, the team should update the matrix shown in Figure 9.4. Third, it is good practice to review both the voting and the responses and tactical actions from time-to-time to ensure accuracy. Fourth, assemble the right balance of stakeholders to participate when using this technique (just like with all the other techniques). A team of all financial experts will likely skew the results toward a financial prioritization. A team of all lawyers will likely skew the results toward a legal perspective. A balanced set of experts is critical to offset the problem. Finally, consider bringing on board a professional facilitator who can help to move the sessions along and ensure that the results are not skewed.

Prioritized Risks	Score
Foreign Hiring Restrictions	34.5
Tariffs	27
Military Takeover	25.5
Contract Violations	25
Terrorism	23
Piracy	22
Increased Regulatory Actions	21
Bureaucratic Delays	20.5
Territorial Conflict	19.5
Expropriation	14

FIGURE 9.4
Summary Matrix Showing Prioritized Risks Using Forced Choice Method.

The forced choice technique can be used at the enterprise level and the country level. It can also be used to compare various assets within the supply chain, e.g., warehouse, information systems, to determine priority and then marry the results to produce a composite chart showing the relative priorities of risks and the supply chain assets. This approach is useful to identify risks and supply chain assets within a country or within a region. Diagram Figure 9.5 is an example of the forced choice method applied to assets of a supply chain combining political risks and assets of a supply chain within a country.

Here is how to apply the technique to assets of a global supply chain. This is how it works. The same process is repeated as was done to create Figure 9.4, only this time the process is applied to assets of a global supply chain, shown in Figure 9.5. Using the strategic goals (whether for an enterprise or business unit or subsidiary), each asset is voted upon the same way and the scores are summed for each one, thereby determining their priority. The assets are ranked in descending order based upon the cumulative scores as shown in Figure 9.6.

A matrix is formed, shown in Figure 9.7, by listing on the top row, in descending order, the threat. On the far axis column (Y-axis), the assets of the supply chain are listed, in descending order based upon the cumulative scores. The values for each threat and each asset are multiplied together to give a cell a numeric product, or value, that represents a risk rating. This process is repeated throughout the entire matrix until a product appears in each cell. The numbers in each cell are to determine what are the top

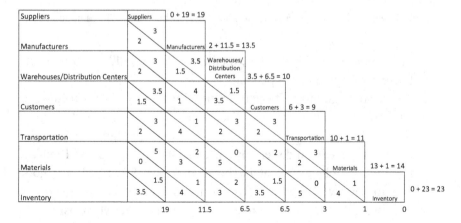

FIGURE 9.5
Forced Choice Method Applied to Supply Chain Assets.

Assets	Score
Inventory	23
Suppliers	19
Manufacturers	14
Materials	14
Transportation	11
Warehouses/Distribution Centers	10
Customers	9

FIGURE 9.6

Summary Matrix Showing Prioritized Risks Using Forced Choice Method.

Assets / Threats ->	Foreign hiring restriction (34.5)	Tariffs (27)	Military takeover (25.5)	Contract violations (25)	Terrorism (23)	Piracy (22)	Increased regulator actions (21)	Bureaucratic delays (20.5)	Territorial conflict (19.5)	Expropriation (14)
Inventory (23)	793 [1]	621 [3]	586 [4]	575 [5]	529 [6]	506 [8]	483 [10]	471 [12]	448 [14]	322 [28]
Suppliers (19)	655 [2]	513 [7]	484 [9]	475 [11]	437 [15]	418 [16]	399 [17]	389 [18]	370 [21]	266 [40]
Materials (14)	483 [10]	378 [20]	357 [23]	350 [24]	322 [28]	308 [30]	294 [32]	287 [33]	273 [38]	196 [57]
Manufacturers (13.5)	466 [13]	364 [22]	344 [26]	337 [27]	310 [29]	297 [31]	283 [34]	277 [36]	263 [41]	189 [59]
Transportation (11)	379 [19]	297 [31]	280 [35]	275 [37]	253 [43]	242 [46]	231 [47]	225 [50]	214 [52]	154 [62]
Warehouses/Distribution centers (10)	345 [25]	270 [39]	255 [42]	250 [44]	230 [48]	220 [51]	210 [53]	205 [55]	195 [58]	140 [63]
Customers (9)	310 [29]	243 [45]	229 [49]	225 [50]	207 [54]	198 [56]	189 [59]	184 [60]	175 [61]	126 [64]

Note: calculated values in cells are rounded to nearest whole number.

Legend

[ ] numeric ranking

( ) risk rating

1–16 = High risk

17–38 = Medium risk

39–64 = Low risk

FIGURE 9.7

Matrix Showing Relationship between Risks and Supply Chain Assets Based upon Priority.

priority (about upper 25 percent), medium priority (middle 50 percent), and lower priority (lower 25 percent).

Here are some good practices to follow when applying this technique. First, assign a scribe to record the discussions; he or she can participate in the deliberations, if necessary. Two, after completing Figures 9.5 and 9.6 revisit it with the team and seek consensus on the voting results. Then, the team should complete the matrix shown in Figure 9.7. Third, it is good practice to review the voting from time-to-time to ensure accuracy. Fourth, assemble the right stakeholders to participate when using this technique (just like with all the other techniques). A team of all financial experts will likely skew the results toward a financial prioritization.

A team of all lawyers will likely skew the results toward a legal perspective. A balanced set of experts is critical for this to succeed. Finally, consider bringing on board a professional facilitator who can help to move the sessions along and ensure that the results are not skewed.

Another qualitative approach is scenario analysis. A scenario is a potential future event that can, if it occurs, have various degrees of impact, such as on an enterprise and its supply chain. It is frequently used in risk management, business continuity, and internal auditing.

Robert McKellar in *A Short Guide to Political Risks* discusses the use of scenario analysis in evaluating political risk. Basically, it entails identifying a series of drivers, e.g., macrotrends, and risk factors and then determine the magnitude or impact, positively or negatively, on an enterprise.

Using scenario analysis is useful to distinguish between variables that are causal, e.g., drivers, and ones that are effects and then assess the impact and the magnitude. Based upon the results, appropriate responses can be developed.[2]

This approach works best when it is difficult to obtain valid and reliable facts and data to determine probability and the degree of impact. Also, this approach while easy and quick to perform can lend itself to being highly subjective. Challenges such as cognitive bias, political sway, and groupthink can influence results. Some ways to offset these challenges is to have reviews by disinterested parties, such as internal or external consultants, or employing a facilitator during group sessions.

Quantitative Risk Analysis

Some risks in a qualitative risk analysis may be useful for the quantitative risk analysis, which is more time consuming and complex than the former. The calculations enable determining the financial impact of a political risk and setting aside contingencies to deal with one should it arise. In other words, it identifies the expected value of a risk. Fundamentally, it entails multiplying the probability times the total amount of an investment deriving the expected value of a risk.

It can, however, become more complex when multiple relationships exist among political risks. These relationships can be independent or dependent. If they are independent, one adds the probabilities using the formula, probability = $P(A) + P(B) + Pn$. If they are dependent, one multiplies the probabilities using the formula, probability = $P(A) \times P(B) \times Pn$. The use of probabilities makes it easier to see the impact of different political risks on one another and the corresponding impacts from a financial perspective. The relationships and impacts often can be reflected in a decision tree, reflecting events and outcomes. The calculations also enable using other statistical measures such as mean, standard deviation (for both individual risks and overall), and variance.

Quantitative risk analysis enables creating several statistical charts, such as tornado diagrams and bubble charts, to illustrate the magnitude of risks. These charts make it easier to see relationships among risks as well as visualize the impacts of relationships among risks from a financial perspective, thereby allowing for an integrated assessment of multiple risks. It also enables effectively using decision trees to demonstrate the relationships.

A matrix can be developed, shown in Figure 9.8, that shows the impact of a political risk on the assets of an enterprise in a global supply chain. An asset can be physical, such as damage to a warehouse, or intangible, such as a damage to reputability in a country. The purpose of the matrix is to show the impact of a risk on a specific asset. This matrix is useful to begin thinking about quantitative analysis of certain risks.

At the top of the matrix is a list of the assets that political risks could potentially affect. Along the left (or Y-axis) is a column showing the

Risks	Asset	Asset	Asset	Asset
Foreign Hiring Restrictions				
Tariffs				
Military Takeover				
Contract Violations				
Terrorism				
Piracy				
Increased Regulatory Actions				
Bureaucratic Delays				
Territorial Conflict				
Expropriation				

Legend (Impact)
Strong
Medium
Low

FIGURE 9.8
Matrix Showing Relationship of Political Risks and Degree of Impact on Supply Chain Assets.

political risks. Inside each cell shows the strength of the relationship between both a political risk and the pertinent asset, which, for example, is a low, medium, or high relationship. Below the matrix includes a legend defining a low, medium, or high impact.

The matrix can be created using a spreadsheet program. It is updated continuously, from the processes assess political risk through perform political risk reporting. Another option is to create a separate matrix for threats and another one for opportunities.

Three additional advantages are attributed to the quantitative risk assessment. One, it leads to effective and efficient use of financial resources when responding to risks. Two, it lays the groundwork for better reporting because one can see the impacts far easier than if simply listed under qualitative risk analysis. Three, it is considered more objective than qualitative risk assessment because it involves calculations based upon numerical data.

A convenient table, shown in Figure 9.9, can show for each risk, its rank, or priority. The chart is useful to determine which risk or risks should have greater focus. The far left column (Y-axis) lists the risks. Along the top of the table are columns for: probability or likelihood; impact; rating (calculated multiplying probability or likelihood times the impact); and the threat's priority (determined by its rating) vis-à-vis other threats. The table should be populated for all risks. The table can be created also for opportunities.

Politics, as discussed in earlier chapters, is interrelated to two other components: economics and sociology; a change in one can cause a change in the others.

Many approaches exist that use mathematical calculations to assess the degree of economic, sociological, and political risk affecting an enterprise. In this book, of course, the focus is on political risks.

Risks	Probability (P)	Impact (I)	Rating (P x I)	Rank (Priority)
Foreign Hiring Restrictions	.1	.7	.7	1
Tariffs	.7	.6	.42	2
Military Takeover	.5	.4	.2	3
Contract Violations	.4	.3	.12	4

FIGURE 9.9
Matrix Showing the Variables Used to Determine Risk Priority.

The goal of mathematical calculation is to have a degree of confidence in the extent of political risk or risks will have on an enterprise. The assumption is that political risk can be reflected in a mathematical model.

Political risk modeling, like all mathematical models, have two major shortcomings.

Mathematical models are based upon assumptions as well as upon facts and data. If assumptions are wrong, the output of the model will likely be wrong.

They incorporate facts and data that are known in a certain point in time. In other words, they are a snapshot in time. The assumption is that current circumstances that exist now will continue in the future. In other words, they are simply projections.

Despite these shortcomings, political risk modeling has two purposes.

Mathematical models provide a way to understand complex phenomena in an orderly manner. The environment may appear complex; however, a model enables to transform the complexity into something understandable, such as a system and the constituent parts and their relationships with one another.

They also enable analyzing relationships among all the constituent parts and the strengths of those relationships. For example, a mathematical model can help to distinguish between the causes and the effects among different variables.

Political risk modeling often takes the following approach.

First, the political risk is broken into categories, such as political stability, which are, in turn, broken into criteria, such as civil strife, guerrilla activities, civil war, etc.

Second, each criterion receives a score based upon a continuum. All variables use the same continuum, such 1 through 10, reflecting the degree of strength, from very weak to very strong, respectively. For example, civil strife might receive a score of 10 points as opposed to guerrilla activities receiving a 5.

Third, each criterion within each category may be weighted in terms of importance by assigning a percentage which, cumulatively, equals 100 percent. For example, civil strife might be assigned a value of 35 percent.

Fourth, the overall value of a criterion's impact is calculated by multiplying the continuum score and the weighted impact. For example, civil strife would be 3.15 (which is a product of .35 times 9). This tally is conducted for all criterion, thereby providing an overall ranking for the category political stability. In fact, the same approach is repeated for all the other categories that have been identified, such as regime stability, international conflict, governmental corruption, and others.

Fifth, all the categories of political are ranked according to its score, indicating their relative risk to one another. Based upon the score, an enterprise can begin determining the most important strategic responses to embrace and determine the tactical actions to take.

Political risk modeling can be combined with other economic and sociological modeling which is frequently the case. The economic and sociological models involve much less judgment by modelers or stakeholders since the variables tend to be more discrete and measurable. That is why political risk modeling involves group participation, such as using the Delphi technique or facilitated group sessions.

CHALLENGES

Several challenges are attributed to performing risk assessment.

Time commitment. Executive and senior management, the main participants in political risk management, have a wide range of responsibilities that consume their time. Performing and evaluating the results of a political risk assessment involves a substantial time due to its complexity. Even with a supporting staff, they can find their time consumed in lengthy meetings when determining probabilities, or likelihoods, impacts, priorities, potential secondary and residual risks, assignment of risk owners, etc. as well as conducting reviews. Long hours and considerable effort are often expended performing a risk assessment.

The learning curve associated with using the tools and techniques. Some stakeholders may experience a learning curve if they had never applied the tools and techniques of a political risk assessment. A steep learning curve often occurs with quantitative risk assessment, which involves mathematical formulas. This does mean that they cannot understand the tools and techniques, but it often requires time understanding the calculation of the results and the meaning behind them.

Facts and data inaccessibility. It might be hard to imagine that in a major enterprise access to facts and data is difficult for executive and senior management when performing political risk management, but it does occur. This circumstance may exist if the facts and data reside in legacy systems or are buried in a cabinet or at an offsite storage facility. Sometimes, even in today's cloud environment, getting access to pertinent facts and data can sometimes prove difficult.

Cognitive bias. As one might suspect, this challenge is ever present throughout political risk management but even more so during a political risk assessment. The tools and techniques applied during this process can help reign in cognitive bias, but it cannot eliminate it, especially when many of the key stakeholders share a common background. Their belief systems, knowledge base, and experiences may all share a commonality leading to groupthink, thereby affecting the results of a risk assessment. A skewed perspective can interfere in the need for objective results due to stakeholders being too eclectic when considering facts and data.

Political sway. That is, the political influences within an enterprise. Jockeying for position and power within an enterprise, especially large ones, can be intense and affect the judgment stakeholders. The tone starts at the top, and it can sometimes affect the judgment of some executive and senior managers, especially in environments where mergers or significant leadership changes have occurred. Naturally, these circumstances can affect the quality of results.

Determining when enough is enough. Some individuals tend to continue on this process with seemingly no end in sight. Facts and data are collected ad infinitum, turning assessment into an endless loop. Sooner or later, a decision must be made, as in all the other risk management processes, to put an end to this process. The payback may reach the law of diminishing returns, meaning the gain from the effort decreases. Usually, it involves one or more very senior executives calling an end to a political risk assessment or the team concluding it by consensus or agreement.

Overconfidence or arrogance (more specifically hubris) of key stakeholders. Overconfidence or arrogance can seize the minds of many executive and senior managers in an enterprise, affecting their judgment and their ability to listen to contrary views. During political risk assessment, they may disagree with results and even alter decisions. Just the mere mention by a powerful executive on a team that he or she disagrees with a particular fact or datum can affect team dynamics. Many who would otherwise speak their minds become bobbleheads.

Lack of feedback from others. Sometimes, executives and senior managers work in a vacuum when performing political risk assessment. They do not attempt to solicit facts, data, or insights from others, such as subject matter experts who are not members of management. They may simply take for granted feedback from each other as they perform the risk assessment; they do not review the results with subordinates to verify the content. This situation is often the case in hierarchical organizations where the chain of command is often rigid and sharing facts and data from a high level is not normal. In this environment, a layered cake affect may exist whereby the top layer is out of sync with the lower levels.

Indecisiveness among executive and senior management. Indecisiveness may be the result of all types of problems. Political infighting, peer pressure, fear of commitment, etc. These and other reasons can result in an incomplete or unreliable political risk assessment. It could also mean that political risk management can come to a sudden stop or die a slow death because of indecisiveness. Fear can play a significant role during political risk assessment due to a reluctance to admit that a certain risk exists and significantly impacts a specific area of responsibility. Some executives, for example, may view it as an admission that they do not have control over their organization or that it is not performing its responsibilities.

Lack of support. Some executives and senior managers may just be there during a political risk assessment but no more than that. Their support is weak or nonexistent. They may feel it is not important, takes them away from their ongoing responsibilities, and view it as the "flavor of the month" and expect it to fade away.

Framing, which involves presenting a question or issue in such a way that structures and simplifies based upon certain attitudes and beliefs. This is associated with cognitive bias, leading to a partial view of a problem or issue. The result is that some risks will seem to naturally rise to the top will others fall below. Few people, let alone executive and senior managers, have the ability or wherewithal to challenge their framing of a problem or issue, let alone their beliefs and attitudes. Framing can filter important facts and data. When framing happens during a political risk assessment, decisions about risk probabilities or likelihoods, impacts, and priorities can be flawed.

Heuristics. Political risk assessment requires solid analysis which can take considerable time and effort. Many executives and senior managers may be impatient performing risk assessments since they are often in the business of making things happen. Consequently, a tendency exists to cut the time and effort to perform a risk assessment by adopting shortcuts or rules of thumb. Sometimes heuristics may be the only way to approach risk assessment when, for instance, of a dearth of facts and data exists; if used too much, however, it will reduce the confidence in the results. The margin of error, for example, whether for probability or likelihood, and impact may be too high to instill any confidence in the outcome.

Data flaws. Data is not meaningful until it is converted into information. The same goes for facts. If data are flawed, therefore, chances are information is also flawed. As one proceeds through risk assessment, flawed data will affect subsequent results. For example, the probability and impact calculations, when performing quantitative risk analysis, may be unreliable when data have been corrupted. The flawed information may then be used to influence judgments, especially when determining risk priorities and responses. Bad data are like bad blood in a body; it can lead to a misdiagnosis and systemic problems. Stakeholders need to maintain a healthy skepticism when any data and corresponding information is presented to them by questioning the validity and reliability.

Treating assumptions as unquestionable facts. The current philosophy of risk management is to treat assumptions as facts until proven otherwise. Unfortunately, many stakeholders do not revisit their assumptions when conducting political risk assessment. They continue to treat assumptions as facts without verification or revisiting them later. The danger is that if an assumption remains untrue but treated as true it can influence logical thinking, calculations, and prioritization of risks. As with data and information, stakeholders should maintain a healthy skepticism of all assumptions and try to prove or disprove their veracity as soon as possible.

Facts and data overload. Sometimes during a political risk assessment, the opposite of inaccessibility of data and information occurs, that is, too much of both are available. Stakeholders can become overwhelmed reviewing volumes of data and information. Under pressure, they may, out of necessity rely on shortcuts, such as heuristics or framing, to reduce the time and effort during a risk assessment. Succumbing to such pressure may cause errors in the results.

Not consider ranges and levels of confidence. A risk involves uncertainty and political risks have a lot of it. That means it can lack accuracy; the concept of an accurate estimate is an oxymoron. Precision is usually not a characteristic of political risk assessment. Granted, some political risks have precision but generally it is not a salient characteristic. Stakeholders in a political risk assessment would find it more valuable to use ranges or levels of confidence level to determine probability or impacts of each risk. It is like using fuzzy logic (basically using imprecise information) to determine probability, or likelihood, and impact or non-numerical data and information when performing qualitative risk assessment.

Overreliance on gut feel or instinct. Gut instinct can prove valuable in some cases, especially when facts and data are inaccurate or inaccessible.

Using gut feel can, however, introduce problems, such as cognitive bias, when assessing political risks. It can produce results having a high level of unreliability. Of course, an argument can be made that any decision boils down using gut feel because there is never enough facts and data; however, strictly relying on gut feel can prove disastrous if the intent is simply to reduce time and effort.

Over-reliance on facts and data. Too many facts and data can bog down a political risk assessment. The obsessive search for facts and data can consume too much time and require needless effort. Insecurities on the part of some executives and senior managers are drivers for this challenge. Ironically, their increase drive for more facts and data increases the desire for more, much like a drug addict seeking another hit. Their insecurities can cause a political risk assessment to become an endless loop.

Relying too much on experience. Experience is a good teacher. However, it depends on the breadth, variability, and depth of that experience. For some stakeholders, their experience may be limited or has hardened their thoughts making it difficult to be open to other views about political risks, such as determining their probabilities or likelihoods, impacts, or priorities. Sometimes the experience of the past can be a good guide; other times it can be obsolete under current circumstances.

Rationalization. While rationalization is common, it can have negative consequences in political risk assessment. It can be used as a cover to accept flawed facts and data or poor calculations of probability, or likelihood, or impacts or prioritization. Rationalizations can serve as an excuse to not follow the risk management plan or take liberties with facts and data to justify a desired outcome. Some rationalizations are not always accurate or even unrealistic despite sounding good.

FINAL THOUGHTS

Assessing political risks helps to focus resources on those political risks that matter the most, meaning having significant impacts to an enterprise's the global supply chain. Probability or likelihood, and impact are the ingredients to determine priority. However, assessing political risks serves little purpose until the results of this process are applied to the next one, prepare political risk responses.

GETTING STARTED QUESTIONS

Questions	Yes	No

1. When assessing risks, are you considering the following?
   a) Engaging a balanced team?
   b) Using multiple sources of facts and data?
   c) Recognizing that sometimes a tradeoff exists between quantity vs. quality of facts and data?
   d) Understanding that uncertainty about risks even after performing the best political risk assessment as possible?
   e) Recognizing the relationship between assessing risks and reporting?
   f) Using risk assessment as the groundwork to develop risk responses?
   g) Attempting to limit the influence of subjectivity?
   h) Using risk assessment to set priorities?
   i) Recording risk assessment results in the risk register?
   j) Being aware of the risk appetite and tolerance of key stakeholders and the enterprise?
   k) Considering both internal and external risks to strategic goals?
   l) Being systemic and systematic when assessing risks?
   m) Documenting assumptions for each risk regarding probability or likelihood, impact, and prioritization?
   n) Recognizing risk assessment results will be imperfect the first time?
2. Have you decided which approach to take when assessing risks?
   a) Qualitative risk assessment?
   b) Quantitative risk assessment?
   c) Combination of both?
3. Whether performing qualitative or quantitative risk assessment, are you keeping in mind the following insights?
   a) Estimate the occurrence of risk to account for uncertainty?
   b) Determine the priority of a risk (whether for a threat or opportunity)?
   c) Record results in the risk listing (also known as a risk register)?
   d) Use the risk management plan to describe the qualitative or quantitative approach taken?
   e) Review continuously and performed iteratively?
   f) Apply under the purview of the strategic goals?
   g) Review assumptions recorded and revisited regularly?
   h) Use as groundwork for better reporting?
   i) Use various methods to solicit input from stakeholders?
   j) Use to provide an integrated assessment of multiple risks?

Questions	Yes	No

4. If using qualitative risk assessment, are you considering the following?
   a) Using a balanced stakeholder team?
   b) Defining scales employed to measure probability or likelihood and impact of risks?
   c) Using multiple sources of facts and data such as:
      1) Interviewees?
      2) Historical facts and data?
      3) Documents, e.g., reports?
      4) Address the challenge of complex linkages among risks?
      5) Determining the basic formats to display the results of the assessment?
5. If using quantitative risk assessment, are you considering the following?
   a) Determining if any risks using qualitative risk analysis candidates for quantitative risk analysis?
   b) Determining which candidate risks have dependent relationships with other ones?
   c) Determining which candidate risks have an independent relationship with other ones?
   d) Selecting which statistical charts to display the results?
6. Are you experiencing any of the following challenges and, if so, determining how to deal with them?
   a) Time commitment of stakeholders?
   b) Learning curves of stakeholders?
   c) Inaccessibility of facts and data?
   d) Cognitive bias exhibited by stakeholders?
   e) Internal political sway?
   f) Completeness of assessment determination?
   g) Overconfidence or arrogance by key stakeholders?
   h) Lack of feedback from others?
   i) Indecisiveness among executive and senior management?
   j) Lack of support of stakeholders?
   k) Use of framing?
   l) Use of heuristics?
   m) Treating of assumptions as unquestionable facts?
   n) Facts and data overload?
   o) Not considering ranges and levels of confidence?
   p) Overreliance on gut feel?
   q) Relying too much on experience?
   r) Rationalizing?

NOTES

1. Ila Manuj and John Mentzer, "Global Supply Chain Risk Management Strategies," *International Journal of Physical Distribution and Logistics*, vol. 3, 2008), 197–198.
2. Robert McKellar, *A Short Guide to Political Risk* (Burlington, VT: Gower Publishing Limited, 2010) 102–109.

10

Prepare Political Risk Responses

After completing the risk assessment, the next process is to develop political risk responses. It involves determining appropriate responses to address political risks and develop any tactical actions. Four activities apply to preparing risk responses. The first activity is to determine appropriate strategies to deal with a risk. The second activity is to determine the tactical actions to implement the strategies. The third activity is to prepare to implement additional tactical actions if the original ones are ineffective. The fourth activity is to assign a risk owner for each risk.

Preparing risk responses applies to both threats and opportunities. This fact is often overlooked because the emphasis is one on the former. While the goal is to minimize the probability or likelihood, and impact of a threat, the opposite is the case for opportunities where the goal is to maximize the probability or likelihood and impact. Threats and opportunities are managed through strategic responses which are implemented through tactical actions (also known as contingencies) to deal with a trigger event or when the risk becomes an issue.

KEY POINTS

When preparing risk responses, keep the following thoughts in mind.

Avoid overkill when determining a response. The idea is to avoid putting out a match with a fire hose; it will only cause more problems or additional political risks which can waste time and monetary resources. When determining a response, consider the impact and priority of a political risk.

Recognize not all responses will be one hundred percent effective; indeed, some may be residual political risks. Some responses may also result in secondary risks. Some responses may be totally ineffective, requiring development of fallback plans.

Recognize responses cannot exceed the circle of control for an enterprise. In some cases, a risk is beyond the ability of an enterprise to respond to an event or issue, requiring the intervention of a third party. That is why it is important to keep the focus on the enterprise-wide goals related to a global supply chain of an enterprise. If an enterprise cannot depend on the support of a third party, an excellent political response is to build alliances with other companies located in a particular country or region. Many petroleum companies communicate and coordinate with one another, such as Venezuela. Hotel chains in foreign countries, such as in southeast Asia, do the same.

Look for linkages among political risks. One may find that a response strategy may address more than one risk. Response strategies are like Venn diagrams; they overlap with one another. The same concept applies for tactical actions which implement response strategies. Knowing these linkages can result in effective and efficient responses.

Record all assumptions when identifying responses. Turnover among stakeholders is common. By recording assumptions in a risk register, for example, the basis for selecting a strategic response for a political risk will be recorded. During political risk management, stakeholders can revisit the assumptions, too, and change to a different response strategy, if necessary.

Ensure that a risk management plan documents how the stakeholders determine the strategic responses and the corresponding tactical actions. It should also list the responsibilities of risk owners assigned to each risk. It should also set thresholds and events that flag when a strategic response and one or more tactical actions may need implementation. The plan contains a general description of major responses and tactical actions and that may suffice; for greater detail, prepare procedures.

Remember that determining strategic responses and tactical actions should involve the participation of all relevant executive and senior managers. This participation can occur via one of many teaming tools and techniques used in political risk management, to include the Delphi technique, brainstorming, and Crawford slip method.

Record all political risk responses and their corresponding tactical actions in a risk register. Even the decision to discard and replace a strategic response or a tactical action should be recorded in the register to provide an audit trail.

Review the strategic responses and tactical actions for each risk continually and iteratively. The environment of an enterprise constantly changes. A strategic response or a tactical action may have become an anachronism which, upon implementation, can cause problems, such as residual or secondary risks.

Assign risk owners for one or more risks. A risk owner watches for the occurrence of political risks by looking for warning signs, such as when conditions exceed thresholds; has responsibility to ensure plans for strategic responses and corresponding tactical actions are maintained, implemented efficiently and effectively; and looking for any unintended consequences e.g., secondary risks.

Avoid the deadly To Be Determined (TBD) when developing strategic responses and tactical actions. TBDs are often forgotten. If a risk is realized and a TBD was not addressed beforehand, then an enterprise will be forced to react to it. When it reacts rather than responds to a risk, an enterprise can often result in confusion, firefighting, ineffectiveness, and inefficiency.

Recognize that not every risk or event can be anticipated and, consequently, no prepared response will be unavailable. Unexpected circumstances may arise that can prove disastrous or catastrophic for an enterprise and its global supply chain. A Black Swan event may occur. Or a risk that was assigned to a watchlist can have an unexpected appearance and have a severe impact to the surprise of executive and senior management; if a wrong or inadequate strategic response and tactical action are applied, it may lack value. Determining strategic responses and tactical actions requires looking into the future, which is associated with some degree of uncertainty. Observes Condoleezza Rice and Amy Zegart in *Political Risk*: "No company, profit, or government can afford to protect everything from every contingency. Risk mitigation requires trade-offs and trade-offs require understanding which assets are the most valuable and most vulnerable."[1]

Strive for agreement or at least consensus among executive and senior management over strategic responses or tactical actions or both. Odds are that agreement will not be reached but consensus which is achievable through understanding, acceptance, and support (UAS), meaning "I understand it, accept it, and support it."

Determine the means to ascertain when circumstances may warrant attention. Look for signals that a risk may become an issue. These signals may include exceeding certain thresholds; a trigger event occurring; or a risk becoming an issue. The assigned risk owner is the person responsible to watch for these signals.

BENEFITS

Several benefits are attributed to preparing political risk responses.

Encourages being pro-active, not reactive. By coming up with advance ways to deal with risks, an enterprise will be prepared if, and when, they become issues and do so effectively and efficiently. They can even act in advance to avoid certain risks.

Serves as a direct linkage with previous political risk management processes, such as identifying risks. Each successive process should build upon the output of a previous one. Ideally, the responses are efficient and effective as well as have executive and senior management support.

Builds confidence among the executives and senior management. If any risks become an issue, they can deal with it, being prepared. They know what responses to implement and the tactical actions to deploy. Even if secondary and residual risks surface, they at least will understand the cause and can take any additional action.

Builds ownership. Executive and senior management as a team prepare strategic responses and develop the corresponding tactical actions to implement; this preparation encourages them to take responsibility for effectiveness when managing risks. Additionally, they have assigned risk owners, which includes executive and senior managers, to keep track of risks, strategic responses, and tactical actions.

Employ a structured approach. Stakeholders determine strategic responses and tactical actions in a consistent, focused, and systematic manner, which increases effectiveness upon implementation. Strategic responses and tactical actions must be clearly understood by key stakeholders. That means they know who does what, when, where, why, and how. Identifying responses and tactical actions is not enough. Responsible individuals must know under circumstances to implement them.

Seize opportunities as well as mitigate threats. Executives and senior managers often overlook the advantage of being prepared to seize opportunities; instead, they focus often on dealing with threats. Anticipating opportunities allows an enterprise to take the initiative in seizing them for their advantage. These opportunities should further improvements of an enterprise's global supply chain. Preparing to deal only with threats is, as an old saying goes, seeing the glass half empty while looking for opportunities is seeing it half full.

Increases risk awareness. By developing risk responses and their corresponding tactical actions as well as assigning risk owners, the alert status for risks, especially medium and high priority ones, cannot help but increase. Communications among stakeholders cannot help but improve, especially when discussing high priority risks. Communications can often intensify, especially among executives and senior managers who see their areas of responsibilities being impacted.

APPROACH

One, focus on the relevant strategic goals impacting the global supply chain. A strategic political response should not go beyond that focus. Otherwise, it could result in inefficiency, ineffectiveness, and unintended consequences for an enterprise. Preferably, stick to the risks already identified since they are based on a global supply chain. Also, identify the practicality of response and its corresponding tactical actions. Avoiding putting out a match with a fire hose. Scalability is key. Otherwise, not only is overkill wasteful but so is the energy and effort expended to execute a strategic response and its corresponding tactical actions. The key is to remain on target. A useful matrix is, shown in Figure 10.1, is one that records the strategic response to take to address each threat confronting a specific element in the global supply chain.

Two, consider the complexity of risks. Not all risks are equal in terms of managing them; this is not the same as priority. Complexity could, for example, be technical or financial. It could also be that a political risk is linked with a series of other risks and when a strategic response is executed it could have a cascading impact on the other ones, positively or negatively.

Three, keep in mind the priority of each risk. Naturally, the highest priority risks should receive the most attention. Strategic responses should focus on descending priorities, such as the following order: high, medium, low, and watchlist. This attention will ensure that resources are deployed efficiently and effectively. Keep in mind, though, that priorities can change over time and new strategic responses and their corresponding tactical actions might be added, deleted, or modified.

Four, look at the pros and cons of each strategic response in the context of the political risk being addressed. For example, one method that can

Threats -> Assets	Foreign hiring restriction	Tariffs	Military takeover	Contract violations	Terrorism	Piracy	Increased regulatory actions	Bureaucratic delays	Territorial conflict	Expropriation
Inventory	Transfer	Etc.	Etc.	Etc.	Etc.	Etc.	Etc.	Etc.		
Suppliers	Mitigate	Etc.	Etc.	Etc.	Etc.	Etc.				
Manufacturers	Mitigate	Etc.	Etc.							
Materials	Etc.									
Transportation										
Warehouses/Distribution centers										
Customers										

FIGURE 10.1

Matrix Showing Relationship among Supply Chain Assets, Threats, and Strategic Responses.

help is to make a list of the advantages and disadvantages, possibly weighing each advantage, each disadvantage, and then tally the scores for each side. The side with the highest score can help to decide whether to implement a strategic response.

Five, be aware that a political strategic response and the corresponding tactical actions may have affects and effects on an enterprise and its global supply chain or even on other risks. For example, a strategic response can have residual effects (not addressing a risk inadequately and, consequently, needs additional attention) or a secondary risk (a new risk is introduced as a result of a strategic response or a corresponding tactical action). In some cases, a strategic response may fail completely; the key is to have a fallback plan to address this eventuality.

Six, know the risk tolerances and attitudes of stakeholders and the enterprise. This knowledge will help to select a strategic response and corresponding tactical actions that are in sync with these tolerances and attitudes. Executive and senior management involvement is crucial when choosing an appropriate response.

Seven, perform the following pattern of activities when applying strategic responses and the corresponding tactical actions. Determine the option or options to deal with risks; select the best option or options; determine which strategic response or responses are necessary to address each political risk if and when it arises; and determine the tactical actions to support the response or responses.

Eight, for high priority risks consider conducting periodic tests on implementing strategic responses and tactical actions. Testing enhances stakeholders' understanding and knowledge on what responses and tactical actions to pursue when a political event occurs. Several types of tests can be employed which are covered in the business continuity section of this chapter.

Nine, prepare flowcharts, procedures, or other documents that require responding to a specific risk. These documents should provide the who, what, when, where, why, and how information and people have access to these procedures; risk owners should be familiar with the content in the documents.

Strategic Responses for Threats

When developing strategic responses for each political threat, choose one or more of the following. Keep in mind these can overlap; they are not mutually exclusive.

Acceptance is doing nothing. An enterprise simply takes the hit, so to speak. Acceptance is one of two forms: active and passive. Active acceptance is developing a contingency plan, such as set aside a contingency reserve, to address the risk; passive is absorbing the impact.

Avoidance is taking action to eliminate a threat. An enterprise may decide, for example, to avoid engaging in a line of business with a specific country, such as China.

Transfer is offloading responsibility of a threat to a third party. An enterprise may decide, for example, to purchase insurance to protect itself from a specific threat when investing in a high-risk project within a developing country, such as Brazil.

Mitigation is reducing the expected value of a threat. An enterprise realizes that a threat can have a financial impact upon occurrence; it decides to set aside funds to help alleviate the impact, such as setting up a contingency reserve to address potential lawsuit settlements for a chemical spill in a developing country, such as India. Rice and Zegart in *Political Risk* suggest employing "excess capacity." Under certain circumstances that may help.[2] The military adheres to this thinking. Major data centers implement matching facilities for disaster recovery purposes. More is better, such as having two manufacturing facilities in case a political event occurs in one of them. Be advised, however, excess capacity requires maintaining two facilities and conducting simultaneous operations.

Sharing is a response whereby an enterprise splits the responsibility to deal with a threat. For example, an enterprise may form a partnership or alliance with another enterprise; both parties can then deal with the impact of a threat, such as petroleum companies operating in Venezuela.

A useful matrix, shown in Figure 10.2, is one that shows the relationship between the relevant strategic goals and the tactical actions. The matrix provides a good idea of how the tactical actions that implement strategic responses will help to protect strategic goals from threats. Where a strategic goal or objective intersect with a tactical action, a cell is created. Within a cell, a check mark can indicate the relationship between the two, or a strategic response, such as mitigation, or the title of a threat or a combination of all three. A separate matrix can also be created for opportunities.

Tactical Actions	Strategic Goal or Objective	Strategic Goal or Objective	Strategic Goal or Objective	Strategic Goal or Objective
Tactical Action	✓	✓		
Tactical Action				✓
Tactical Action		✓		
Tactical Action				
Tactical Action	✓			
Tactical Action			✓	✓
Tactical Action				

FIGURE 10.2
Matrix Showing the Relationship of Tactical Actions with Strategic Goals.

Negotiating in good faith from the start by seeking a win-win result, not a win-lose. That is perhaps the best way to lower the chances of a political threat. The key is to align interests, especially if an enterprise seeks to remain in a country and preserve its international reputation. Otherwise, the probability increases of a host country's government may start interfering in business operations.[3]

Negotiating in good faith from the start by seeking a win-win result not a win-lose one. That is perhaps the best way to lower the chance of facing a political threat. The key is to align interests, especially if an enterprise seeks to remain in a country and preserve its international reputation. Otherwise, the probability increases that a host country's government may start interfering in business operations.[4]

Strategic responses overlap with one another, like Venn diagrams. A specific tactical action can satisfy one or more responses. Some of the tactical actions are proactive, meaning that one or more of them can be implemented before a threat occurs. Other tactical actions are a response taken to a specific threat event. Below is a partial list a of financial and operational tactical actions that can be applied to deal with political threats pertaining to a global supply chain:

- Adopt asset and flow redundancy
- Alliance among enterprises in a host country
- Compliance with import and export laws
- Compliance with regulations
- Continual monitoring of the host government
- Contractual protection addressing:

- Agreement changes
- Dispute resolution
- Guarantee of foreign exchange
- Inventory control and maintenance
- Liquidated damages
- Political force majeure
- Sovereign immunity
- Supplier warranties
- Decide not to invest in a country
- Gradual transfer of asset to a local company
- Hold collateral in offshore accounts
- Increase involvement with local communities
- Independent professional performance reviews
- Information sharing among partners
- Innovative financial investment strategies
- Joint venture with a local company
- Local equity ownership
- Negotiate long-term contracts
- Negotiate win-win results
- Obtain progress reports on operational performance
- Offshore payments to deal with convertibility issues
- Payment in foreign currency in an offshore account
- Performance testing between global enterprise and firm in host country
- Preferential listing of firms within host country
- Purchase political insurance
- Seek foreign suppliers with reliable performance record
- Seek multilateral institution guarantee
- Self-insure
- Set up assets in different countries
- Sovereign guarantees, such as performance failure of a firm
- Spread investment risk
- Transfer higher costs to customers

Strategic Responses for Opportunities

When developing strategic responses for opportunities (also known as positive risks), choose one or more of the following strategic responses. As with political threats, keep in mind these can overlap; they, too, are not mutually exclusive. In many respects, they are mirror images of each other.

Acceptance is once again to do nothing; an enterprise accepts the opportunity, either actively or passively. Active acceptance may involve increasing contingency reserves to take advantage of an opportunity. Passive acceptance is simply taking no action at all, such as a military takeover in a less developed country, such as Jamaica, which may prove advantageous to an enterprise.

Escalate is recognizing an opportunity but not having the authority or power to seize it. Instead, the opportunity is elevated up the organizational chain of command to take advantage of economies of scale. A department or business unit may see an opportunity but can do nothing other than escalate it, for example, to the board of directors to decide whether to take advantage of an opportunity. Or an aerospace company may elevate a potential sale its government to put pressure on another country, such as India, to purchase airplanes.

Exploit is furthering an opportunity and do whatever it takes to gain the advantage. For example, an enterprise may try to reduce the uncertainty surrounding an opportunity by influencing the environment in such a way to seize the advantage. For example, enterprises might seek to take advantage of a thaw in relations between two countries after a long period of hostilities, such as participating in the textile trade, which occurred between the Vietnam and the United States.

Share is allocating a portion of the gains of an opportunity with a third party. For example, an enterprise may share profits with another business entity to seize an opportunity, such as BP, Anadarko Petroleum, and MOEX Offshore sharing ownership in Deepwater Horizon before it turned into an issue impacting the United States.

Enhance is increasing the probability and impact of an opportunity. An enterprise does what it can to increase the chance for an opportunity to occur and increase the gain. An enterprise may decide to outsource a business process to gain a competitive advantage. Aerospace forms sometimes engage in offset agreements which essentially serves as an exchange of aircraft to another country at a discount in exchange for consulting services.

It is often handy, whether for threats or opportunities, to capture information about risk responses and corresponding tactical actions in a risk register. Typically, the register includes a column for political risk and, strategic responses, and cells for tactical actions.

Matrix can be developed, shown in Figure 10.3, showing the relationship between political risks and strategic responses from a global supply chain perspective. The purpose of the matrix is to ensure that significant risks have been addressed by a strategic response. At the top of the matrix is a list of the strategic responses potentially applicable to political risks. Along the left (or Y-axis) is a column showing the political risks. Inside each cell shows the tactical actions to execute a response for each risk if it occurs.

The matrix can be created using a spreadsheet program. It is updated continuously, from the processes assess political risks through perform political risk reporting. Another option is to create a separate matrix for threats and another for opportunities.

Some people do not like to use matrices. Instead, they prefer a decision tree. It presents a panoramic view of the relationships among the variables, from the probability or likelihood of political impacts, responses, tactical actions for each political risk, such as the one shown in Figure 10.4. Moving from left to right, a political risk is identified, for example, such as increased tariffs by China, and a "limb," or branch, follows for each likelihood of occurrence (low, medium, and high). A limb moves to a political risk impact, such as increased tension between the Chinese and US government. A response is reflected at the end of another limb that might be mitigation and the corresponding tactical action or actions, such as working closely with the US Trade Representative with China. Frequently, a decision tree can have only one path through it and at the end of each limb

Political Risks	Strategic Response	Strategic Response	Strategic Response	Strategic Response
Foreign Hiring Restrictions	Tactical Action(s)			
Tariffs				
Military Takeover				
Contract Violations				
Terrorism				
Piracy				
Increased Regulatory Actions				
Bureaucratic Delays				
Territorial Conflict				
Expropriation				

FIGURE 10.3
Matrix Showing Relationships between Political Risks and Strategic Response.

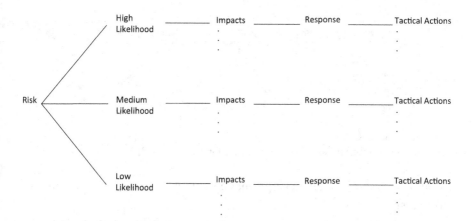

FIGURE 10.4
Decision Tree Showing the Decision Paths for a Risk.

a list of impacts, responses, and tactical actions are listed. Again, the advantage of a decision tree is that it provides a good integrated, visual perspective of each risk.

Decision trees work very well when performing quantitative risk analysis. Probability is used more than likelihood and is multiplied against the total value of the investment in a country related to its global supply chain to determine the financial impact, and then listing the appropriate responses, e.g., transferring the risk, and a corresponding tactical action, such as pursuing political risk insurance.

A useful matrix is one, shown in Figure 10.5, showing the relationship between each threat and the impact, such as low, medium, or high. The matrix helps to ensure that all impacts of a threat are addressed by a strategic response. The cell created by the relationship between a threat and an impact records the strategic response, such as avoidance, transfer, or mitigation. The matrix can be developed also for opportunities.

Ila Manuj and John Mentzer in the *International Journal of Physical Distribution and Logistics Management* take a somewhat different approach in responding to threats that affect a global supply chain. They identified several risk management strategies to pursue in a global supply chain. These are postponement, speculation, hedging, control/share/ transfer, security, and avoidance.

Postponement is deliberately delaying the commitment of resources to ensure reducing costs and increasing flexibility. A common action supporting this risk management response is offshoring. The authors state

Threat: Expropriation   Impact

Risk Strategy	High	Medium	Low
Accept			
Avoid			
Transfer	✓		
Mitigate			

FIGURE 10.5
Matrix Showing the Strategic Response to Take for Managing a Risk.

that this is mainly a fallback option; however, it can also serve as a mitigation response.

Speculation involves a different approach. It involves moving goods to forward inventories. Common action supporting this risk management response might be accumulating resources or goods. Again, this might be considered a mitigation response.

Hedging requires dispersing suppliers and other supply chain assets, such as warehouses, across the globe to mitigate the impact of a threat. Like speculation, it can be expensive but hedging does offer flexibility in response to a threat. This response might be generically considered a transfer response.

Control/share/transfer entails offloading some of the impact of a threat to other entities. Common actions to support this risk management strategy include implementing partnering strategies throughout a supply chain to deal with threats in a global business environment. The challenge with this risk management strategy is having an integrated supply chain. Another challenge exists that the entanglements may reduce flexibility when responding to a changing business environment. Again, this response might be considered generically as a transfer response.

Security, according to the authors, involves dealing with a wide range of topics, from information technology security, criminal activities, and working with governmental authorities. The response and supporting actions primarily seek to deal with delays in the global supply chain resulting from simple negligence to purposeful intent. The actions can be expensive but so can ignoring them. This response might be considered generically as an avoidance or acceptance response.

Avoidance is a response that requires acting but over to what extent. The authors identify two types of avoidance. Type 1 is an avoidance response that allows for no probability of occurrence of a risk. Any occurrence of a risk is unacceptable; actions are taken to ensure the risk does not occur. Type 2 is an avoidance response to minimize the probability of occurrence of a risk but does not eliminate uncertainty as is the case with Type 1. Examples of Type 2 risk avoidance tactical actions include audits, pre-approvals, and setting quality baselines. Type 1 and II responses obviously fit within the avoidance category.[5]

CHALLENGES

Several challenges present themselves when preparing political risk responses.

Assigning risk owners. If executives and senior managers see themselves personally impacted by a risk, they may be reluctant to accept the role of risk owner. They have other responsibilities that require keeping their departments or business units operational. Being a risk owner requires devoting time and resources which, in many cases, also increases over-head costs. Under certain circumstances, however, they may enthusiastically want to be a risk owner which increases their commitment to ensure responses and tactical actions are implemented efficiently and effectively, especially if it involves their areas of responsibility.

Having risk owners following through on responsibilities. Time constraints and managing their department or business unit often compete with performing as a risk owner. Under such circumstances, being a risk owner fades into the background due to other responsibilities.

Maintaining awareness of trigger events. This responsibility requires being regularly vigilant. A disciplined follow-through is required to monitor risks for trigger events, just as the other responsibilities of being a risk owner. This responsibility can fade into the background again due to other responsibilities.

Determining what is in the circle of control for an enterprise. No enterprise controls everything involving that happens to its global supply chain. Ideally, all the political risk management processes are consistently focused on political risks affecting a global supply chain. That is why it is important to focus on these strategic goals that relate to the global supply chain; otherwise, political risk management processes from a supply chain perspective may not be too effective or efficient.

BUSINESS CONTINUITY 101

With a more complex global supply chain and unstable globalization, resiliency becomes critical. Resiliency is the ability of an enterprise to respond or recover from the impact of events. The road to resilience is business continuity which is the discipline of developing, deploying, and maintaining strategies and procedures to ensure that an enterprise survives by increasing the likelihood of responding and recovering from an event crippling or destroying in part or whole its critical business processes. A critical business process is a series of procedures and activities key stakeholders have identified as vital to the survival of an organization. In most multinational companies, one or more of its global supply chains are considered a critical business process. If one or more significant events, including political ones, impact any element of a critical global supply chain, it affects an enterprise's profitability, perhaps even its existence.

Several drivers exist for business continuity to apply to global supply chains. Global sourcing has increased in the presence of international trade disruption due to political situations. Recent political events from Covid-19 to Brexit to Chinese-United States relations have presented significant challenges to global supply chains. Regional trade alliances and partnerships have become strained over issues of immigration and national defense. Terrorism, war, and political turmoil continue to interfere with global supply chains. Regulations and nationalizations by developed, developing countries, and less developed countries all have, to one degree or another, disrupted global supply chains. Global supply chains increasingly rely upon a more complicated weave of transportation and information systems; connected by free flow of international capital; and legal barriers. The circumstances are present in the face of interdependence and integration. One disruption, even a mild one, and the dominos in a global supply chain can fall. Business continuity, as a component of political risk management, can increase the resilience of a global enterprise in the face of such circumstances.

In our book, *Business Continuity Planning*, by CRC Press, we present a hierarchy of events which is the occurrence of an incident impacting a critical business process. An event can range in intensity and impact, such as very mild to being catastrophic. A political event can span the entire continuum. The five types of events are incident, emergency, disaster, crisis, and catastrophe. An incident is an event having an inconsequential impact such as a repelled cyberattack by Russian government against an enterprise's information system located at the corporate headquarters in Hollywood; an emergency threatens usually life, safety, and property and requires immediate attention, such as a terrorist bomb is set to explode inside an enterprise's headquarters of a business unit located in Paris, France; a disaster has severe consequences for a considerable time unless an immediate action is taken, such as a guerrilla group seizes power from a regime in Chile and threatens to expropriate a significant production facility; a crisis exceeds normal expectations of disruption and necessitates recovery actions which, if not taken, threatens the survivability of an enterprise; and a catastrophe exceeds the ability and capability of an enterprise to respond and recover from an event and leads to devastating consequences.

Ideally, an enterprise can respond effectively to an event (short of a catastrophe) by resuming normal operations as soon as possible. Normal operations, also known as business as usual, is the state of business operations prior to the occurrence of an event. When an event occurs, a response may be necessary which is applying processes, procedures, and actions quickly to prevent, mitigate, or avoid a negative impact. Recovery is the actions taken to lead to the resumption of a business process and eventually to a return to normal operations. Resumption is the processes, procedures, and actions to restart a critical business process when recovery actions are completed after the disruptive event.

There are essentially three components to business continuity: business impact analysis, the business preparedness plan, and testing. All three components have a direct tie to enterprise risk management.

The business impact analysis (BIA) requires identifying the critical business processes, such as a global supply chain, within an enterprise and the impact of risks should they occur. It also provides guidelines to determine when to initiate recovery procedures that are in the business preparedness plan. It is conducted at the strategic level, such as at the executive and senior management levels, and within each critical business process. Two goals are to establish the relationship between risks and critical business processes and assess the impact of the risks on them. The BIA takes a more enterprise wide perspective.

The business preparedness plan (BPP) is a document capturing the necessary information to guide what are known as recovery teams and enhance the ability of a critical business process to recover from a disruptive event, such as political dissidents in Nigeria capture key executives from a petroleum company and demand the firm to leave or they will execute the captives; a catastrophe exceeds the ability and capability of a firm to recover, such as war between two regional nations, resulting in maximum casualties and destruction, such as what could occur between North and South Korea or Pakistan and India. The plan includes lists of the members of a recovery team and their roles and responsibilities, the resources to enhance recovery, and the time required for their availability and instructions on executing a call tree. The BPP is prepared at the business unit or operational level of an enterprise.

Testing is a systematic approach to verify and validate the effectiveness of an enterprise's ability to respond to, and recover from, an event using the BPP. The purpose of testing is to increase the accuracy of the plan, keep it current, and add to the recovery team's knowledge about the plan. Testing requires coming up with a scenario that presents a set of conditions and impacts challenging a recovery team's ability to respond to it. Typically, testing may be one of the following, table topic or simulation. A table topic exercise entails applying the contents of a BP plan to a scenario using discussion and not acting. A simulation exercise is having the recovery team apply the specific content of their BP plans against a scenario. The scenario should progress according to degrees of intensity. A simulation exercise is having recovery team members apply specific content of their BPP against a scenario by acquiring or applying resources and exercising the content of the plan. The emphasis is on action, less discussion. Testing is often done at the business unit or operational level.

Often overlooked, but as important as the business impact analysis, business preparedness plan, and testing is maintenance of the BPP. The BPP can be updated during testing but also periodically such as every six months or once a year. The reason is due to organizational changes, the business environment may have changed, or recovery team members have departed. Once updated, the BPP should be reviewed, approved, and distributed by key stakeholders. Maintenance of the BPP is usually done at the business unit or operational level.

FINAL THOUGHTS

Identifying and assessing political risks are useful processes; however, the real payoff comes from performing these processes by having responses and tactical actions ready to implement once risks become issues. Enterprises can then respond proactively, not reactively, to political circumstances affecting their global supply chain. Of course, knowing when to respond depends on performing the next process, perform political risk monitoring and controlling.

GETTING STARTED QUESTIONS

Questions	Yes	No

1. When preparing risk responses, are you considering the following?
   a) Avoiding overkill when determining a response?
   b) Recognizing not all responses will be one hundred percent effective?
   c) Recognizing responses cannot exceed the circle of control for an enterprise?
   d) Looking for linkages among risks?
   e) Recording all assumptions when identifying responses?
   f) Ensuring that a risk management plan describes how the stakeholders determine the strategic responses and the corresponding tactical actions?
   g) Remembering that determining strategic responses and tactical actions should involve the participation of executive and senior management?
   h) Recording all risk responses and their corresponding tactical actions in a risk register?
   i) Reviewing the strategic responses and tactical actions for each risk continually and iteratively?
   j) Assigning risk owners for one or more risks?
   k) Avoiding the deadly To Be Determined (TBD) when developing strategic responses and tactical actions?
   l) Recognizing that not every risk or event can be anticipated and, consequently, no prepared response exists?
   m) Striving for agreement or at least consensus among executive and senior management over strategic responses and tactical actions?
   n) Determining means to ascertain when circumstances, e.g., events, may warrant attention?
   o) Focusing on the enterprise-wide goals?
   p) Considering the complexity of risks?
   q) Keeping in mind the priority of each risk?
   r) Looking at the pros and cons of each strategic response in the context of the risk being addressed?
   s) Recognizing that a strategic response and its tactical actions may affect an enterprise and have effects on its profitability?
   t) Knowing the risk attitudes and tolerances of the stakeholders and the enterprise?
   u) Performing this pattern when applying strategic responses and actions:
      1) Determine options to deal with risks?
      2) Select the best option or options?
      3) Determine which strategic response or responses are necessary to deal with a risk?
      4) Determine the tactical actions to support the response or responses?

Questions	Yes	No

2. When developing strategic responses for each threat, are you considering these strategies:
   a) Acceptance?
   b) Avoidance?
   c) Transfer?
   d) Mitigation?
   e) Sharing?
3. When developing strategic responses for each opportunity, are you considering these strategies:
   a) Acceptance?
   b) Escalate?
   c) Exploit?
   d) Share?
   e) Enhance?
4. Are you experiencing any of the following challenges and, if so, determining how to deal with them?
   a) Assigning risk owners?
   b) Having risk owners follow through on responsibilities?
   c) Maintaining awareness of trigger events?
   d) Determining what is in the circle of control for the enterprise?

NOTES

1. Condolezza Rice and Amy Zegart, *Political Risk* (New York: Twelve, 2018), 192.
2. Rice and Zegart, *Political Risk*, 199.
3. William T. Irwin "Political Risk: A Realistic View Toward Assessment, Qualification, and Mitigation," in Managing International Political Risk, ed. Theodore H. Moran (Oxford: Blackwell Business, 1998) 68.
4. William T. Irwin "Political Risk: A Realistic View Toward Assessment, Qualification, and Mitigation," 68.
5. Ila Manuj and John Mentzer, "Global Supply Chain Risk Management," *International Journal of Physical Distribution and Logistics*, vol. 3 (2008): 192–223.

11

Perform Political Risk Monitoring and Controlling

Performing monitoring and controlling is maintaining awareness of any imminent political risks and ensuring, if applicable, responses have been implemented and are effective. It entails tracking risks; looking for trigger events to forewarn of a risk occurrence; ensuring the effectiveness and efficiency of risk responses; maintaining risk awareness among key stakeholders; adhering to and updating of a risk management plan and other pertinent policies and procedures; and following up with risk owners to verify their exercise of risk owner responsibilities.

KEY POINTS

When performing risk monitoring and control, keep these thoughts in mind.

Occurs continuously. Monitoring and controlling requires keeping a pulse on an enterprise's environment to determine whether one or more political risks have occurred and the effectiveness of their corresponding responses. It involves collecting and compiling facts and data regularly so that an enterprise can respond to risks if they arise.

Requires good communications up and down the chain and command, from the board of directors to operational levels. Broken communications can lead to misinformation, lost information, etc. that could indicate over-looking the occurrence of high priority threats and opportunities or not knowing about the effectiveness of responses.

Requires good follow-up. A combination of continuous monitoring and controlling as well as solid communications are fine; however, when executive and senior management make a decision regarding a response, for example, follow-up becomes critical. Key stakeholders need to answer whether the decision, such as responding to a political risk, has been implemented and, if so, was effective. Sometimes, follow-up on decisions is often overlooked when a political risk occurs; few people are aware of the results.

Details should be documented in a risk management plan. It should cover topics such as key threshold levels; significant trends and variances regarding facts and data; trigger event tracking; facts and data collection (to include source and capture); risk assessment and response strategies; roles and responsibilities; and updates to the risk listing.

Take an integrated perspective of an enterprise. The different levels of an enterprise, such as strategic and business unit levels, share facts, and data regarding risks confronting it. The facts and data are "rolled up" to a strategic level to allow for determining the overall effectiveness of monitoring and controlling risks.

Consider the history of the risk attitude and tolerances of an enterprise as well as for current executive and senior management. Risk attitude and tolerance can influence the degree of monitoring and controlling that occurs.

Requires following the relevant risk management policies and procedures of an enterprise and, just as importantly, the content of a risk management plan. As already mentioned, it does not make sense to devote the time and effort to create a risk management plan and then having it sits on a shelf with no one following it. If such circumstances exist, the risk management plan needs revision to reflect reality and then receives approvals of key stakeholders.

Maintain focus on the priorities. If following the political risk management processes described in this book, focus should be predetermined unless a black swan or unk unk occurs. Without focus, the facts and data collected may not pertain to a risk because stakeholders have broadened their scope, possibly without realizing it. That is why it is important to focus on goals relevant to a global supply chain.

Question all facts and data received during monitoring and controlling. Some of the facts and data may be slanted to force a perspective; be inaccurate; or dated. This situation is not easy as it seems if the environment is dynamic, such as in a country experiencing high levels of violence that could disrupt a global supply chain.

Keep communications opened, free of riffraff. The key is to use both formal and informal channels of communications. Formal channels may be from inside an enterprise, such as the board of directors, and outside of it, such as IGOs and government sources. Informal communications might include maintaining communications with local leaders of a locale within a country. Also, consider using alternative instruments to collect facts and data, such as using surveys and questionnaires.

BENEFITS

Several benefits are attributed to risk monitoring and controlling.

Reflects being proactive, not reactive. Monitoring requires maintaining continuous awareness of what is occurring in an environment, and controlling involves responding to, not reacting to, risk events and conditions. In other words, both monitoring and controlling require taking the initiative; that is, making a deliberate decision to be vigilant and to act.

Builds confidence among key stakeholders. They exhibit less fear even if something does happen negatively. An enterprise is ready and able to deal with the threat or event. Or if something positive arises, the enterprise is ready and able to seize an opportunity.

Enhances the effectiveness of an enterprise in its pursuit to achieve its strategic goals related to global supply chains. Keep in mind that the scope of political risk management is focused on dealing with threats and opportunities through the lens of the strategic goals of an enterprise. Monitoring and controlling helps to ensure that any political risks impacting those goals are dealt with to further their achievement.

Encourages integration and interdependence among all the major stakeholders throughout an enterprise. This activity, to be effective, requires sharing and communicating facts and data up and down and across the enterprise. This cooperation also helps to demonstrate how well political risk management provides value to key stakeholders.

Leverages on other political risk management processes, such as defining and assessing risks, that are also efficient and effective. Risk monitoring and controlling concentrates on those threats and opportunities affecting the global supply chain of an enterprise.

Provides the means to collect and compile facts and data to generate reports. Facts and data are provided to perform statistical calculations (such trends and variances as well as exceeding thresholds); track the use of contingency reserves; look at key performance indicators; evaluate response effectiveness; and monitor the impact of secondary and residual risks.

APPROACH

The bottom line of performing risk monitoring and controlling is to maintain constant awareness of an enterprise's business environment to accomplish three purposes: identify when risks arise; ensure relevant responses are executed; and determine the effectiveness of responses.

As mentioned earlier, monitoring is keeping a pulse on an enterprise's business environment, to include political risks. It requires solid communications throughout an enterprise to ascertain what is occurring and how well it adapts to any circumstances monitoring requires effective communications vertically and horizontally throughout an enterprise. The communications derive from line management, functional departments, business units, and corporate. It is important to determine the level of accuracy and granularity of the of facts and data needed to conduct effective monitoring. It is also important to have continuous verification, review, and approval of the facts and data for use in decision-making by executive and senior management. Some facts and data used during monitoring include the current status of risks from identifying risks, to include residual and secondary ones; this status includes the probability or likelihood, impact, and priority. Additional facts and data might include indicators or warning signs, such as trigger events and threshold metrics, to indicate when to gain attention or escalate to appropriate stakeholders, e.g., risk owners. These requirements are defined in a risk management plan.

Again, as mentioned earlier, controlling is using facts and data from monitoring to determine how well an enterprise is managing its risks and issues. The facts and data tells whether any risks have become issues and, if so, whether the responses are effective, need improvement, or some other action is necessary, such as a workaround (which is an unplanned response to a threat whereby specific resources are unavailable) or corrective action (which is a response to address, for example, an ineffective response). Improvement in a response is pursued if a response is significantly deviating or varying from expectations, such as exceeding a threshold or using too much of a contingency reserve. All actions are recorded in a risk listing. Remember, controlling does not guarantee success in managing risks. It only offers what auditors consider as reasonable, not absolute, assurance of effectiveness. Too many variables exist that are hard to manage, such as judgments and breakdown in procedures.

CHALLENGES

Several challenges present themselves when performing risk monitoring and controlling.

Fear. Most people do not want to be the bearer of bad news, especially when involving threats that have not been addressed as planned. Yet, someone needs to deliver negative as much as positive news. Both positive and unwelcomed facts and data are necessary to allow for good decisions and to evaluate the effectiveness of their implementation. Often, though, some stakeholders communicate what executive and senior management what it wants to hear, not what it needs to hear. Unfortunately, some people know that sometimes the messenger gets shot. Such an atmosphere inhibits the sharing of important facts and data.

Inaccurate and unreliable facts and data. Closely tied to the previous challenge, this one addresses more directly the quality of the facts and data about risks and the effectiveness of their corresponding responses. For facts and data to be of value for monitoring and controlling risks, both must be scrubbed for errors; collected and compiled consistently; not slanted to affect results; satisfy criteria as described in the risk management plan; and provide the basis for the next risk process, perform risk reporting.

Incompatible information systems. This challenge is especially difficult to overcome for enterprises with facts and data residing in legacy systems (which are dated hardware, application, and operating systems). Facts and data must be extracted and reconciled from disparate systems. This effort can be an inefficient and arduous process which can cause significant delays in relaying important facts and data to key decision makers when performing risk monitoring and controlling.

Subjectivity in feedback. Cognitive bias and behavioral sway by executive and senior management can influence the presentation of facts and data. Quite often, as information moves up the chain of command, its content gets "massaged," presenting a picture that might be unrealistic or an inaccurate portrayal about risks and responses, leading to poor decisions.

Cultural factors. Risk monitoring and controlling can be influenced by cultural factors, especially for global enterprises. People in some cultures do not want to share facts and data, especially if it means losing face or causing displeasure with executive and senior management. The style of communication may also be different which can affect how facts and data are presented, such as face-to-face or via written document. This challenge can affect the quality and reliability of facts and data.

Restrictions on access to facts and data for review. Some facts and data may be proprietary, thereby restricted to certain stakeholders. Some facts and data may be restricted as to who can view it, such as foreign contractors participating on governmental contracts. Such constraints can make it difficult to for some stakeholders to receive an accurate picture about the risks and responses concerning an enterprise's global supply chain or make it difficult for them to participate effectively.

Internal political posturing when seeking facts and data about political risks. In a large corporation, fiefdoms are not uncommon as executives and senior managers jockey for positioning among themselves. Power plays may entice them not to share facts and data about any risks; this situation is especially the case if the facts and data is about risks concerning their organization, e.g., business unit, that tarnishes its reputation. The desire to appear to be or appear to be in control can influence what facts and data are shared, especially among peers.

Not responding early enough to risks. Collecting facts and data when performing monitoring and controlling can consume considerable time and effort, especially for large enterprises. Taking too much time and effort may result in late collection and compilation to determine which political risks have occurred and whether the corresponding responses have been effective. Timely and sufficient collection and compilation of facts and data regarding corrective actions and workarounds are also important but can be challenging, too, in obtaining facts and data on their effectiveness.

FINAL THOUGHTS

Having reliable facts and data to determine whether a risk has become an issue is important. If it has become an issue having reliable facts and data about the effectiveness of responses and corresponding tactical actions are just as important, if not more so. The feedback is essential for situational awareness about the impacts to an enterprise's global supply chain. The facts and data are collected and compiled for the next process, perform political risk reporting.

GETTING STARTED QUESTIONS

Questions	Yes	No
1. When performing risk monitoring and controlling, are you considering the following?		
a) Keeping a pulse on your enterprise's environment to determine if one or more risks occurred and the effectiveness of the responses?		
b) Ensuring good communications is occurring up, down, and across the hierarchy?		
c) Following up on decisions made regarding risk responses?		
d) Describing the risk monitoring and controlling process in the risk management plan?		
e) Taking an integrated perspective of the enterprise?		
f) Considering the risk attitude and tolerance of the enterprise as well as that of current members of executive and senior management?		
g) Following the relevant risk policies and procedures of the enterprise and the content of the risk management plan?		
h) When performing risk monitoring and controlling, are you performing these actions:		
2. Are you determining the effectiveness of responses by considering the following?		
a) Ensuring relevant responses are executed?		
b) Maintaining good communications with stakeholders?		
c) Conducting continuous verification, review, and approval of facts and data?		
3. Have you faced any of the following challenges and, if so, determining how to deal with them?		
a) Overcoming the fear of being the bearer of good news?		
b) Having access to accurate and reliable facts and data?		
c) Using incompatible information systems?		
d) Removing subjectivity in feedback?		
e) Dealing with cultural factors impacting the validity and reliability of facts and data?		
f) Dealing with restrictive access to facts and data?		
g) Overcoming internal political posturing that impedes the quantity and quality of facts and data?		
h) Responding early enough to risks?		

12

Perform Political Risk Reporting

Risk reporting involves providing information to key stakeholders on how well an enterprise is managing its political risks. The overall goal is to provide the right information in the right quality in the right format to the right people. Risk reports provide status on risks, responses, and any other pertinent topics, such as trigger events and residual risks.

KEY POINTS

Keep the following points in mind when performing political risk reporting.

Be skeptical of any facts and data received. Check the validity and reliability prior to generating a report. Some stakeholders will try to game facts and data, regardless of format. The reality is that people prefer not to report negative news, especially if it reflects poorly upon themselves or their organization.

Question the sources of facts and data. This point is especially critical when dealing with facts and data regarding political risks and their events. Stakeholders providing facts and data may have good, honest intentions; however, their prejudices can interfere with the validity and reliability of facts and data that they provide. The subject of politics is not always something measurable and, when not, it can be tainted with misinformation, disinformation, or misinterpretation as already discussed in previous chapters.

Be consistent in reporting facts and data. Consistency can help offset the problems discussed in the last two points. Through consistency in presentation comes a perception of validity and reliability about facts and data. A consistent series of reports will engender confidence in the content and, just as importantly, the deliverer.

Keep the audience in mind when generating reports. Stakeholders have their preference about the way facts and data are presented, e.g., tabular vs. graphical format. Therefore, avoid sending a "data dump" to recipients. Focus on the contents to meet the requirements of the recipients.

Remember that facts and data in most reports are lagging indicators. That is, reports reflect what is known up to a specific point in time. Ideally, a report should reflect content that is as close to real time as possible. In political risk management, flaws in the currency of the content can result in poor or anachronistic decision making. Political risk reporting may especially confront this situation because the content often needs additional verification and validation.

Never send a report without it first being subjected to a rigorous review. The time and effort expended will prevent embarrassing the creator of a report and a loss of credibility. A peer review is one useful approach, whereby a small team of experts and managers conduct a deep dive into the contents, questioning the validity and reliability of each fact and datum. It also helps in overcoming biases that may enter a report.

BENEFITS

Several benefits are attributed to perform risk reporting.

Keeps key stakeholders, such as the board of directors, aware of the risks confronting an enterprise and its global supply chain as well as the effectiveness of any responses. In other words, it raises awareness of the value of political risk management through continuous reporting.

Enables an enterprise to respond more quickly and effectively to changing circumstances that may pose political threats or offer opportunities. Clear and current facts and data in reports enables executives and senior management to become better decision makers, having to rely less upon guess, innuendo, or assumptions. They can focus on managing political risks, knowing what the actual impacts are on an enterprise's global supply chain.

Provides an audit trail of any decisions by executive and senior management regarding political risks and the responses. Reports provide a record to help stakeholders acquire an understanding of why and how decisions were made and other information, such as why some political risks are either a lower or higher priority or why certain residual and secondary risks exist. Reports also help in legal proceedings, serving as a source of facts and data.

Places visibility on political risk owners by showing their names on reports. Executive and senior managers will know who is responsible for which political risks and the execution of responses. Risk owners cannot hide since others will see their name on reports.

Gives visibility to political risks and responses, especially ones with a high probability, or likelihood, and high impact. Stakeholders will also see the other risks relative to one another as well as any residual and secondary risks. This visibility places pressure on risk owners to develop a game plan to implement responses and ones not previously identified. If a report contains a high priority risk but no formulated response, key stakeholders can pressure the applicable risk owner to develop one. A report can also show which risks have risen or declined in priority over time, especially ones that had a low priority or were on a watchlist. The assigned risk owner can then investigate the causes and develop recommendations for responses.

APPROACH

The two main media for risk reports are documents and meetings. Whether using one or both channels, the contents share the same qualities.

One, content must be timely, accurate, clear, and concise. The medium must communicate topics like priorities; consequences of decisions; actions; and other pertinent facts and data.

Two, a report must be consistent in content and format. Consistent in content means facts and data should cover the same categories from one reporting period to the next, except for any significant changes. For example, content should present high priority risks and their status, etc. Consistent in format might include common charts, such as 5 x 5 charts, and statistics. A standard format should be used from one reporting period to the next.

Three, the content might need tailoring to the needs of a recipient. One size usually does not fit all. Both the content and the structure should be tailored to the needs of the audience, just as with all reporting. Usually, executive and senior managers want summary facts and data in uncluttered charts and diagrams while others in the hierarchy might prefer greater detail. Ideally, before a presentation or report comes before executive and senior management, the content and format are vetted by other stakeholders.

Four, the content is objective, meaning it relies strictly on facts and data, unless, of course, the audience expects one or more recommendations. If the content of a presentation or report reflects too many assumptions or unsubstantiated opinions, credibility of the content will suffer. Both presentations and reports must contain content that is consistently represented, vetted by stakeholder, and relies on facts and data.

A typical political risk management presentation or report includes:

- Executive summary
- Assessment of risks and responses
- Description of significant residual and secondary risks, status, and actions taken
- Help Needed
- Impacts to strategic goals
- Key Accomplishments
- Next Steps
- Overall risk assessment status
- Significant trigger events and conditions
- Summary Metrics

One of the most effective ways to communicate the state of political risk management for an enterprise is to create a heat map, shown in Figure 12.1. A heat map shows the status of each political risk in two charts. This chart can be developed at any level within an organization; however, this format works best at the business unit or enterprise level.

Risk ID	Risk	Likelihood	Impact	Risk Rating (Score)
A	Foreign Hiring Restrictions	5	5	25
B	Tariffs	4	2	8
C	Military Takeover	2	3	6
D	Contract Violations	5	1	5
E	Terrorism	2	2	4

Likelihood Scale	Impact	Risk Rating Score
High = 5	High = 5	High Priority = 16-25
Medium = 4-3	Medium = 4-3	Medium Priority = 6-15
Low = 2-1	Low = 2-1	Low Priority (watchlist)= 1-5
No Likelihood = 0	No Impact = 0	No Impact = 0

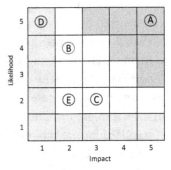

Legend
(A) Foreign Hiring Restrictions
(B) Tariffs
(C) Military Takeover
(D) Contract Violations
(E) Terrorism

FIGURE 12.1
Heat Map (Operational Level).

Goal or Objective:					
Risk	Foreign Hiring Restrictions	Tariffs	Military Takeover	Contract Violations	Terrorism
Enterprise-wide (rollup)	Y	G	B	R	B
Business Unit	Y↑	G	B	R	G
Business Unit	G	G↓	B	Y↑	B
Business Unit	G	G	B	R	B
Subsidiary	Y↓	G	G	R	G

Legend
Red (R) = High Risk
Yellow (Y) = Medium Risk
Green (G) = Low Risk
Blue (B) = No Longer a Risk
↑ = Improving
↓ = Deteriorating

FIGURE 12.2
Summary Heat Map.

Two charts exist to the heat map. One chart is the 5 by 5 chart, such as one shown in Figure 12.2 and the other chart shows more information about each risk. It uses a unique designator for each risk, the risk title, description, likelihood (or probability), impact, and overall risk rating. For each cell related to likelihood (or probability), impact, or risk rating, a color-coding scheme is shown, such as red, yellow, green, or blue. (Red is often used to represent negative; yellow for warranting attention but no action necessary; green for put on watchlist, and blue for no longer applicable). In some cases, even using color, a capital letter is used, too, for people who might be color blind. A legend is at the bottom or side of the chart to define what the colors represent.

At the enterprise level, a summary heat map is created for reporting, shown in Figure 12.2. It is a matrix providing an overall summary for the enterprise and for each business unit and subsidiary regarding each applicable political risk. Along the top row is a list of the political risks. The left column lists the entities within the enterprise, starting with the parent corporation. Within each cell intersecting with a political risk and a business unit a color scheme to reflect overall status. Red, yellow, green, and blue are common colors and, for the color blind, a large capital letter appears in a cell to represent the color. A common practice is to place an up or down arrow in the cell to indicate if the political risk is improving or getting worse, such as going from red to yellow or yellow to green, respectively. For the parent company (or corporate level) represents an overall summary of each risk; it is an overall assessment based upon the cumulative reporting of the business units. Again, a color code scheme is used to represent the overall summary for the enterprise. A legend is at the bottom or side of the chart to define what the colors represent.

CHALLENGES

Several challenges present themselves when performing risk reporting.

Difficulty in acquiring timely and accurate facts and data. Reports are only as good as the reliability and validity of the information contained in them. If facts and data are "corrupted" or late, then the usefulness of a report will diminish, and executive and senior management will lack confidence in the contents. A balance must exist among the necessary content of the report; the time required to generate it; and when it must be available to the recipients.

Getting access to the necessary facts and data to produce a report. In large enterprises, getting access to data and information can prove challenging, as previously discussed. Both can reside in incompatible legacy systems, which are hidden in enterprise fiefdoms. Under such circumstances, it can delay producing reports due to reconciliation and verification of facts and data.

Maintaining objectivity. A tendency will always exist among key stakeholders to impose their view in the content of reports, sometimes valid and sometimes not. Their biases can influence what the report contains and how the content is portrayed. The value of a report then declines.

Tailoring a report to the specific needs of recipients. Reports can sometimes be voluminous which will only frustrate recipients, unable to determine what is important. Such reports often take the form of one size fits all. Burrowing into needless detail can also lead to making bad decisions or being indecisive.

FINAL THOUGHTS

Performing political risk reporting requires providing the right stakeholders with the right information in the right time, and in the right format. This process is really about communications to enhance the situational awareness about political conditions and events facing an enterprise's global supply chain and the effectiveness of responses. Political risk reporting can be complicated due to the mercurial nature of political phenomena. It requires verifying and reverifying as best as possible the validity and reliability the facts and data and the understandability of the content before reports are sent so that key stakeholders can make decisions having confidence in what is presented to them.

GETTING STARTED QUESTIONS

Questions	Yes	No

1. When performing risk reporting are you keeping the following points in mind?
   a) Being skeptical of any facts and data received?
   b) Questioning the sources of facts and data?
   c) Being consistent in the facts and data being reported?
   d) Keeping the audience in mind when generating reports?
   e) Remembering that facts and data in most reports are lagging indicators?
   f) Never sending out a report without it first being subject to a rigorous review?
2. When performing risk reporting, are you taking these actions?
   a) Ensuring the contents is timely, accurate, clear, and concise?
   b) Being consistent in content and format?
   c) Tailoring the content is the needs of the recipients?
   d) Ensuring the content is objective?
3. Does the risk management presentation or report contain this content?
   a) Executive summary?
   b) Summary metrics?
   c) Overall assessment status?
   d) Impacts to strategic goals?
   e) Key accomplishments?
   f) Assessment of other risks and responses?
   g) Description of significant residual and secondary risks, status, and actions taken?
   h) Significant trigger conditions?
   i) Help needed?
   j) Next steps?
4. Have you faced any of the following challenges and, if so, determining how to deal with them?
   a) Acquiring timely and accurate facts and data?
   b) Accessing facts and data?
   c) Maintaining objectivity?
   d) Tailoring reports to the specific needs of recipients?

13

Maintain Political Risk Management

For political risk management to prove of value to an enterprise, its processes need to keep current. Otherwise, stakeholders will view the processes as ineffective and inefficient; they will likely not participate in executing the processes.

Maintenance requires a three-fold approach. First, the processes require updating because the internal and external environments of an enterprise change. Second, the updates to the processes require updates to the political risk management plan, which is the primary artifact of political risk management. Third, the contents of the revised political risk management plan need to be communicated to stakeholders.

KEY POINTS

Keep the following points in mind when maintaining the political risk management processes.

Apply configuration management. Once a political risk management plan has been updated and approved by key stakeholders, the document should be under configuration management which prevents people from making random changes. Any changes must be managed so that stakeholders follow the same processes executed. They will also know if they have the most current version of the document.

Provide ongoing accessibility to the document. The best approach is to store a soft, or electronic, copy of the plan on a server or provide access via groupware. If the plan contains restricted content, controlled access is necessary.

Remember that the agreed upon political risk management processes and the plan reflect what is occurring at a specific point in time. If the enterprise and its environment changes significantly, both the processes and the plan will need updating. Again, configuration management can prove of value by controlling changes to both processes and the plan.

Be aware that a change to one political risk management process may impact one or more of the other processes. For example, a decision to forego political risk quantitative assessment may require changing the contents of political risk reports delivered to stakeholders.

Update the glossary in the plan. New terminology regarding political risks, economics, security, etc. often arise from professional associations and parent organizations within an organization. Existing processes may adopt a new procedure or technique that uses its own terminology. New terminology and changes to existing terminology need to be recorded in the glossary.

Establish a regular schedule to conduct a review of the political risk management processes and the plan. This schedule might require an in-depth review of processes and the plan, such as every six months. A regular review of only the plan might be monthly or quarterly and mainly focuses on making minor changes, such as the names of people arriving or departing.

Review all relevant facts and data captured on previous responses to political risks. Ideally, the facts and data are captured in debriefings and lessons learned, or hot washes. The facts and data should provide insight on the successes and challenges responding to political risks and indicate ideas for revising a process.

BENEFITS

Three principal benefits are attributed to maintaining political risk management processes and the plan.

Stakeholders will have current, relevant, and accurate knowledge of political risk management processes applicable to their enterprise and its global supply chain. Every stakeholder will apply the same procedures, tools, and techniques.

The awareness of the political risk management processes and the plan will increase among stakeholders. Periodic reviews of processes and the plan will require each stakeholder to refresh his or her awareness and knowledge, especially if they are required to participate in a review and approval of any changes.

Process and plan reviews encourage communications among stakeholders. During regularly scheduled reviews, stakeholders will contact others just to verify if any changes to the processes or the plan involves them. The plan will circulate for review and, for a few, for signature of approval.

APPROACH

Many approaches exist to maintain political risk management processes.

One, apply project management to help keep the political risk management processes and the risk management plan updated. Applying project management is often light, meaning at a high level. All that might be required is a bar or milestone chart showing summary start and finish dates or a symbol reflecting completion dates, respectively. These charts would also indicate who is responsible for which activity to update the processes and the plan.

Two, establish a regular update cycle for the political risk management processes and the plan. The key is to keep to the schedule and ensure that all stakeholders participate in updating processes and the plan.

Three, assign a single point of contact for each process and the plan. The single point of contact should have responsibilities to maintain awareness of any changes to their respective processes and have an idea of what content in the political risk management plan is affected. The single point of contact collects the input from the other points of contact for each process, updates the plan, and sends it to the appropriate stakeholders for review and approval.

Four, apply change management to the processes and the plan. Stakeholders should seek approval from the executive sponsor or a steering committee, before deviating from an agreed upon process that is described in the plan. If a process is changed, the new process should be followed, and the plan placed under configuration management.

Five, conduct regular and ad hoc performance reviews of the political risk management processes. Ideally, metrics and data on cycle time, defects, and other performance criteria are collected as well as interviews conducted with stakeholders helps to provide insight on what processes have gone well and ones needing improvement.

Six, reflect all changes to political risk management processes in the risk management plan. Upon approval by key stakeholders, the plan should be distributed or accessible to individuals or organizations to ensure stakeholders are applying political risk management consistently. A good practice is to hold periodically a group information sharing session among stakeholders explaining what has changed and why and to answer any questions.

Seven, remember that the chief artifact describing the political risk management processes is the risk management plan. The document should be kept current as much as possible to help ensure the efficient execution of those processes, especially from a communication and coordination perspective.

Eight, once a change is to process and has received formal approval, communicate the changes to all relevant stakeholders. This action will have stakeholders following the same process and enable efficient and effective execution of political risk management.

Nine, train people on the newly revised process. Not only will they know the content but they will also have the opportunity to ask questions. During training, they can practice or test the revised political risk management process.

CHALLENGES

Maintaining political risk management processes does present some challenges.

Keeping the importance of political risk management in the forefront of stakeholders' minds. Most stakeholders participate in political risk management not because they want to do so but because of some requirement originating from the strategic level of an enterprise. Many stakeholders have other priorities which can cause some stakeholders to drop the topic from their immediate attention. Add the flow time of a political risk management project, for example, the topic can, at least for a while, not be their top priority.

Allocating administrative overhead to maintain political risk management processes. Participating on a political risk management project, for example, to develop and deploy processes will likely have a budget and a cost baseline. The challenge comes when the processes exist on an ongoing basis and the plan needs occasional updating. In many enterprises that may be considered an overhead activity that can consume time, effort, and especially money. Charging issues can then become an issue, especially in public enterprises providing services to a government.

Maintaining knowledge about political risk management. Some stakeholders concentrate on other priorities. Consequently, their knowledge of political risk management may fade. When a scheduled review is upcoming, these stakeholders will either need to relearn the processes or refresh their memories. This situation is rare and, when it occurs, can slow the maintenance of political risk management processes and the plan.

Keeping the political risk management processes current. Most enterprises, internally and externally, have changing environments. Executives and senior managers are constantly moving around. Applying political risk management processes consistently and keeping the plan updated can become difficult.

Changing strategic goals, strategies, and the global supply chain. Laws and regulations may change, impacting business strategies goals. Such changes and many others can impact political risk management processes which, in turn, affect a global supply chain. The review and approval of changes may take too much time. By the time the updated plan is released, it may, ironically, be outdated.

FINAL THOUGHTS

Enterprises and their global supply chains operate in a dynamic environment, meaning internal and external circumstances change. People, processes, data, systems, policies, laws, regimes, etc. change, necessitating re-evaluation of all processes, just political risk management ones. It is important, therefore, to re-evaluate regularly political risk management processes to determine the relevancy to an enterprise. If changes to these processes are necessary, the political risk management plan must be updated to reflect the current state of the processes.

GETTING STARTED QUESTIONS

Questions	Yes	No

1. When maintaining political risk management processes and the risk management plan, have you considered the following?
   a) Placing the updated political risk management plan under configuration management?
   b) Providing ongoing access to the updated political risk management plan?
   c) Remembering the agreed upon political risk management processes and the risk management reflect what is occurring at a given point in time?
2. Are you taking the following actions?
   a) Applying project management to keep political risk management processes and the risk management plan updated?
   b) Establishing a regular update cycle for the political risk management processes and the plan?
   c) Assigning a single point of contact for each process and the plan?
   d) Applying change management and configuration management to the political risk management processes and the risk management plan?
   e) Conducting a regular and ad hoc performance reviews of the political risk management processes?
   f) Reflecting all changes to the political risk management processes in the risk management plan?
   g) Remembering the chief artifact of the political risk management processes is the risk management plan?
3. Are you experiencing any of the following challenges and, if so, determining how to deal with them?
   a) Keeping the importance of political risk management in the forefront of stakeholders' minds?
   b) Allocating administrative overhead to maintain political risk management processes?
   c) Maintaining knowledge about political risk management?
   d) Keeping political risk management processes current?

14

Seven Keys to Success

Enterprises and their global supply chains operate in a dynamic world. Politics adds to that complexity. Predictability is difficult enough from an economic and sociological perspective. Throw politics into the mix and the challenge to thrive in such an environment increases dramatically. What adds to the complication and confusion is that politics is as much an art as it is a science. How an enterprise handles a political risk can determine whether its global supply chain remains standing like a line of dominoes or one domino falls and collapses all the subsequent ones which can impair or imperil business performance.

A QUICK SUMMARY

However, enterprises do not have to operate in a fog when faced with political risks. Political risk management is one way to manage the complexity as discussed in the previous chapters. What follows is a quick overview of the processes (Figure 14.1).

The first process is to establish an infrastructure to support building and deploying political risk management. In some enterprises, the infrastructure may already exist in a risk management organization. In other enterprises, the infrastructure may require being built from the ground up. Whether an enterprise can capitalize on what has already been done or needs to build or deploy a new infrastructure, project management is the discipline to apply. Project management plays a key role in ensuring political risk management is developed, deployed, and sustained in an enterprise.

The second process is to identify the strategic goals of an enterprise. However, that is not enough. An enterprise must know which goals might

FIGURE 14.1
Political Risk Management Processes.

be impacted by political risks. By making that determination, an enterprise can focus on what matters the most from a political risk perspective and identify key stakeholders to participate in political risk management.

The third process, which occurs concurrently with the second one, is to identify stakeholders. These are people or organizations who have an interest in political risk management. These stakeholders can range from the board of directors to executive and senior management of business units and subsidiaries. The relevant strategic goals help to narrow the number of stakeholders to participate when developing, deploying, and maintaining political risk management.

The fourth process is to prepare the political risk management plan. Stakeholders play a key role in developing this document. The document delineates the rules of the game, describing the who, what, when, where, why, and how for each political risk management process. Key stakeholders review and approve the document which is then followed by every person and organization involved with political risk management.

The fifth process is to identify political risks. Stakeholders identify threats and opportunities that could arise using the strategic goals that pertain to an enterprise and its global supply chain. Stakeholders can pursue several approaches to identifying risks. The result is a comprehensive risk listing and a risk tree.

The sixth process is to assess political risks. The ultimate objectives of this process are to determine the probability or likelihood of a risk, its impact, and priority. Two approaches, qualitative and quantitative, can be applied separately or together to achieve the objectives. This risk management process consumes the most time and effort because it requires considerable discussion among stakeholders as well as requires collecting facts and data to perform quantitative risk analysis.

The seventh process is to prepare political risk responses. Using the output from the previous processes, stakeholders determine which strategic responses to pursue if a specific risk arises. Each response requires one or more tactical actions to execute it. The ultimate objective is being proactive, rather than being reactive, when dealing with a risk.

The eighth process is to perform political risk monitoring and controlling. This process involves gathering facts and data regarding the status of risks, their relative priorities, and the effectiveness of their responses. Risk owners assigned to each risk are responsible to provide facts and data about risks for which they are responsible. If a risk arises, the risk owner communicates the status, whether it a risk remains one or becomes an issue.

The ninth process is to perform political risk reporting. Facts and data are compiled and presented to key stakeholders to determine if any decision or action is required. Often the reports go to an audit or risk management committee for an enterprise and, if a risk or issue is serious enough, then a presentation is delivered to the board of directors to make a decision or take action.

The tenth process is to maintain political risk management. The objective of this process is to ensure that all the other risk management processes are executed efficiently and effectively. The risk management plan provides the new baseline that the stakeholders follow once approved and updated.

The important lesson from this overview is take a strategic, integrated perspective of political risk management. What has been presented in this book is a framework, not a methodology, which, provide a series of steps. A framework provides an overall structure and allows adapting its contents to the specific needs of an enterprise. In some enterprises, emphasis may be more on one process as opposed to another one. In other enterprises, all the processes are equally important. In the end, like political risk analysis, judgment is required because the answers are not all black and white but most of the times, gray.

SEVEN KEYS TO SUCCESS

The ten processes cannot and do not guarantee successful implementation of political risk management; they only give reasonable assurance of success. They simply increase the odds of success. To increase the odds, what follows are keys to consider when developing and applying political risk management as it pertains to an enterprise and its global supply chain.

Key #1: Put cognitive bias aside. An old saying goes that never discuss politics in a bar. The subject can quickly turn into a brawl. While it may not be that extreme in business enterprises, cognitive bias can easily creep into discussions. When that happens, objectivity is replaced with subjectivity and stance taking, making it difficult to respond to a political event in a way that furthers the business goals pertaining a global supply chain. Ideally, the goal is to set aside one's political prejudices and think in terms of the interests of the enterprise. Such an approach does not mean doing something illegal or immoral. Rather, it means that an enterprise's leadership in the global marketplace needs to maintain its objectivity so it can respond to an event in a way that does not circumvent its own goals. Two ways to achieve that objectivity is to follow the processes of political risk management as described in this book and maintain situational awareness free of biases.

Key #2: Take a collaborative approach. Working collaboratively in any enterprise is essential for success. Collaboration is even more important in an enterprise with a global supply chain. The number of assets and their interaction to deliver goods and services to a customer can become quite complex. The number of stakeholders and their relationships can also become quite complicated. When politics affects a global supply chain, the complexities can augment dramatically. The government of a host country can implement tariffs or regulations that can cause inefficiencies as well as puta supply chain in disarray as if it were a series of falling dominoes. Political risk management requires both the strategic and operational levels of an enterprise to collaborate when dealing with, for example, an IGO or a government. If the strategic level operates without working with the operational level, not only does it weaken the response to a political risk but also disrupts the global supply chain.

Key #3: Create a balanced team of stakeholders. As discussed, politics is interlinked with other disciplines, especially with economics and sociology. For that reason, a team developing, deploying, and executing political risk management should be a multidisciplinary one. Stakeholders should come from different areas of an enterprise have representatives, not just from one organization, such as the legal department, but also from other areas like audit, security, human resources, supplier management, finance, information systems, etc. At a minimum, they should be consulted if they do not directly participate on a team but have a tangential interest. Such a team will not only help in overcoming cognitive bias but also increases collaboration.

Key #4: Translate political risk into business terms. Stakeholders will be more receptive toward viewing political risk as meaningful if its impact can be discussed in business terms. Quantitative risk assessment lends itself to demonstrating a political risk's impact financially. Qualitative risk assessment is often used because the impact is hard or impossible to quantify. Nevertheless, the impact should demonstrate, at least logically, the consequences to a supply chain in a way that business professionals can appreciate inherently. Determining a political risk's impact in business terms is similar when conducting a business case analysis. Some of the analysis is not financially tangible but requires discussing how a benefit can have a business impact, e.g., reduce shareholder value.

Key #5: Maintain situational awareness about the world. Enterprises with global supply chains need to develop and maintain awareness of what is occurring politically across the globe, especially in regions of interest. Politics is dynamic, meaning that actors and events are constantly changing. Failure to develop and maintain awareness can result in an enterprise's supply chain being broadsided. Key stakeholders need to identify and understand events occurring in a host country or its region. Developing and regularly distributing fact sheets about political events can help. Often, a government affairs organization produces such documents but also stakeholders can have access to online sites. Keeping abreast of politics in a supply chain's areas of operation will help further understanding of events as well as enhance situational awareness.

Key #6: Be flexible; not fluid. Being flexible involves having structure and direction when dealing with events. Being fluid entails having little structure or sense of direction when responding to events. Because most political events are dynamic, even making it difficult to determine if a risk is an issue, flexibility becomes crucial. How a team of stakeholders respond to events will determine its effectiveness. If the team follows a set of processes; its roles and responsibilities have been defined and understood; and its goals identified, the chances for success increase dramatically. Without these characteristics, political risk management will become a free for all. A good political risk management plan should help provide this direction along with leadership exhibited by executive management.

Key #7: Use a disciplined approach. Political risk management, as described in this book, provides discipline by serving as a framework. A disciplined approach does mean regimentation; rather, it means providing just enough structure necessary to perform efficiently and effectively. If stakeholders follow an approach, a team can identify, assess, and respond to risks in an organized and focused manner. A tendency in many organizations is to create or adopt an approach, whether dealing with political or other risks, and then few following it. Instead, people scatter like marbles. For example, if a corporate decides to respond to political events affecting its supply chain in a host country and the business unit operating in that location responds differently confusion can occur among stakeholders. However, if stakeholders follow the same framework, responses to political events will be more efficient and effective.

FINAL THOUGHTS

In theory, political risk management appears quite simple. Realistically, not quite so. Political actors and their relationships are constantly changing. Events on one side of the globe can have an impact 180 degrees away. Some political events can have multiple impacts and can be affected by other events. The same can be said about risks. The complexity can be mindboggling especially when politics disrupts a global supply chain. Each part within the supply chain can easily topple, impacting its operations. A revolution here; a revolt there. A war here; an assassination there. A regime overthrow here; an expropriation there. All these political events and more can cause a global supply chain to fall like a row of dominoes.

Appendix A

A CASE STUDY ON POLITICAL RISK MANAGEMENT

da Vinci Aerospace Industries, Inc., founded in 1987, is headquartered in Wichita, Kansas. With 22,000 employees and business operations and dealings spread across the globe, it generates $30 billion revenue each year, thanks in large part to the sale of its line of business jets called Cielo models, starting with the Z100 back in the late 1980s to the current Z900. Despite being a moderate player in the private jet aerospace market, it has been gaining market share, until lately, over the years, surpassing many of its competitors. The Z800 and Z900 models have received wide praise for their cabin features, such as width, length, and height; the size of its baggage capacity; and its airspeed and maximum flight time. Both aircraft received excellent reviews and substantial sales after its participation at the Farnborough and Paris Air Shows. As a result, da Vinci's stock has doubled over the last year but is starting to decline.

The quality of the aircraft is just part of the story. The enterprise had bought another aerospace company, Crozier Aerospace, in Ireland to enhance its technical expertise in aerospace technology, especially in building embedded systems. Crozier provided the necessary expertise to develop advanced flight management systems as well as enable fly-by-wire systems for the Z800 and Z900 models. Additionally, the Z800 and Z900 models consist of composite materials which substantially reduced fuel costs and enabled increasing flight time, thanks to outsourcing to Australian firms.

da Vinci Aerospace industries has also streamlined its processes for building aircraft. It has improved each phase for building its aircraft: understanding the customer's needs and wants; negotiating contracts; procuring materials; fabricating parts and tools; executing subassembly and final assembly processes; painting aircrafts; performing flight test; delivering aircraft to the customer; and providing ongoing service. The enterprise accomplished this achievement through a series of quality improvement activities as well as transitioning to just-in-time delivery and computer-aided design. As a result, it can provide three types of models of an aircraft, such as a Z900, to its customers. The standard, out of the box, is called Model I. If a customer has some specific requirements but does not radically change Model I, then mass customization processes can satisfy certain customer's needs and wants, creating Model II. If a customer wants to make substantial changes, da Vinci will create what it calls Model III. Naturally, Model I costs less than a Model II and the latter less than a Model III.

Another reason for the success of the da Vinci is that it has increased its outsourcing to companies across the globe. As a result, 50 percent of its planes are sold in North America, down from 80 percent. Its international business is now 20 percent with Asian and Central Asian countries; 10 percent with the European Union; 10 percent in Latin America; and 10 percent in Africa. It attributes part of its success to outsourcing because it builds relationships with those countries which eventually has led to selling airplanes to them and negotiating offset agreements related to technological support.

Making the transition described above was not without its challenges. Earlier, da Vinci was an enterprise stuck into the traditional manufacturing processes and its earlier models reflected that approach. The company was very hierarchical and its attitude to the customers was often construed as arrogant and its manufacturing costs consumed a large percent of its revenues. Shareholders, institutional and private, and the board of directors knew something had to change. Consequently, the board of directors developed a vision statement and promulgated it throughout the ranks of the enterprise:

- Become a premier aerospace systems integrator by adopting
- A customer focus orientation
- Just-in-time tools and techniques
- State-of-the-art information and engineering technologies
- The highest ethical standards

As mentioned earlier, da Vinci outsources to companies within the United States and others from these nations: Japan, Mexico, China, Australia, and Ireland. What follows is an overview of those products and services.

United States. Primarily, the factory buildings in the outskirts of Wichita are reserved for subassembly and final assembly for its product lines as well as performing subassembly and integration testing among just a few of the major operations within the walls of its factories. Subsystem testing is performed, such as wing to body joins and forward aft and body joins. Subsystem integration testing occurs for example which includes wings, body sections, nose gears, and elevators. Final assembly and integration testing include the engines, flaps, empennage, as well as electrical connections.

Additionally, the airfield, located near the factory buildings, has warehouses that store components as they are delivered from their suppliers. The components include ones from other countries as well as from other suppliers within the United States. For example, tires come from a supplier in Detroit; carbon brakes from Missoula; black box and voice recorders from Seattle; and nose gear from Chicago.

The paint hangar lies just outside of the factories adjacent to the airfield where flight testing occurs, such as takeoff and landing. While in flight, testing occurs such as related to depressurization and turbulence. Down the runway is a delivery center where the customer takes possession of an aircraft.

Japan. Several companies, mainly in Yokohama, have responsibilities to provide the following components for each of the da Vinci's models. These relate to the empennage, wings, and control surfaces. Some specific deliverables include radar, spars, doors, hatches, elevators, stringers, slats, ailerons, flaps, and spoilers. These components are stored in several warehouses after being built and sub-assembled in factories owned by subcontractors spread across the country.

Mexico. Several companies, mainly outside of Mexico City, have responsibilities for rebuilt spares, consumables, panels, and shields. Some specific deliverables include blades, pressure bulkheads, tail skids, lights, fans, gyroscopes, galley and toilet components, nose gear wells, and position lights on wings. These components are stored in several warehouses after being built and sub-assembled in factories owned by subcontractors spread across the country.

China. Several companies, mainly in Shanghai (except circuit boards which are manufactured in Shenzhen, north of Hong Kong), build fuel tanks, and pneumatic systems. Some specific deliverables include electronic components, auxiliary power units, and power receptacles. These components are stored in several warehouses after being built and sub-assembled in factories owned by subcontractors spread across the country.

Australia. One major company, located in Melbourne, is responsible for building fuselage components. Some specific deliverables include composite empennage, floor beams, stringers, and fuselage sections. These components are stored in a major warehouse after being built and sub-assembled in a large factory.

Ireland. Located just outside of Dublin, Crozier Aerospace, a subsidiary of the da Vinci, is responsible for the control cabin for all aircrafts. It has responsibilities, for example, flight kits, flight deck avionics, such as the flight management system, and cabin entertainment. Crozier has an "embedded systems factory" and the results are electronically delivered to Wichita.

Of course, da Vinci does more than build aircraft. It also provides several support services out of Wichita. The enterprise, in an effort to demonstrate its customer-focused orientation, ensures that rotables (that is, reusable items), such as landing gear and generators; expendables (that is, items where the cost of repair exceeds its cost of replacement); and consumables (that is, items not cost effective to replace replacement), such as engine oil. The company also provides AOG (air on ground support), such as sending engineers and mechanics as well as dispatch parts to help aircraft resume service. It also provides technical services to customers, such as pilot training, to include using flight simulators; providing operations flight training; offering maintenance training; and distributing up-to-date hard and soft documentation.

To build the aircraft and provide the services, da Vinci has the following organizational structure.

At the top of the organization is Board of Directors (BoD), as shown in Figure A.1. It consists of the following executives, from the chairman and chief executive officer (CEO) to executive vice presidents:

- Jose Alvidrez, Chief Executive Officer and Chairman
- Tanya Salinksi, Chief Operating Officer
- Daniel Jones, Chief Financial Officer
- Roger Binstrim, Executive VP, Customer Relations
- Tabitha Fullerton, Executive VP, Operations
- Robert Coloson, Executive VP, Finance
- Hazel Smithton, Executive VP, Legal

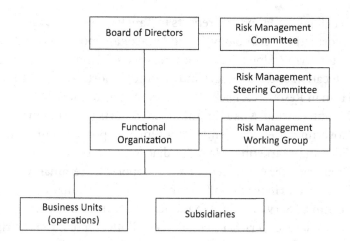

FIGURE A.1
Organizational Chart for da Vinci Aerospace Industries.

- Irwin Stein, Executive VP, Public Relations
- Viktor Zeinmann, Executive VP, Chief Engineer, Technology
- Frank Morelli, Executive VP, Employee Relations
- Riku Tanaka, Executive VP, Internal Governance

Reporting to the BoD are several committees, one of which is the risk management committee which consists of four members. It has responsibility to provide options and recommendations regarding all risks to the BoD.

Beneath the risk management committee is a risk management steering committee which consists of several executives. It has the responsibility to provide direction and oversee the work of the risk management working group which consists of representatives from the functional organizations. It has the responsibility to provide direction and support to the corporate risk management organization throughout da Vinci.

Below the BoD are the functional organizations and their senior vice presidents at the corporate level that report to their respective executive vice presidents and ultimately to the chief operating officer and the chairman and CEO:

- Risk Management, Eric Smith, reports to Tanaka
- Finance, Donna Gapone, reports to Coloson
- Supplier Management, Iris Zakava, reports to Fullerton
- Procurement, Dick Hebert, reports to Fullerton

- Legal, Janine Francona, reports to Tanaka
- Information Technology, David Laracona, reports to Zeinmann
- Engineering, Howard Schwarz, reports to Zeinmann
- Education and Training, Cindy Laford, reports to Binstrim
- Human Resources, Nick Dzysinski, reports to Morelli
- Manufacturing, Mike Zorankowski, reports to Zeinmann
- Government Affairs, Jenifer Houseman, reports to Smithton
- Sales and Marketing, Mary Sundale, reports to Stein
- Propulsion Systems, Henry Saleno, reports to Zeinmann
- Structures, Heinrich Volksturm, reports to Zeinmann
- Technical Services, Cindy Saderford, reports to Binstrim
- Customer Delivery Services, Rafael Dilotte, reports to Binstrim
- Public Relations, Frank Luger, reports to Stein
- Flight Operations, Serge Dimotrov, reports to Fullerton
- Quality Assurance, Rhonda Tellini, reports to Tanaka
- Internal Audit, Hank Packurt, reports to Tanaka

Within the functional organization is the corporate risk management group, managed by Eric Smith who reports to Riku Tanaka, Executive Vice President. The group consists of three sections: risk analysis and assessment; risk modeling and tools; and risk processes and maintenance. The risk analysis and assessment section has operations risk specialists, business risk specialists, and market risk specialist. The risk modeling and tools consist of data analysts and tool specialists. The risk processes and maintenance consist of process specialists, documentation specialists, and office administrators.

As shown in Figure A.2, the business units and the subsidiaries report to the corporate organization. Each business unit and the subsidiary mainly replicate the corporate's functional structure. For example, these operational organizations also have their own risk management section which coordinates with the corporate risk management organization.

Underneath da Vinci's blanket of success are some underlying serious problems. These problems could jeopardize future growth and opportunities to dominate the aerospace market.

First, the move from traditional manufacturing to just-in-time and direct ship operations has caused labor problems within the United States. Its US workforce has been cut by more than 30 percent as work moved to other countries. The morale of the domestic workforce declined and tension has increased between itself and dealing with other nationalities. This

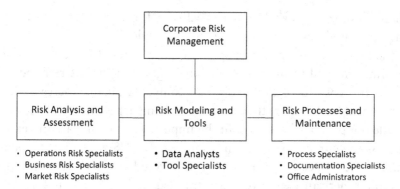

FIGURE A.2
Risk Management Organization Chart within da Vinci Aerospace Industries.

situation is especially the case over the purchase of Crozier Aerospace, resulting in laying off information technology professionals at da Vinci. Tension between the Americans and the Irish has increased and bridging the cultural differences has been challenging.

Second, the pressure to reduce labor costs for the enterprise to remain competitive has led to reducing benefits for existing and new employees. Salary increases have not kept pace with inflation and other benefits related to medical care and retirement have declined. Consequently, negotiations with domestic labor unions have been tumultuous over the last few years as they see work shifting to other countries like China where labor costs are substantially lower.

Third, reducing the workforce has affected the overall craftmanship of da Vinci Aerospace. Its US workforce was considered one of the best in the aerospace industry. Due to the competitive nature of the industry and the desire to increase stock value, many engineers and other technical professionals were laid off. Not only did this action cause a "brain drain" but it also allowed competitors to hire former employees. The result is that other aerospace firms, including foreign ones, are capitalizing on the newly acquired expertise and are beginning to encroach upon da Vinci's market share.

Fourth, and perhaps just as complicated, are the international political tensions which are beginning to impact relations with overseas suppliers. Protectionism, both within the United States and other countries, such as China, that da Vinci does business with has introduced political risks that could and have impacted its global supply chain. In other words, supply chain optimization has declined as delivery delays from foreign suppliers have increased, resulting in production schedule slides.

The tension with China is a special case in point. The US government has implemented tariffs and the Chinese government has responded in kind. The costs of these tariffs have only marginally increased each component cost but further tariffs could impact manufacturing costs. While not proven, the defects in the imports from China are increasing, such as the circuit boards from Shenzhen. The US government has also raised other concerns with da Vinci that could lead to substantial fines. Several American executives have traveled to China who had received substantial gifts from leaders in the Chinese government which violates US federal law. Additionally, two executives are under federal investigation for taking laptops into China containing information that may have military value which again violates federal law. da Vinci has noticed, too, the cyberattacks originating from China have increased.

da Vinci Aerospace has also experienced tension with Japan but over cultural differences between itself and the United States. On numerous occasions, Japanese suppliers have received poor written specifications from engineers at da Vinci. When the suppliers delivered components to Wichita, they failed to meet the expectations of the Americans. Several US executives expressed concern which was leaked to the newspapers and embarrassed the Japanese. In addition, the Japanese wanted to work face-to-face with the Americans; however, the latter preferred working remotely to reduce costs. The Japanese viewed such a working relationship as an affront.

Tensions have also increased between the US and Mexico over immigration issues and the illegal drug trade. The US government threatens to restrict imports between the two countries as well as increase tariffs. Mexican suppliers to da Vinci have responded accordingly. The labor force of some of the smaller suppliers have walked off their jobs as well as sabotaged and pilfered the central warehouse. The Mexican government has threatened to deport company liaisons from Mexico.

The relationship with the former Crozier Aerospace workforce has a strained relationship. The cultural differences in information technology practices and having many more holidays posed a challenge. The differences in programming of embedded systems by the Irish were not in sync with those of the practices of American counterparts and often resulted in long meetings for which the latter lacked patience. Also, the Americans found it difficult to create delivery schedules due to the lengthy and number of vacations or holidays observed in Ireland. Finally, the fate of Ireland and Brexit created doubt about the reliability of future production and delivery schedules.

Australia, too, was not without its challenges. The Australian government has expressed concerns to the US about Chinese expansion in the Pacific Ocean and especially in the Philippine Sea. Its government is fearful that US trade is serving as catalyst for China's expansion, economically and politically, with Southeast Asian countries and has successfully eclipsed Australian trading opportunities. The government has threatened tariffs against the US imports of aerospace parts from China. In addition, within Australia, the principal supplier to da Vinci has been the target of cyberattacks allegedly from China.

Because of all the above challenges, internally and externally, supply chain optimization is gradually declining. Data collected show that components and software delivery times from suppliers has become longer and more frequent. The quality from suppliers has also deteriorated, reflected in data such as defect rate. Communication problems have been more frequent because the relationship between some da Vinci and foreign suppliers has become quite tense, especially between Americans and Japanese. The reputation of da Vinci is becoming increasingly negative, within the US and abroad due to the increasing perception by the international press that some defects are threatening passenger safety. da Vinci has also come under fire from environmental groups for not doing enough to suppress methane emissions from its aircraft; it also has come under attack from international human rights groups for not doing anything about Chinese suppliers employing political prisoners to build parts for da Vinci components.

da Vinci soon realized it was getting broadsided with too many political risks and needed to gain some control over the circumstances. Institutional investors in the enterprise were getting frustrated since the stock was declining in value, approximately 20 percent and the dividends were getting smaller. One institutional investor threatened to withdraw its investment if the enterprise did not get its act together when dealing with political risks. It felt da Vinci did fine dealing with economic and technical risks but not political ones.

The board of directors decided to act immediately. It directed the risk management committee to come up with a set of recommendations by March 1, six weeks away. The four members of the committee were Hazel Smithton (chairperson), Tabitha Fullerton, Robert Coloson, Daniel Jones, and

Riku Tanaka. The committee decided that it needed a situation-target-proposal (STP). It directed Eric Smith, vice president of the Risk management organization, to draft the STP and present it to the committee in a week.

Smith decided to meet with Hazel Smithton to ascertain any issues or concerns that she and the committee wanted addressed specifically. He sought to ensure that the STP met the expectations of the committee members and answer any questions regarding the STP.

Smith formed a team, consisting of multidisciplinary group from the strategic and operational levels of da Vinci Aerospace. The ore team consisted of people with knowledge, expertise, and experience in one or more disciplines related to legal, engineering, government affairs, internal audit, flight operations, and, of course, risk management. The core team developed a milestone chart when the feedback to the team was required and when the final STP must be drafted for presentation to the risk management committee. Smith assigned a project manager to follow up with each team member and ensure the information was collected from each stakeholder.

Smith had received feedback from all the participants. The information was compiled in the form of an STP. He verified and cleaned up the information with the aid of his risk management staff He then presented the revised version of the STP to the team for final review. Upon receiving approval, Smith scheduled a meeting with the risk management committee. Prior to the meeting, however, Smith requested a preliminary session with Smithton to present a preliminary copy of the STP. He wanted to ensure that the STP answered all the issues and concerns of the committee. Smithton provided some feedback which he incorporated. He then communicated her feedback to the team.

On January 14, Smith presented the STP to the risk management committee. In a nutshell, the situation presented background information and identified the causes of the political risk management challenges that da Vinci faced. The target described what successful political risk management would look like for da Vinci as it applied to its global supply chain. The proposal presented several options to achieve the target for the board which decided that the best one was using the existing risk management governance structure but adopt enterprise risk management as a framework to manage political risks. Smithton, assuming the position of executive sponsor, attended the quarterly board meeting which gave the go ahead to proceed with the program. Smith was present to answer any technical questions that board members had.

Immediately, Smith scheduled a meeting with the risk management steering committee which consisted of vice presidents from selected functional organizations, business units, and subsidiaries. He communicated the STP results to the risk management steering committee (which usually met every six months but also on an ad hoc basis) expressing the need to form a program team. The steering committee approved and recommended that the members of the risk management working group (consisting of managers and risk management professionals) serve on the program team or their selected representatives.

Smith convened an ad hoc meeting of the risk management working group. He presented the STP and the decisions of the BoD and the risk management steering committee. He then designated a core team (the working group giving its assent to the team members) to draft a charter, a program announcement, work breakdown structure, cost and time estimates, communications management integrated schedule, roles and responsibilities, a program governance structure, and reporting requirements. Project managers were assigned to each of the functional areas at the strategic level and the business unit, and subsidiaries selected their own project managers and core teams which were responsible to produce a project plan within the parameters set by the program plan. The high-level work breakdown structure, serving as the scope, included modifying the existing risk management governance structure, training, and developing and deploying all ten of the risk management processes. Each political risk management process had its own schedule that made up the entire enterprise schedule. The program set up a weekly reporting cycle at the program, steering committee, and risk management committee levels. The program level was bi-weekly; steering committee monthly; and risk management committee quarterly. All these activities were integral to complete the first process of political risk management which is to establish infrastructure and project. To complete the process, all team members received high-level training on political risk management from the context of the STP. The training described what is political risk management, its goals, and how it will help da Vinci enterprises. The training also provided the opportunity to answer any questions.

The second process that the program team executed according to the program plan was to review the pertinent strategic goals of the enterprise as they relate to da Vinci's global supply chain. A sub-team was formed to perform this exercise. The sub-team conducted a comprehensive review of strategic and operational plans as well as other related documentation and interviewed selected senior executives. Some goals were eliminated, being perceived as having no relationship to political risk. The sub-team then prioritized the remaining goals according to an agreed upon criteria and reflected the results in a matrix showing the relationship between strategic goals and their supply chain impact. The program manager captured lessons learned from all stakeholders involved in this process to identify what went well and what needed improvement; this feedback was used to revise the political risk management plan.

Using the list of goals, the sub-team executed the third political risk management process, identify stakeholders, which was performed concurrently with identify strategic goals. These stakeholders are the people and functional organizations that have a direct or indirect interest in the outcome of the program. The sub-team mapped the goals to the stakeholders and then created a chart displaying the risk profile of each stakeholder. The sub-team then presented the results to the program team for feedback and consensus. The program manager captured lessons learned from all stakeholders involved in this process to identify what went well and what needed improvement; this feedback will eventually be used to revise the political risk management plan.

The fourth process that the program executed was to prepare the political risk management plan. Again, a sub-team was formed with the responsibility to determine if a separate plan for political risk management was necessary or that revisions to the existing risk management plan were necessary. The sub-team identified the advantages and disadvantages of each one, weighing each criterion. The sub-team decided that since the risk management committee's decision to leverage on the existing risk management process, the best approach was to update the existing risk management plan for the enterprise. The sub-team presented recommendations to the team for feedback and consensus. The proposal was then presented to the risk management steering committee for approval.

Having received the approval of the steering committee, the program team started to identify the revisions to the risk management plan. These revisions included changes on how each of the subsequent processes recorded in the current risk management plan would be revised, from identifying risks to maintaining risk management processes. The revisions were made after a series of program and project meetings with stakeholders across the enterprise, from the strategic to operational levels. The risk management plan was updated to reflect the political risk management and eventually presented to the steering committee for review and approval.

Now that the plan was approved, the program team was ready to pursue the fifth process, identify political risks. Using the list of strategic goals of the enterprise and a description of the global supply chain, another sub-team was formed which comprised of at least one team member representing key stakeholders from the strategic and operational levels. The sub-team held meetings using brainstorming to identify all the political risks that could impact each goal, creating a matrix showing which goals were impacted by which risks. It also created another matrix showing the relationship between supply chain assets and threats. It also "affinitized" the list of risks into categories and built a political risk register. The team then married the list of stakeholders with the risks to help determine where in da Vinci Aerospace the political risks could have the biggest impact. The sub-team presented the results to the rest of the program team for feedback and consensus. The program manager captured lessons learned from all stakeholders involved in this process to identify what went well and what needed improvement; this feedback was used to revise the political risk management plan. At the end of this significant achievement in the program, Smith presented the highlights of the process to the steering committee along with program cost and schedule performance. Of note, Smith was not hesitant to communicate to the steering committee for any help needed to overcome any obstacles in completing the program.

The program team was now ready to perform the sixth process, assess political risks, which was the most challenging and took the longest time in the program schedule. The first activity was to identify for each risk any trigger events that indicated it might become an issue. Next an important judgment was necessary, whether to perform a qualitative or quantitative risk assessment. The team agreed to perform a qualitative risk assessment. It then decided if any risks would be to candidates for conducting a quantitative risk assessment.

For the qualitative risk analysis, the team needed to decide whether to develop a 5 × 5 chart or conduct a forced choice exercise. The team decided initially to create a 5 by 5 chart but the effort proved more difficult than anticipated. The team had too many disagreements over the priority of each risk relative to one another. The team decided not, however, to applying a forced choice technique. The approach would require extensive preparation. Instead, the team operationalized what was meant by high, medium, and low priority by defining ranges within each one; it did the same for high, medium, and low impact. These definitions reduced the subjectivity and made it easier to calculate the risk rating for each risk. The team then created a matrix showing the probabilities, impact, risk rating, and relative rank of each risk. The information was then reflected in a 5 by 5 chart and used to update the risk listing. The team proceeded to determine how each risk impacted the global supply chain and recorded this information in the risk listing. The team reviewed the risks to determine the ones to perform quantitative risk analysis and recorded the results in the risk listing. The program manager captured lessons learned from all stakeholders involved in this process to identify what went well and what needed improvement; this feedback was used to revise the political risk management plan. The results of this process were then presented to the steering committee.

The team was now ready to perform the seventh process, prepare political risk responses. The goal was to determine in advance what to do if a political risk arose. This process requires considerable "blue skying," meaning it requires thinking in advance about how to respond to an event that may not occur using the limited availability of facts and data. The team listed each risk and, for each one, determined the appropriate one or more strategic responses to apply. For each risk and strategic response, the team determined one or more tactical actions to implement. For each risk, the team also determined if any linkages could possibly arise with other risks and what responses and tactical actions to pursue. Also, for each risk, the team determined what one or more responses and tactical actions were required for any residual and secondary risks. The team captured the results in the matrix showing the relationship between political risks and tactical actions. It also decided to draw a risk map showing the relationships among the risks and updated the risk listing. The results were reviewed one more time by the team to achieve consensus. Smith then identified risk owners for each of the risks; the risk owners were recorded in the risk listing. The program manager captured lessons learned from all stakeholders involved in this process to identify what went well and what needed improvement; this feedback was used to revise the political risk management plan. The results of this process were then presented to the steering committee, along with the performance baseline of the program.

The program team was now ready to turn political risk management into a reality by identifying a specific timeframe to perform risk monitoring and controlling, the eighth process, according to what was defined in the risk management plan. China was selected as a pilot study during this timeframe. The program emphasized collecting facts and data about any political risks that arose; the effectiveness of the strategic responses and tactical actions; and the challenges risk owners faced when implementing their responsibilities. Additional emphasis was on the effectiveness of the activities collecting facts and data about risks and the responses to them. The results were reviewed by the team to determine the reliability and validity of the facts of data collected. The program manager captured lessons learned from all stakeholders involved in this process to identify what went well and what needed improvement; this feedback was used to revise the political risk management plan. The results of this process were then presented to the steering committee, along with the performance baseline of the program.

Referring to the risk management plan, the team was ready to execute ninth process, perform political risk reporting. The goal was to determine the effectiveness of communicating political risk information to various stakeholders. The team emphasized the importance of preparing presentation formats and status documents that met the needs of specific stakeholders. These needs ranged from more detailed information for business units and subsidiaries spread across the global supply chain to summaries for higher levels of management at the strategic levels. Several program team members delivered presentations and reports to members of the corporate staff as well as the executive and operations personnel working in the business units and subsidiaries to collect feedback was collected from these stakeholders and the results captured in a lesson learned document. The results of this process were then presented to the steering committee, along with the performance baseline of the program.

Smith, along with selected stakeholders, compiled the lessons learned that were documented at the end of each process which had been treated as phases in the program schedule. The document included a performance review from a program management perspective as well as recommendations to improve each of the political risk management process. Smith then submitted it to the steering committee which accepted with minor changes. The committee then requested that the risk management plan be updated and resubmitted for review.

Smith and the rest of the team felt this request was good for testing the tenth process, maintaining the political risk management plan. The single points of contact had the opportunity to practice their responsibilities. They incorporated any changes relevant to their areas of responsibilities, to include obtaining reviews and approvals of their respective process. The risk management plan was updated; Smith submitted the updated plan for review and approval by the steering committee which requested that Smith present it to the risk management committee of the board of directors along with a presentation about the successes and challenges. He submitted the risk management plan in advance to the members of the risk management committee to provide sufficient time to prepare questions and provide their insights. He also reviewed the presentation with Smithton as a heads up and to obtain any feedback before the final presentation. She emphasized keeping it at a high level which he did. The presentation had five slides, each one addressing a separate topic: cover; background information; notable successes; challenges; and help needed.

Smithton submitted the results of the program to the risk management committee on March 1. The BoD granted final approval.

Bibliography

Arnold, Tony J. R. 1991. *Introduction to Materials Management*. Englewood Cliffs, NJ: Prentice Hall.

Barber, Benjamin R. 1996. *Jihad vs McWorld*. New York: Ballantine Books.

Barnes, James C. 2001. *A Guide to Business Continuity Planning*. Chichester: John Wiley & Sons.

Barton, Thomas L. 2001. *Making Enterprise Risk Management Pay Off*. Morristown, NJ: Financial Executives Research Foundation, Inc.

Biegelman, Martin T. and Joel T. Bartow. 2006. *Executive Roadmap to Fraud Prevention and Internal Control*. New York: John Wiley & Sons.

Blanchard, David. 2007. *Supply Chain Management*. Hoboken, NJ: John Wiley & Sons.

Bowersox, Donald J., David J. Closs, and M. Bixby Cooper. 2010. *Supply Chain Logistics Management*, 3rd ed. New York: McGraw-Hill/Irwin.

Brawley Mark, R. 2003. *The Politics of Globalization*. Peterborough, Ontario: Broadview Press.

Calleo, David P. 2001. *Rethinking Europe's Future*. Princeton, NJ: Princeton University Press.

Caralli, Richard A., Jukia H. Allen, and David White. 2011. *CERT Resilience Management Model*, Version 1.1. Upper Saddle River, NJ: Addison-Wesley.

Caramani, Daniele, editor. 2014. *Comparative Politics*, 3rd ed. Oxford: Oxford University Press.

Chouhan, T. R. et al. 2004. *Bhopal: The Inside Story*. New York: The Apex Press.

Christopher, Martin. *Logistics and Supply Chain Management*, 4th ed. Harlow, England: Pearson.

Clark, William, Matt Golder, and Sona Nadenichek Golder. 2013. *Principles of Comparative Politics*, 2nd ed. Los Angeles: CQ Press.

Cohen, Shoshanah and Joseph Roussel. 2005. *Strategic Supply Chain Management*. New York: McGraw-Hill.

Crouhy, Michel, Dan Galai, and Robert Mark. 2006. *The Essentials of Risk Management*. New York: McGraw-Hill.

David, Pierre and Richard Stewart. 2008. *International Logistics*, 2nd ed. Southbank, Australia: Thomson.

DesJardins, Joseph. 2006. *An Introduction to Business Ethics*, 2nd ed. Boston: McGraw-Hill.

Dezenhall, Eric and John Weber. 2007. *Damage Control*. New York: Portfolio.

Dodds, Klaus. 2007. *Geopolitics*. New York: Oxford University Press.

Dorner, Dietrich. 1997. *The Logic of Failure*. Cambridge, MA: Perseus Books.

Doughty, Ken, editor. 2001. *Business Continuity Planning*. Boca Raton, FL: Auerbach.

Eiteman, David K., Stonehill, Arthur L., and Moffett, Michael H. 2001. *Multinational Business Finance*, 9th ed. Boston: Addison Wesley.

Fearn-Banks, Kathleen. 2010. *Crisis Communications*, 4th ed. New York: Routledge.

Ferraro, Gary P. 1998. *The Cultural Dimension of International Business*, 3rd ed. Upper Saddle River, NJ: Prentice Hall.

FitzGerald, Jerry and Ardra F. FitzGerald. 1990. *Designing Controls into Computerized Systems*. Redwood City, CA: Jerry FitzGerald & Associates.

Franklin, Daniel with John Andrews. 2012. *Megachange*. London: Profile Books.

Friedman, George. 2010. *The Next 100 Years*. New York: Anchor Books.

Friedman, George. 2015. *Flashpoints*. New York: Anchor Books.

Friedman, Thomas L. 2008. *Hot, Flat, and Crowded*. New York: Farrar, Straus and Giroux.

Friedman, Thomas L. 2000. *The Lexus and the Olive Tree*. New York: Anchor Books.

Fulcher, James. 2004. *Capitalism*. New York: Oxford University Press.

Ghemawat, Pankaj. 2007. *Redefining Global Strategy*. Boston: Harvard Business School Press.

Gilpin, Robert. 2003. *Global Political Economy*. Himayatnagar, India: Orient Longman.

Glenny, Misha. 2008. *McMafia*. New York: Alfred A. Knopf.

HBS. 2000. *Harvard Business Review on Corporate Governance*. Boston: Harvard Business School Press.

Hebron, Lui and John F. Stack, Jr. 2017. *Globalization*, 3rd ed. Lanham, MD: Rowman & Littlefield.

Hult, Tomas, David Closs, and David Frayer. 2014. *Global Supply Chain Management*. New York: McGraw-Hill.

Huntington, Samuel P. 1997. *The Clash of Civilizations and the Remaking of World Order*. New York: Touchstone.

Ireland, Ronald K. with Colleen, Crum. 2005. *Supply Chain Collaboration*. Boca Raton, FL: J. Ross Publishing, Inc.

Irwin, Douglas A. 2005. *Free Trade Under Fire*, 2nd ed. Princeton, NJ: Princeton University Press.

Jacobs, Daniel. 2016. *BP Blowout*. Washington, DC: Brookings Institution Press.

Jonathan, Kirshner, editor. 2006. *Globalization and National Security*. New York: Routledge.

Judge, David and David Earnshaw. 2003. *The European Parliament*. London: Palgrave MacMillan.

Kendrick, Tom. 2003. *Identifying and Managing Project Risk*. New York: AMACOM.

Kildow, Betty A. 2011. *A Supply Chain Management Guide to Business Continuity*. New York: AMACOM.

Kliem, Ralph L. and Gregg D. Richie. 2016. *Business Continuity Planning*. Boca Raton, FL: CRC Press.

Kliem, Ralph L. 2016. *Managing Lean Projects*. Boca Raton, FL: CRC Press.

Koller, Glenn R. 2007. *Modern Corporate Risk Management*. Boca Raton, FL: J. Ross Publishing.

Korten, David C. 2015. *When Corporations Ruled the World*, 3rd ed. Oakland: Berrett-Koehler Publishers, Inc.

Kunreuther, Howard and Michael Useem. 2009. *Leaning from Catastrophes*. Upper Saddle River, NJ: Wharton School Publishing.

Lamy, Steven L., et al. 2013. *Introduction to Global Politics*. New York: Oxford University Press.

Loch, Christoph H., Arnoud De Meyer, and Michael T. Pich. 2006. *Managing the Unknown*. New York: John Wiley & Sons.

Mansbach, Richard W. and Kirsten L. Taylor. 2012. *Introduction to Global Politics*, 2nd ed. London: Routledge.

McKellar, Robert. 2010. *A Short Guide to Political Risk*. Surrey, England: Gower Publishing Limited.

Moran, Robert T. and William E. Youngdahl. 2008. *Leading Global Projects*. Oxford: Butter-Heinemann.

Moran, Theodore H., editor. 1998. *Managing International Political Risk*. Oxford: Blackwell Publishers Ltd.

Myers, Kenneth N. 1999. *Manager's Guide to Contingency Planning for Disasters*. New York: John Wiley & Sons.

O'Neil, Patrick H. 2013. *Essential of Comparative Politics*, 4th ed. New York: W. W. Norton & Company.

Pickford, James, editor. 2001. *Mastering Risk*, Vol. 1. London: Pearson Education Limited.

Pinder, John and Simon Usherwood. 2001. *The European Union*. New York: Oxford University Press.

Pritchard, Carl L. 2005. *Risk Management*, 3rd ed. Arlington, VA: ESI International.

Reinert, Erik S. 2008. *How Rich Countries Got Rich … and Why Poor Countries Stay Poor*. London: Constable & Robinson Ltd.

Rice, Condoleezza and Amy B. Zegart. 2018. *Political Risk*. New York: Twelve.

Russo, Edward J. and Paul J. H. Schoemaker. 1990. *Decision Traps*. New York: Simon and Schuster.

Sayer, Natalie J. and Bruce Williams. 2012. *Lean for Dummies*. Hoboken, NJ: John Wiley & Sons.

Shapiro, Jeremy F. 2001. *Modelling the Supply Chain*. Pacific Grove, CA: Duxbury.

Sheffi, Yossi. 2005. *The Resilient Enterprise*. Cambridge, MA: The MIT Press.

Simchi-Levi, David, Philip Kaminsky, and Edith Simchi-Levi. 2003. *Designing and Managing the Supply Chain*, 2nd ed. Boston: McGraw Hill/Irwin. Simchi-Levi.

David, Philip Kaminsky, and Edith Simchi-Levi. 2004. *Managing the Supply Chain*. New York: McGraw-Hill.

Steger, Manfred. 2009. *Globalization*. New York: Oxford University Press.

Rose-Ackerman, Susan and Palifka, Bonnie J. 2016. *Corruption and Government*, 2nd ed. Cambridge, UK: Cambridge University Press.

Stiglitz, Joseph E. 2007. *Making Globalization Work*. New York: W. W. Norton & Company.

Taleb, Nassim N. 2010. *The Black Swan*. New York: Penguin Books.

The Committee of Sponsoring Organizations of the Treadway Commission. 2004a. *Enterprise Risk Management – Integrated Framework (Executive Summary Framework)*. Jersey City, NJ: AICPA.

The Committee of Sponsoring Organizations of the Treadway Commission. 2004b. *Enterprise Risk Management – Integrated Framework (Application Techniques)*. Jersey City, NJ: AICPA.

The Committee of Sponsoring Organizations of the Treadway Commission. 1994a. *Internal Control – Integrated Framework (Executive Summary)*. Jersey City, NJ: AICPA.

The Committee of Sponsoring Organizations of the Treadway Commission. 1994b. *Internal Control – Integrated Framework (Evaluation Tools)*. Jersey City, NJ: AICPA.

Toksoz, Mina. 2014. *Guide to Country Risk*. New York: Public Affairs.

Wagner, Daniel. 2012. *Managing Country Risk*. Boca Raton, FL: CRC Press.

Wilkinson, Paul. 2007. *International Relations*. Oxford: Oxford University Press.

Williams, Maurice J. 2002. *Challenges of Globalization for America*. New York: Xlibris.

Wincel, Jeffrey P. 2004. *Lean Supply Chain Management*. New York: Productivity Press.

Zakaria, Fareed. 2008. *The Post American World*. New York: W. W. Norton & Company.

Zolli, Andrew and Ann Marie Healy. 2012. *Resilience*. New York: Free Press.

ARTICLES

Manuj, Ila and Mentzer, John T. "Global Supply Chain Risk Management Strategies." *International Journal of Physical Distribution and Logistics*, Vol. 3, 2008.

Glossary

Acceptance: one of the type of strategic responses to threats or opportunities; it involves taking acceptance or passive acceptance; the former entails setting aside contingency reserves while the latter taking no action.

Analyze: one of four parts of a framework on political risk by Rice and Zegart; collecting and evaluating information about political risk and using that information to make business decisions.

Assumptions: suppositions or perceptions assumed to be facts until proven otherwise.

Audit Committee: a subset of the board of directors to help certain functions, such as internal audit, remain independent from management.

Avoidance: (1) one of the type of strategic responses to threats involving taking action to eliminate a threat; (2) a risk management strategy by Manuj and Mentzer regarding taking action in one of two ways:

Type 1 which allows for probability of occurrence of a risk and Type 2 that does not eliminate uncertainty.

Benchmarking: a technique used to compare the performance of a process to another one in a similar organization to determine its efficiency and effectiveness.

Black Swans: events that are totally unanticipated, explainable only in hindsight, and have a catastrophic impact.

Board of Directors (BoD): group of executives that oversees performance, sets the strategic direction of an enterprise, and looks after shareholder interests.

Brainstorming: a facilitated group discussion session that encourages free generation of creative ideas to solve a problem or provide alternate solutions.

Breach: a failure, in whole or part, to perform according to contract.

Bribe: the exchange of something of value, often money but not necessarily, to influence decisions or actions.

BRIC: an acronym consisting of these emerging countries: Brazil, Russia, India, and China.

Business Case: a study demonstrating the value of political risk management to an enterprise; it covers both tangible and intangible benefits.

Business Continuity: the discipline of developing, deploying, and maintaining strategies and procedures to ensure that an enterprise survives by increasing the likelihood of responding to and recovering from a risk event.

Business Impact Analysis (BIA): analyzing operations within an organization to identify critical business processes and the impact of potential risks.

Business Preparedness Plan: a document capturing the necessary information to guide recovery teams and enhance the ability of a critical business process to recover from a disruptive event.

Business-to-Business (B2B): an enterprise sells to another enterprise.

Business-to-Consumer (B2C): directly selling products and services to customers.

Butterfly Effect: a small change in a nonlinear system having a large impact somewhere else in it.

CAGE: an acronym for cultural, administrative, geographical, and economic; four distances, or differences, that add complexities to global business relationships as identified by Ghemawat.

Catastrophe: one of 5 types of events; an event exceeding the ability and capability of an enterprise to respond and recover.

Change Management: part of the organizing process of project management; it is detecting, analyzing, evaluating, and implementing changes to all baselines.

Charter: part of the defining process of project management; it is a high-level document, not more than two or three pages, signed by key stakeholders that defines the scope of a project and gives the project manager the necessary authority to proceed.

Cherry Picking: deliberately selecting facts and data to prove one's point.

Chief Risk Officer: an individual, usually at the executive or senior management level, responsible for strategic oversight of risk management throughout an enterprise; responsibilities may also include serving as an advisor to an audit committee or the board of directors.

Closing: a project management process; it is actions taken to complete all activities and tasks and informing stakeholders of the results.

Cognitive Bias: the influence of subjectivity in decision-making and actions taken based upon perception of reality.

Communications Management: part of the organizing process of project management; it is providing the facts and data at the right time in the right format to the right person to make the right decisions and take the right actions.

Configuration Management: part of the organizing process of project management; it is maintaining the baseline of deliverables and tracking changes to them.

Consensus stakeholders understand, accept, and support a decision or action despite reservations.

Control/Share/Transfer: a risk management strategy by Manuj and Mentzer which entails offloading some of the impact of a threat to other entities.

Controlling: part of the monitoring and controlling process of project management; it is taking preventive or corrective actions to achieve the goals and objectives of a project.

Corporate Veil: legally protecting a corporation's shareholders from liability, such as the actions of a subsidiary.

Cost Baseline: the criterion to evaluate the financial performance of a project.

Cost Management: part of the organizing process of project management. It is allocating and managing funds for initiating, defining, planning, organizing, executing, monitoring and controlling, and closing a project.

Crawford Slip Technique: a variant of brainstorming that with the aid a facilitator, defines a problem or issue and then records thoughts on slips of paper, which are compiled, grouped, and summarized.

Crisis: one of 5 types of events; an event; an event exceeding normal expectations of disruption and necessitates recovery actions which, if not taken, threatens the survivability of an enterprise.

Critical Business Process: a series of procedures and activities key stakeholders have identified as vital to the survival of an organization.

Defining: a project management process; it involves creating the authority document for a project and the assigned project manager to commit resources, performing stakeholder analysis, and defining roles, responsibilities, and authorities.

Delphi Technique: sending a questionnaire or survey to key stakeholders asking them a series of questions or ratings on topics, issues, risks, or a combination thereof of all until reaching a consensus.

Demand Risks: one of four categories of supply chain risks identified by Manuj and Mentzer; ones concerning outbound flows to satisfy customer requirements.

Emergency: one of 5 types of events; an event; an event threatening life, safety, and property and requires immediate attention.

Enhance: one of the type of responses to opportunities; it involves increasing the probability and impact of an opportunity.

Enterprise Risk Management: a formal framework for identifying and responding to risks potentially impacting the goals and objectives of an enterprise.

Escalate: one of the type of strategic responses to opportunities; it involves elevating opportunity up the chain of command to take advantage of economies of scale.

European Union (EU): a political and economic organization of nations guaranteed fundamental rights and free trade among its membership.

Executing: a project management process; it is implementing the project according to the performance measurement baseline.

Exploit: one of the type of responses to opportunities; it involves furthering an opportunity and do whatever it takes to gain the advantage.

Export Administration Regulations (EAR): as opposed to ITAR which deals with defense related items, EAR applies to commercial items appearing on the Commercial Control List to ensure export control and treaty compliance.

Facilitator: a neutral individual who helps team members to collaborate in an environment that enables open communications and trusting relationships.

Forced Choice Method: choosing between two (sometimes more) options, such as A or B.

Foreign Corrupt Practices Act (FCPA): a federal law makes it illegal to bribe a government official or another country with the expectation of receiving or keeping business; it requires keeping records and providing a system of internal control.

Framework: an adaptable structure, such as an outline, as opposed to a methodology, that serves as a guide.

Fuzzy Logic: making a choice or selection according to degrees or continuum, rather than a dichotomous choice, such as yes or no.

Game Theory: a view that people are motivated by self-interest by making rational choices, especially regarding material payoff.

General Data Protection Regulation (GDFR): a European Union (EU) law; protects data privacy, including transfer of data outside the EU.

Globalization: enterprises with supply chains transcending national boundaries.

Goal: a broad aspiration that is difficult to define but has some inherent meaning which may be interpreted differently, as opposed to an objective.

Governance: frameworks, processes, procedures, methods, and techniques of an infrastructure within an enterprise to determine goals, implement strategies, and monitor performance results.

Groupthink: peer pressure that is so intense that it alters individuals' judgment even in the presence of contrary facts and data.

Hedging: a risk management strategy by Manuj and Mentzer whereby suppliers dispersing suppliers and other supply chain elements across the globe to mitigate the impact of a threat.

Heuristics: rules of thumb or an educated guess based upon assumptions and insufficient data and information.

Human Resource Management: part of the organizing process of project management; it is identifying the people resources required for a project, its team organization, staffing management plan, and the roles, responsibilities, and authorities.

Illegal Acts: violating laws and regulations.

Incident: one of 5 types of events; an event having an inconsequential impact.

Independence: freedom from influence that can impact judgment.

Infrastructure: an organizational structure that supports political risk management for an enterprise at the strategic and operational levels.

Integration: the degree to which each component interacts with the other.

Interdependence: the degree of reliance the output of a component has on another component.

International Governmental Organization (IGO): two or more countries collaborating to deal with one or more issues by forming a separate reality.

International Traffic in Arms Regulations (ITAR): restricts and controls export of military and defense technologies that potentially involves US national security and foreign policy.

Just-in-Time (JIT): a system that provides the right amount of resources at the right time, at the right place, thereby reducing inventories and so allow for continuous flow.

Kanban: a signal that manages or regulates the flow of resources through a value stream by notifying upstream, for example, production or activities.

Known Unknowns: identifiable risks that have a probability or likelihood of occurrence.

Leading: motivating people to achieve the goals and objectives of a project.

Lean: a customer-focused approach that concentrates on providing value by eliminating waste and increasing quality.

Legacy System: outdated information technology incompatible with more contemporary ones.

Lessons Learned: identifying what did and did not go well and provide suggestions for improvement.

Mitigate: one of four parts of a framework on political risk by Rice and Zegart; managing exposures to risks.

Monitoring and Controlling: a project management process; it is observing, measuring, assessing the performance of a project, and taking corrective action to achieve the goals and objectives of a project.

Monitoring: part of the monitoring and controlling process of project management; it is observing, measuring, and assessing the performance of a project.

Network Diagram: part of the planning process of project management; it is a tool that displays the interrelationships among activities that are identified in the work breakdown structure.

Nongovernmental Organization (NGO): a citizen-based group acting independent of a government.

Nonlinear Thinking: looking at the world as a series of complex relationships that occur simultaneously and proportionally.

Normal Operations: also known as business as usual; the state of business operations prior to the occurrence of an event.

Office of Foreign Assets Control (OFAC): administered by the US Department of Treasury and enforces economic and trade sanctions applied against other countries and nongovernmental organizations.

Operational Risks: one of four categories of supply chain risks identified by Manuj and Mentzer; ones affecting the internal performance of an enterprise to produce products and provide services which ultimately affect profitability.

Opportunities: positive risks.

Organizing: a project management process; the project management process that it brings together all aspects of a project, setting up its infrastructure, and conducting meetings.

Outsourcing: exchange of payments or offsets for the services of external companies or other organizations.

Parent Company: controls a subsidiary through stock ownership.

Performance Measurement Baseline: it provides the basis for reporting progress on a project; it costs of cost, scope, and schedule.

Planning: a project management process; it defines in greater detail the scope of a project and ultimately the performance measurement baseline.

Political Actor: an individual, business, government, nongovernmental organization, and intergovernmental organization that can interact in a complex, nonlinear manner.

Political Risk Assessment: one of the political risk management processes; it involves determining which risks are more important than others.

Political Risk Controlling and Monitoring: one of the political risk management processes; it involves monitoring whether a risk has occurred and implementing the requisite response to deal with it.

Political Risk Identification: one of the political risk management processes; it involves developing a list of possible risks that could impact strategic goals and objectives.

Political Risk Management Plan Preparation: one of the political risk management processes; it involves documenting the overall approach, tools, and techniques to conduct political risk management, resulting in a political risk management plan.

Political Risk Management Plan: a document that describes the procedures, tools, and techniques used to conduct political risk management.

Political Risk Management: understanding the context, accumulating facts and data, assessing situations, and responding effectively to political behavior in a manner that minimizes loss and maximizes gain.

Political Risk Modeling: a systemic approach to understand complex political phenomena by identifying the constituent components and their relationships.

Political Risk Reporting: one of the political risk management processes; it involves compiling facts and data about the effectiveness of risks concerning an enterprise.

Political Risk Responses: one of the political risk management processes; it involves identifying the strategies and tactical actions to take should a risk occurs.

Political Risk: an event or condition that can negatively or positively affect a business investment.

Politics: the art and science of one or more political actors seeking, holding, or accumulating power to achieve tangible or intangible goal.

Portfolio: a collection of projects and programs that are aligned with the vision, goals, and objectives of a parent organization.

Postponement: a risk management strategy by Manuj and Mentzer which involves deliberately delaying the commitment of resources to ensure reducing costs and increasing flexibility.

Power: the enabler to satisfy a desire; it is having the capability or authority to execute actions to achieve some tangible or intangible goal.

Procurement Management: part of the organizing process of project management; it is obtaining the appropriate products or services to complete a project.

Program: a collection of projects supporting the achievement of common goals and objectives.

Project Announcement: part of the defining process of project management; it is a brief one-page memo (or email) announcing the existence of a project.

Project Life Cycle: a series of phases that, upon completion, produce a product or deliver a service to the customer.

Project: a set of processes performed to achieve a specific result.

Qualitative Risk Analysis: determining the likelihood, impact, and priority of a risk using scales; considered a "subjective" technique.

Quality Management: part of the organizing process of project management; it is determining the standards for quality on a project and ascertaining whether they are being met and, if not, take the necessary corrective actions.

Quantitative Risk Analysis: a systematic, mathematical approach to determine the impact of a risk, usually financially; considered an "objective" technique.

Racketeer Influenced and Corrupt Organization Act (RICO): a federal law to address fraud, extortion, and illegal activities and allowing an injured party to recover damages.

Reasonable Assurance: providing a significant degree, but not 100 percent, confidence in a decision, assessment, or results.

Recovery: actions taken to lead to the resumption of a business process and eventually return to normal operations.

Requirements Management: part of the organizing process of project management; it is determining and documenting the needs and wants of the internal or external customer which will be used to ascertain the scope of a project.

Residual Risk: part of a risk remains after implementing its response.

Resilience: the ability of a corporation to respond to or recover from conditions or events.

Resource Requirements Estimating: part of the planning process of project management; it is determining the types of and number of labor and non-labor needs to complete a project.

Respond: one of four parts of a framework on political risk by Rice and Zegart; learning from what they call "near misses" by asking about the effectiveness of a response and identifying ways to improve.

Resumption: processes, procedures, and actions to restart a critical business process when recovery actions are completed after disruptive events.

Risk Attitude: a person's or organization's degree of perception about uncertainty.

Risk Management: part of the planning process of project management; in the context of managing a project and not to be confused with political risk management, it is identifying potential threats and opportunities that may impact a project and the responses implemented to deal with them.

Risk Rating: the product or score of a risk by multiplying the probability or likelihood by the impact.

Risk Tolerance: a person's or organization's degree of willingness to face uncertainty.

Sarbanes-Oxley Act: passed in 2002, this law requires executives disclose information that can materially impact an enterprises financial statement; the chief executive officer and chief financial officer play key roles.

Scenario Analysis: a technique that employs a potential future event having an impact on an enterprise, such as its global supply chain.

Schedule Management: part of the organizing process of project management; it is determining the type of schedule, the types of relationships among activities, and updating status.

Scheduling: part of the planning process of project management; it is determining when activities start and stop in a project schedule.

Secondary Risk: the occurrence of one risk causes another risk to occur.

Security Risks: one of four categories of supply chain risks identified by Manuj and Mentzer; ones concerning personnel, information systems, and other functional responsibilities of an enterprise.

Security: a risk management strategy by Manuj and Mentzer to preclude threats regarding information technology, criminal activities, and working with governmental authorities.

Sharing: one of the type of responses to threats; it involves an enterprise splits responsibility to deal with a threat.

Simulation: having a recovery team apply the specific content of a business preparedness against a scenario.

Situational Awareness: knowledge and understanding of an environment and avoid reacting to it in way that is detrimental to the performance of an enterprise whether its supply chain occurs locally, e.g., within a country, or across multiple countries in a global economy.

Situation-Target-Proposal (STP): a report explaining the current circumstances, the desired end state, and the means to achieve the vision.

Speculation: a risk management strategy by Manuj and Mentzer involving moving goods to forward inventories.

Stakeholder Identification: one of the political risk management processes; it entails identifying and involving the right people or organizations when performing political risk management.

Stakeholder Matrix: part of the defining process of project management; it records information about individuals or organizations having an interest in the outcome of a project.

Stimulus-Organism-Response: a theory that people respond to their environment in a less than predictable manner which is largely psychological in nature.

Stimulus-Response: a theory that people react to their environment in a predictable, causal way to stimulus, such as a physical one.

Strategic Goals Identification: one of the political risk management processes; it involves collecting, compiling, and reviewing facts and data to ascertain an enterprise's overall goals and objectives.

Supply Chain: an integrated network of suppliers, manufacturers, warehouses, distribution centers, and retail outlets that either operate within the political jurisdiction or boundaries of a government or across several governments, necessitating compliance with laws, regulations, decrees, etc. Of these public entities.

Supply Risks: one of four categories of supply chain risks identified by Manuj and Mentzer; ones concerning inbound supplies coming into a global enterprise which can impact an enterprise's ability to meet customer requirements.

SWOT Analysis: an acronym for strengths, weaknesses, opportunities, and threats; an analytical technique to determine which decision to make.

Systematic: applying a consistent framework that all stakeholders follow to avoid inconsistency in results.

Systemic: viewing an enterprise as an interacting set of components working together to achieve strategic goals and objectives.

Table Topic: applying the contents of a business preparedness plan to a scenario using discussion and not acting.

Testing: a systematic approach to verify and validate the effectiveness of an enterprise's ability to respond to, and recover from, an event using a business preparedness plan.

Threats: negative risks.

Time Estimating: part of the planning process of project management; it is determining how long an activity will likely take to complete.

Tone at the Top: the general "atmosphere" or operating style established by executive management of an enterprise.

Total Quality Management: an organizational approach by forming cross-functional teams to develop recommendations that address defects and ineffectiveness and inefficiencies related to organizational processes.

Transfer: one of the type of responses to threats; it involves reducing the expected value of a threat.

Tree Diagram: displaying data and information at various levels of abstraction, from general to specific detail.

Understand: one of four parts of a framework on political risk by Rice and Zegart; looking at the risk appetite of stakeholders and increasing alertness about "blind spots."

Unknown Unknowns: unidentifiable risks.

Vision Statement: a high-level guide stating the goals of an enterprise that represents its overall philosophy on conducting business.

Work Breakdown Structure (WBS): part of the planning process of project management; it is a detailed listing of activities and deliverables required to complete a project and defines the scope of a project.

Index

Printed in the United States
by Baker & Taylor Publisher Services